THE AMERICAN NOVEL

THE
AMERICAN
NOVEL

FROM JAMES FENIMORE COOPER
TO WILLIAM FAULKNER

Edited by WALLACE STEGNER

BASIC BOOKS, INC., PUBLISHERS
New York   *London*

810.9
666

4982

The Authors

DANIEL AARON, Mary August Jordan Professor of English at Smith College and Director of its American Studies Program, has edited an Emerson anthology and Robert Herrick's *The Memoirs of an American Citizen.*

CARLOS BAKER, Woodrow Wilson Professor of Literature at Princeton University, is the author of fifteen books, including two novels, a collection of poems, and a forthcoming biography of Ernest Hemingway.

JOHN BERRYMAN, Professor of Humanities at the University of Minnesota, has published two books of poems and a biography of Stephen Crane.

CARVEL COLLINS, Professor of English at Massachusetts Institute of Technology, has written several books and edited two collections of William Faulkner's early works.

ROBERT LEE HOUGH, Associate Professor of English at the University of Nebraska, is the author of *William Dean Howells: The Quiet Rebel.*

KAY SEYMOUR HOUSE, Assistant Professor of English at San Francisco State College, will publish her critical study of James Fenimore Cooper's fictional America in 1965.

LEON HOWARD, Professor of English at the University of California in Los Angeles, is the author of *Literature and the American Tradition* and studies of Herman Melville, James Russell Lowell, and Jonathan Edwards.

IRVING HOWE, Professor of English at Hunter College, is the author of numerous books, including *Politics and the Novel* and *A World More Attractive.*

DAVID LEVIN, Professor of American Literature at Stanford University, is the author of *What Happened in Salem?* and *History as Romantic Art.*

ARTHUR MIZENER, Professor of English at Cornell University, is the author of *The Far Side of Paradise: A Life of F. Scott Fitzgerald*.

THOMAS C. MOSER, Professor of English at Stanford University, is the author of *Joseph Conrad: Achievement and Decline* and *"Wuthering Heights": Texts, Sources, and Criticism*.

RICHARD POIRIER, Professor of English at Rutgers University, is the author of *The Comic Sense of Henry James*.

CLAUDE M. SIMPSON, JR., Coe Professor of American Literature at Stanford University, is the editor of *The Local Colorists* and *Masters of American Literature*.

HENRY NASH SMITH, Professor of English at the University of California at Berkeley, is the author of *Virgin Land: The American West as Symbol and Myth* and *Mark Twain: The Development of a Writer*.

WALLACE STEGNER, Professor of English at Stanford University, is the author of eighteen books, including *The Big Rock Candy Mountain, A Shooting Star, Beyond the Hundredth Meridian*, and *The Gathering of Zion: The Story of the Mormon Trail*.

FRANKLIN WALKER, Aurelia Henry Reinhardt Professor of American Literature at Mills College, has published a book on Frank Norris and is at work on a biography of Jack London.

Preface

A book on the American novel by sixteen scholars, many of whom are the foremost authorities on the authors they treat, is unlikely to develop a thesis or maintain a consistent point of view. This one does exactly the opposite, and that may be its virtue. For if it fails to achieve concentration and singleness, it also avoids tendentiousness and the bending of evidence to fit a line; and, if it risks diffusion, it gains a rich variety.

No attempt is made here to present a history of the American novel. Designed as they were for oral presentation over the Voice of America, to listeners often imperfectly prepared to follow a historical or generic discussion involving wide knowledge of American culture, these essays began and remain talks about single novels. The authors did not compare notes, nor did I, as coordinator and editor, attempt to put critical gaskets between their meeting surfaces. Though the book does demonstrate considerable coherence of approach, it is the coherence that is inevitable when well-informed minds work within a known tradition.

That, and the coherence I may have enforced simply by my selection of titles. I am aware that another might have picked differently at a number of points, but I am convinced that the bulk of this list of nineteen novels is inescapable. I needed a substantial group of novelists who seem now, after the passage of some years, to have expressed significant aspects of the developing American tradition; since I was limited to a single novel from each writer, I wanted that one to be not only the best but if possible the most representative. To carry the selection all the way to the present would have forced us to deal with an unwieldy number of novels from an increasingly tentative judicial base. I therefore stopped at the year 1929, selecting that date because the year of the stock market crash, the beginning of the Great Depression, the catastrophic nose dive of the old thoughtless American confidence, seemed a more decisive dividing line than any other—more decisive than the naturalist movement just before the turn of the century, more decisive than World War I or the Treaty of Versailles. After 1929 America had to begin to grow up, and its literature changed to reflect a changed national consciousness and conscience.

Given these general principles of selection it was unavoidable that some good books had to be left out. Charles Brockden Brown asserts a claim as our first novelist and as the ancestor of the American Gothic: I omitted him because Hawthorne, with greater skill and much greater profundity, adapted the Gothic manner to American uses. Harold Frederic, in *The Damnation of Theron Ware* (1896), wrote a book with much sand and iron in it: if there had been room, I would have liked to include it. And Henry Adams, though less a novelist than a historian, nevertheless wrote, in *Democracy* (1880), a novel that sticks in the mind. I wish I had put it on the list. I cannot think why I did not.

Apart from these few possibilities, I doubt that I would select a different list if I started afresh. I would certainly come up with the same novelists, and I do not think that my taste and understanding would be better represented by other books than those discussed here. There is no leaving out *The Scarlet Letter, Moby Dick, Huckleberry Finn, The Red Badge of Courage, My Antonia, Winesburg, Ohio, The Great Gatsby,* or *Look Homeward, Angel.* Some might choose another Leatherstocking Tale—probably *The Prairie*—to represent Cooper; some might want *A Hazard of New Fortunes* to represent Howells; there could be considerable dispute about what single novel of Henry James most expresses his mind, and some, though not quite so much, about the proper choice among the novels of Edith Wharton. As Daniel Aaron rather wistfully says, there are critics who prefer *Babbitt* to *Main Street;* there are likewise critics who prefer *The Sun Also*

Rises to *A Farwell to Arms*. Among the novels of Faulkner, *As I Lay Dying, Light in August, Absalom, Absalom!*, and *The Hamlet* would all receive votes. Nevertheless, I believe that the list as constituted has served to allow discussion of the major achievements and the major themes of the American novel prior to 1930.

Those achievements and themes have been analyzed and explicated in many places and at length. To attempt here to do more than suggest a few relationships would be to risk serious oversimplifying, for the course of development of American civilization, including the American character, the American "idea," and the American language, as well as the literature that reflects them, has been complex, tentative, and full of contradictions and reversals.

One currently fashionable attempt to define the American character is in terms of its "innocence"; rebaptism in the symbolic waters of the New World is its characteristic rite, and measurement against corrupt or decadent Europe its characteristic test. The newness was reinforced by successive frontiers, each farther from European influence; the comparison with the Old World by new immigrations, cultural pilferings, feelings of inferiority, critical books by British travelers, and persistent expatriation of the literary. D. H. Lawrence remarked that the American son compulsively killed the European father, and that the Leatherstocking Tales brilliantly reflect the American experience by moving from wrinkled age to radiant youth, and from the settlements to the pure wilderness. But quite as often as the rebellious son has repudiated Europe, he has been reclaimed by it. More of our novelists have been expatriates than have been hundred percenters. Yet even, perhaps especially, as expatriates they have felt the need of personal and national definition.

In the novels before us we observe several faces of the persistent American innocence. We cannot avoid seeing it in Natty Bumppo, in Huck Finn, in Carrie Meeber, in Jay Gatsby, in Benjy Compson; without too much straining we may sense it in Silas Lapham, Lily Bart, even McTeague. The dialogue with Europe, persistent from Cooper to Fitzgerald,

Hemingway, and Wolfe, might be indefinitely expanded by expanding the list of novels, but it is plentifully present in these nineteen. Echoes of the backwoods brashness of *The Innocents Abroad* reverberate in the conversations between Huck and Jim, and in the cultural pretensions of the "King" and the "Duke." Our nineteen novels give us yearners toward the Old World as various as Isabel Archer, Ántonia Shimerda, and the culture-craving Carol Kennicott. And the antagonism between innocence and experience, between the wilderness and society, finds expression not only in *Huckleberry Finn*, with its contrasts between idyllic river and sordid towns, but in *The Pioneers*, with its conflict between responsible freedom and rigid law, and in *The Great Gatsby*, where innocence is made an attribute of the Midwest, and corruption once thought of as European has been transplanted among the careless rich of the eastern seaboard.

Allied with the theme of American innocence is the theme of freedom, and inseparable from the theme of freedom is that of moral responsibility. Here our novels show a progression from moral certainty to ambiguity, doubt, or denial. Calvinistic determinism, however much it may have bent the character of early New England, does not much figure in novels, since Calvinists neither wrote nor read them. Instead, our early novels assert the freedom of the will, a freedom intensified by the lack of a society capable of restraining individual action with its forms. Sin and guilt and error are acts in the teeth of the moral law. The adultery of Hester Prynne, Ahab's monomaniac pursuit of the whale, Isabel Archer's reckless insistence on living according to her own choice, are not only acts of will, but acts of a romantic and Promethean will that remains defiant. For Hester's guilt is compounded by her lack of contrition, Isabel refuses the last-minute rescue offered by Caspar Goodwood as she has ignored the warnings of Ralph Touchett, our final image of Ahab's "Pequod" is the arm that reaches up out of the whelming sea to nail the flag higher on the mast. And the moral and dramatic crux of such novels as *Huckleberry Finn* and *The Rise of Silas Lapham* and *The House of Mirth* is an ethical choice, deliberately made.

In many later novels faith in the autonomy of the will has crumbled before the ugliness and the human diminishments of industrialism, before the pressures of the jungle city, and before the sad persuasions of the naturalistic philosophy imported from Europe and nourished by evolutionary thought. Despite William Dean Howells' belief that any American writer who sounded Dostoevsky's dark note would do a "false and mistaken thing," despite his belief that "the more smiling aspects of life" are the more American,* the dark note has been sounded increasingly since the 1890's. Pessimism about the validity of the moral law and the possibility of justice or happiness has been accompanied by a loss of faith that the individual human will has any strength against the forces of life. In the experimental way that novels have of stating and dramatizing possibilities, we have gone the whole way from will to no-will, and some of our novels have asserted a determinism as harsh as Calvin's ever was. Instead of that defiant arm thrusting upward from the "Pequod's" foundering, we have McTeague, helpless to control the animal in him and helpless to resist society's hostility, stumbling through the desert chained to death and with the cosmic commentary of a twittering bird in a gilded cage. Instead of elected damnation we have the fall of Carrie Meeber, soft as a squashing custard, a fall without a thought or a qualm or a feeling. Instead of romantic spirits challenging the universe we have Lieutenant Henry with his burning ants and his nihilistic bleakness:

> They threw you in and told you the rules and the first time they caught you off base they killed you.

When our discussion ends, at the year 1929, neither the Depression nor World War II with its bestialities had added their chilling evidence of the puniness of the individual will against cosmic or social force, and the population explosion had not, by doubling the world's numbers, reduced the individual to computer fodder. Nevertheless it would be an error to say that belief in the will has disappeared even now, and certainly it had not disappeared in 1929. In *Look Homeward,*

* *Criticism and Fiction* (New York: Harper, 1892), p. 128.

Angel and *The Sound and the Fury,* both published in that fatal year, neither Thomas Wolfe nor William Faulkner had given an inch on that issue. They are still there on their last tidal rock in the last red sunset, and still talking. It is an act equivalent to nailing the flag higher up on the mast.

In this, as with other themes that might be extracted from our group of novels, the emphasis changes, the ground shifts, but the debate is likely to go on. It has been said that the "Success Story" is the truest American myth, and surely our literature has displayed it in every form from the Alger story to savage anti-Alger fables such as Nathanael West's *A Cool Million* and Nelson Algren's *A Walk on the Wild Side.* If we wish, we may see *Huckleberry Finn* and *the Rise of Silas Lapham* as success stories stated in moral terms, *The Red Badge of Courage* as a success story stated in terms of physical bravery, *Sister Carrie* as a success story expressed in the vocabulary of blind chance, *The Great Gatsby* as a success story that celebrates "romantic readiness" and the "capacity for wonder." But to go this far is to risk the fate of the man who tried to wrap three watermelons in one package.

It is enough to point out a few cross-references. Among these nineteen books are two early fictional treatments of the Civil War that later expanded into a myth and an industry. There are several versions of the Revolt from the Village that exercised the twenties: half-affectionate in *Winesburg, Ohio* and *My Ántonia,* acid in *Main Street,* polarized into contradictory impulses of sanctuary and escape in *Look Homeward, Angel.* The non-English-speaking immigrants who through the latter nineteenth century transformed our ethnic composition enter our literature as Dreiser's Germans and Willa Cather's Czechs and Swedes. The color problem that has lain like a snake among the roots of our national life for three hundred years is stated in some of its aspects in *Miss Ravenel's Conversion,* and dramatized in both *Huckleberry Finn* and *The Sound and the Fury,* in each of which a black person is essentially the hero.

As for the American language, which is one element of our character, it breaks into literature in *Huckleberry Finn* and is a persistent, if interrupted, stream thereafter. The native voice, as distinguished from traditional literary English, is to be heard most strongly in *Winesburg, Ohio, A Farewell to Arms,* and *The Sound and the Fury,* and in *Main Street* it appears as a quacking caricature.

The condition of American life has been an extravagant pluralism, and our writers have vacillated between the assumption that out of the many must surely come one and the feeling that such variety and richness should not be flattened out and monochromed. In reading such a collection of essays as this, one barely becomes aware of some of the unifying possibilities before one is dispersed again by the multiplicity of character and approach displayed in any group of our novels. In the end, it is not for their reflections of American life, not for their sociological or economic or political associations, not for their rendering of history that we read them, but for their imaginative re-creation of human beings in the act of living within a comprehensible society. Each novel is its own justification, and that justification is literary. I suggest that each essay in this book is likewise its own justification, and that among the many points of view and the many facets of American life represented, the reader will find his own cross-references and make his own synthesis—if indeed synthesis is either possible or necessary.

Stanford, California   WALLACE STEGNER
January 1965

Contents

THE AMERICAN NOVEL

1 JAMES FENIMORE COOPER
The Pioneers

Kay Seymour House

After the death of James Fenimore Cooper in 1851, the American historian, George Bancroft, predicted, "Another like Cooper cannot appear, for he was peculiarly suited to his time, which was that of an invading civilization." Being so suited required, of course, that the novelist know not only the German, Scotch, and Irish peoples who were coming to America, but also the Negroes, the Dutch, the Indians, the French, and the English who had been in the country for many years. To do more than describe—to create a coherent fictional world as Cooper did—required further a deep feeling for the land being invaded and an intelligent interest in the process of civilization itself. A man of immense physical and intellectual vitality, Cooper was temperamentally suited to the task. Moreover, his mind was at once liberal and analytic, and he was to prove a perceptive observer. Later in his career, almost eight years of residence in Europe would increase his understanding of America's cultural heritage from the Old World, but none of his later works contradicts, or even seriously questions, the America he portrayed in *The Pioneers,* the first of the Leatherstocking Tales.

During the years in which he wrote, from 1820 to 1850, Americans were obsessed with their composite national character—or lack of it. Back in 1782 (a long time ago, by American standards), Crèvecoeur had boasted that America would shortly show the world "a new man, who acts upon new principles." If the world was still waiting to see what this new

1

man would look like and how he would act, so were Americans themselves. Hence Daniel Webster placed "national character" first on a list of the nation's needs in 1831. The obsession with national character was further documented, and America's sensitivity about it increased, by a stream of European visitors—hostile, friendly, or merely curious—who kept coming over to see how the great American experiment was getting on. For all these, Americans and Europeans alike, the question of American character became a metaphor for general concern about the quality and goals of American life. Could individual liberty be preserved against tyranny imposed either by the state or by the majority? Would democracy mean a lowering of standards? Or, as Victor Hugo and others at the International Peace Conference of 1848 wanted to know, did the United States' disparate population point to the possibility of a commonwealth of nations? That these "American" questions were also Europe's, Cooper and other intelligent Americans knew, and Cooper has recently been described as "one of the clearest and perhaps one of the last political thinkers to insist that a country's form of government affects its culture." [1]

Further complicating the problem of American character was the rapidity with which Americans, particularly those on the frontier, were changing the face of their portion of the earth before it had really become familiar to them. Cooper believed that these changes were so rapid and discontinuous as to call for unremitting judgment, and he wrote in 1829, "To see America with the eyes of truth, it is necessary to look often." To survive the chaotic present and to emerge into a future they had chosen rather than chanced upon, Americans needed to understand the forces that were shaping American life. "The nation is passing," Cooper wrote in 1821, "from the gristle into the bone." The sense of urgency implicit in his statement was authentic, and Cooper wrote his first two American romances, *The Spy* and *The Pioneers*, to help Americans understand themselves by examining their own

[1] Sebastian de Grazia, *Of Time, Work, and Leisure* (New York: The Twentieth Century Fund, 1962), p. 291.

history. *The Spy* is obviously indebted to the methods and materials of Sir Walter Scott, but with *The Pioneers* Cooper began to create for Americans what Van Wyck Brooks was to call a "usable past." Generally speaking, the book is a paradigm of early American life; it tells what it is like to build towns and clear farms where only trees and beasts had been; it describes the passing of Indians and colonial officials and the turning of other soldiers and hunters to civilian vocations and settlement living; finally, it tries to relate the abstraction of democracy to daily life.

The Pioneers was written rapidly and the prose is frequently tangled; yet the novel stands as an impressive and seminal work, one clearly relevant to the main body of American literature. Cooper had few theories about the novel as a form of art, and criticism of his earlier work had been contradictory. Lacking guidance, he decided, as he tells us in the preface, to write *The Pioneers* exclusively to please himself.

Cooper took for his novel's setting his own boyhood home in northern New York State. His father, Judge William Cooper, boasted of having settled more acres of land than any other man in America, and had owned over 750,000 acres at one time or another. He differed from the usual land agent, however, by moving to the frontier and advising the new settlers in person. He was the first judge of his county and was twice elected to Congress; Judge Temple, one of the main characters in *The Pioneers*, is undoubtedly based on Judge Cooper.

The setting itself, a frontier village carefully described during the four seasons of a year, explains this novel's appeal for many readers. D. H. Lawrence, for one, wrote of it,

> Perhaps my taste is childish, but these scenes in *Pioneers* seem to me marvellously beautiful. The raw village street, with wood-fires blinking through the unglazed window-chinks, on a winter's night. The Inn, with the rough woodsmen and the drunken Indian John; the church, with the snowy congregation crowding to the fire. Then the lavish abundance of Christmas cheer, and turkey-shooting in the snow. Spring coming, forests all green, maple-sugar taken from the trees; and clouds of

pigeons flying from the south, myriads of pigeons, shot in heaps; and night-fishing on the teeming, virgin lake; and deer-hunting.

Pictures! Some of the loveliest, most glamorous pictures in all literature.[2]

These pictures are interspersed through a narrative that was meant to be held together by a conventional love story. Judge Temple's daughter Elizabeth is the heroine, and as Cooper's heroines go, she is one of the best; for Cooper's readers, in 1822, her romance and adventures were the central interest. (A scene in which she is threatened by a panther, published in advance as an advertisement for the novel, probably accounted for the record 3500 copies sold in America the first day of publication.) By keeping the hero's identity a mystery and by creating a series of misunderstandings, Cooper contrived to keep the lovers apart until he could use their marriage to close off the main plot. The union of Elizabeth Temple with young Oliver Effingham promises a peaceful and fruitful continuation of responsible leadership for the young community.

Against this conventional happy ending, however, Cooper set a discordant coda, a final chapter in which Natty Bumppo, the old hunter otherwise known as Leatherstocking, leaves the settlement and turns away into the forest. For Cooper's early readers, the book ended affirmatively with the marriage; for us today it ends with the alienation of Leatherstocking and the beginning of the Leatherstocking myth. Extruded by the opposition of Judge Temple's household to Natty Bumppo's, the myth expands, finally to contain such fundamental antitheses as settlement and wilderness, law and liberty, society and the individual, conservatism and anarchy.

To say what The Pioneers is specifically about, then, we need to examine the relation of Leatherstocking to the rest of the community. As Cooper presented it, the little settlement of Templeton is composed of representatives from many ethnic groups. Irish, French, German, Negro, Indian, Cockney English, Tory Anglo-American, Dutch—each group has at

[2] Studies in Classic American Literature (New York: Doubleday & Co., 1953), p. 65.

4

least one representative figure in the narrative. Each contributes uniquely to the community so that stereotyped traits —French vitality, German deliberation, Indian patience—are shown as enriching social life rather than embarrassing it. Were any one of these characters to be lost, by that much would Templeton be impoverished. The prevailing mood is one of welcome, and although some persons are clearly more valued than others, no one is excluded and the temper of the community is benign.

Cooper was a careful historian, and his fictional village encloses a fair sampling of the various peoples then living in the northeastern states. Most of the inhabitants are unlike the earlier description sent abroad by Crèvecoeur, who had written:

> He is an American who, leaving behind him all his ancient prejudices and manners, receives new ones from the new modes of life he has embraced, the new government he obeys, and the new rank he holds.[3]

By contrast, Cooper put in his American novels many characters who were formed abroad and who landed with their "prejudices and manners" intact. In the aggregate (drinking together from one cup before the tavern fire in *The Pioneers,* for instance), they are a cosmopolitan group. The novel approves their holding fast to their heritage, for the "new modes of life" Crèvecoeur wrote of have yet to be defined clearly, the new government is remote, and they have no rank from which to derive an identity. Cooper saw that for the average man a cultural vacuum meant danger as well as opportunity. Blind imitation, undue reliance on public opinion, willfulness, active evil—all these could thrive in the absence of familiar standards.

He made his point in *The Pioneers* by portraying variants of a stereotype character generally recognized as "The Yankee." Cooper's fictional characters are exercises in definition, and his usual method was to specify first what "class" (mean-

[3] J. Hector St. John de Crèvecoeur, *Letters from an American Farmer* (New York: E. P. Dutton & Co., 1957), p. 39.

ing by this what cultural group) a character belonged to, then to show how that character differed, if at all, from other members of the class. In *The Pioneers,* as in the geographical area Cooper knew best, the dominant class in numbers and political power was made up of white, male Protestants born in the northeastern states of predominantly Anglo-Saxon stock. The Yankee stereotype that had already gone abroad from this group was represented as quick-witted (but unscrupulous), energetic (but largely in his own behalf), militantly Protestant (but basically irreligious), and acquisitive (without knowing the end for which he acquired).

Five men, all coming from the cultural group that produced the Yankee, wield some notable power in the community: Richard Jones, Billy Kirby, Hiram Doolittle, Judge Temple, and Natty Bumppo. Natty is immediately set apart as different because he has abandoned his proper group and lives with an Indian. Yet, by comparing all five of these characters, by examining the principles by which they live and the values they honor, we approach Cooper's judgment of American society and discover the American dilemma as he saw it.

If, as some people believe, the male American is notable for incessant activity and technological efficiency, then Richards Jones, the cousin of Judge Temple, would be the typical American of this group. Richard has unflagging energy, seems to be perpetually in motion, and assumes that all motion is progress. His lack of concern about the consequences of anything he does follows logically from his naïve faith in his own abilities. Ingenious rather than creative, he tries to imitate on the frontier the famous European edifices he has heard praised but has never seen. Excellence, so far as Richard is concerned, is quantitative rather than qualitative, and he shoots a cannon at flocks of pigeons and fishes with a seine. Richard is irresponsible and a fool, but because he is restrained by his cousin, the Judge, he damages the community most by setting a bad example for his admirers to emulate.

His two colleagues, Billy Kirby and Hiram Doolittle, are more clearly dangerous types. Billy bases all ethical decisions on what seems "fair" to his common-sense view; consequently, his great physical power is largely governed by his mood at the moment. In spite of a certain disarming boyishness, he is a crude—even cruel—man to whom political freedom means that he can kill, burn, maim, chop down, or otherwise destroy anything not specifically protected by law. America's natural resources are so abundant that he feels justified in wasting them, and he slashes his way through the forests, declaring that trees "are a sore sight, unless I'm privileged to work my will on them."

Hiram Doolittle, the cowardly town constable, works his own will against men rather than trees. He is the provocative agent in Natty Bumppo's conflict with the community; the trouble begins with a locked door. Natty and his Indian friend Chingachgook are secretly caring for a senile British major who had once been Natty's superior officer. Because of his condition, they keep the hut's door locked, but Hiram considers a closed door a personal affront. His resentment builds until, by attributing his own values to Natty, he convinces himself and others that the hut's owners must have discovered a silver mine and that the closed door can only guard a great treasure. Hiram uses his public position as constable to vent his personal frustration and cupidity. Through this bumptious functionary who exceeds his authority, Cooper chillingly represents the harassment of a police state and indicates that legalism is no better than license.

As society works in *The Pioneers*, Hiram's opportunity comes about because of people like Billy Kirby and Richard Jones. They and other settlers seem to have forgotten that they once nearly starved in that same valley; their wastefulness has caused Judge Temple to obtain game laws. Since Leatherstocking and Chingachgook follow the Indian custom of killing only what they need, the laws are not directed at them. But Hiram Doolittle, wishing to break into Natty's hut, cuts loose the watchdogs who then chase a deer into the lake where Natty kills it. Having failed to break into the cabin, Hiram uses this infraction of the game law to obtain a search warrant. Thus confronted, Natty confesses the killing

7

and offers to pay the small fine, but he resists arrest and refuses to let Hiram search the hut.

These are the events that, when considered with the relative guilt of each man, dramatize two warnings Cooper repeated throughout his career. As he saw it, the man who relinquishes his own natural means of protection (such as Natty's deadly ability to shoot) deserves government protection for his rights. Cooper once recommended that:

> it be written in letters of brass in all of the highways and places of resort in the country, that A STATE OF SOCIETY WHICH PRETENDS TO THE PROTECTION THAT BELONGS TO CIVILIZATION, AND FAILS TO GIVE IT, ONLY MAKES THE CONDITION OF THE HONEST PORTION OF THE COMMUNITY SO MUCH THE WORSE, BY DEPRIVING IT OF THE PROTECTION CONFERRED BY NATURE, WITHOUT SUPPLYING THE SUBSTITUTE.[4]

In a state of nature, Natty Bumppo could make short work of Hiram Doolittle. Because some men, like Hiram, are evil, and others are irresponsible, like Billy Kirby and Richard Jones, society needs laws. Yet, in *The Pioneers*, law becomes the weapon that lets Hiram defeat a morally better and naturally stronger man.

Second, Cooper here dramatizes a belief he also stated in *The American Democrat*:

> He is the purest democrat who best maintains his rights. . . . There is getting to be so much public right that private right is overshadowed and lost. A danger exists that the ends of liberty will be forgotten altogether in the means.

In other words, there were whole areas of a man's experience over which the public could have no legitimate control. Privacy, one of the most obvious personal rights, is represented by the locked door, and Cooper reinforced the argument by portraying Natty as an individual who imposes on himself

---

[4] James Fenimore Cooper, *The Redskins* (New York: G. P. Putnam's Sons, n.d.), p. 367.

restrictions even more stringent than those society asks. While tolerant of the shortcomings of others, Natty judges his own performance severely and compares it with humanly possible excellence. Society's requirements are heaped on Natty's own self-imposed restraints (of which his silent laugh is a sign). A simple-minded and uneducated man like Natty easily runs afoul of the net of legalisms spread against the visionary schemes and multiple aggressions of Jones, Doolittle, and Kirby.

In realizing the necessity of law, Cooper agreed with Judge Temple, but in feeling its insufficiency to guarantee justice, he also understood the appeal of anarchy. He set up the contrast cleanly by making the settlement's wealthiest citizen, Judge Temple, and its poorest, Natty Bumppo, the two most responsible men in the novel. In making Natty a gentleman in every way but wealth and education, Cooper displayed the warmth of his faith in the common man's ability to act nobly. Both Natty and the Judge are, as gentlemen should be, disinterested. They have no designs on anyone else's person or property. Both remember the virgin beauty of the country prior to settlement, and both decry the settlers' waste and destruction. Both are grateful for the country's abundance and consider themselves stewards to whom the land has been entrusted.

With the question of land use, however, we reach an end to the area of agreement, large though it is. The Judge wants to conserve resources and ration them to future generations; Natty never accumulates more than he can use immediately and trusts to his own abilities and a merciful Providence to provide for the future. The Judge is dedicated to communal interdependence, Natty to individual self-reliance. Their differences ultimately are expressed in terms of conservatism and anarchy, of artificial law and natural justice.

Natty's most significant act is to burn his hut shortly after his altercation with Hiram Doolittle. With its burning, he severs his connection with much of his own past, with settled society, and with fixed property; property is the means through which society's agents can make his personal life miserable. As he stands watching his hut burn to embers, a posse comes to arrest him and Natty blurts out his bitterness:

> You have driven me, that have lived forty years of my appointed time in this very spot, from my home and the shelter of my head, lest you should put your wicked feet and wasty ways in my cabin. You've driven me to burn these logs, under which I've eaten and drunk . . . for the half of a hundred years; and to mourn for the ashes under my feet as a man would weep and mourn for the children of his body. You've rankled the heart of an old man, that has never harmed you or your'n, with bitter feelings toward his kind, at a time when his thoughts should be on a better world; and you've driven him to wish that the beasts of the forest, who never feast on the blood of their own families, was his kindred and race; and now, when he has come to see the last brand of his hut, before it is melted into ashes, you follow him up, at midnight, like hungry hounds on the track of a worn-out and dying deer. What more would ye have? for I am here—one to many. I come to mourn, not to fight; and, if it is God's pleasure, work your will on me.

Natty is seeing society anew. It is true that he has never been gregarious, has always chosen his companions carefully. Yet, until Hiram Doolittle took advantage of what Natty calls the "twisty ways of the law," Natty never thought of men as animals that hunt in packs, or of himself as their helpless quarry. His acknowledgement that he is "old and helpless" and "one to many" violates his lifelong feeling of self-sufficiency. Alone in the forest he is strong; alone in society he is weak. Natty's recognition of the difference is supported by Judge Temple's surprise that an "old, friendless man like him would dare to oppose the officers of justice."

Natty's own idea of justice has a catholic complexity that admits gradations and mitigation, and he is hurt when Judge Temple, sentencing him, seems to have forgotten a personal obligation. The old hunter cannot grasp the complex power embodied in the Judge. The man who personally owes his daughter's life to Natty is powerless to repay the debt when wearing robes; yet only when he acts as judge has he more power than anyone else in the settlement. All this denies the testimony of Natty's senses, and he cannot relate the abstract ideal to its effect on human life. When the Judge upholds the law and says, " 'the dignity of the law requires an open exhibition of the consequences of your crime,' " Natty translates the punishment into human terms as " 'showing off a man in his seventy-first year, like a tame bear, for the settlers to look on!' " The Judge worries about the dignity of the law, Natty about the dignity of man, and Cooper, sympathizing with both positions, could only wish they did not seem to be mutually exclusive.

The threat of the settlements, then, is most dangerous to Natty's idea of himself as a human being. Once he has done his duty (*not* his legal duty) by his dying friends, the Indian and the Major, he turns to the wilderness. He feels that he must, and explains, " 'I lose myself every day of my life in the clearings.' " Natty's self, painfully formed from the experiences of a lifetime, is threatened by society. To justify what remains of his life, to bolster his shaken sense of human worth, he falls back on his favorite doctrine ("Use, but don't waste") and applies it to himself. In rejecting the young Effinghams' offer of charity, Natty insists, " 'The meanest of God's creatur's be made for some use, and I'm formed for the wilderness; if ye love me, let me go where my soul craves to be ag'in!' " To civilization, which hoards its cash, squanders its natural resources, and places law as a weapon in the hands of the greedy and cunning, Natty Bumppo is himself so much waste. His survival involves more than the clearing of the forests and the consequent scarcity of game. To survive as Natty Bumppo, he must leave the settlements and go where his integrity can be preserved. Asking us to admire not only the Effinghams and Temples, who represent the best of society, but also the Natty Bumppo who rejects it, Cooper acknowledges a basic dilemma in American life.

From this time on, which is to say in the next four novels Cooper wrote about him, Leatherstocking lives in a buffer state between raw primitivism and encroaching civilization. Like Virgil's Arcadia it is, in Bruno Snell's words, "a half-way land . . . where currents of myth and empirical reality flow into one another." [5] With the other four books (*The Last of the Mohicans, The Prairie, The Pathfinder,* and *The Deerslayer*), the character of Leatherstocking becomes more complete, but *The Pioneers* offers the essence of the character and defines the central conflict. Compounded of America's legendary past and its apparent future, an embodied truce of conflicting impulses, Natty is one of the great synthetic characters in literature. He clearly reveals Cooper's conviction that an American's primary function was to build a character consistent with ancient values and the truths taught by contemporary experience. If, as Richard Chase said, Natty "seems ultimately to deny the whole idea of society," we see why he does. Natty's business is to form himself, to find his place in the universe, and this is essentially a religious (rather than political) activity. It is also by its nature a solitary one, and Natty leads us into the territory of antithesis, for a successful quest after perfection of individual character was the desire of democratic society. Yet Cooper wanted us somehow to manage to have it all—liberty and law, individual integrity and social harmony, the wilderness and the invading civilization.

Formed as he is out of conflict, Natty Bumppo elicits varying responses, but the affirmation was caught by D. H. Lawrence when he described Leatherstocking's progress as the "onward march of the integral soul." In subsequent novels, Leatherstocking marches backward through time until the last of the series, *The Deerslayer,* shows him as a young man undergoing his first tests of character and confronting the widest number of choices ever available to him. The whole series, as Lawrence said, goes "backwards, from old age to golden youth. That is the true myth of America." The American character who finally emerges as Deerslayer is then a new man, after all. Unencumbered, mobile, and plastic, he is free to form himself.

[5] *The Discovery of the Mind* (New York: Harper & Brothers, 1960), pp. 283, 301.

2 NATHANIEL HAWTHORNE
The Scarlet Letter

David Levin

Nathaniel Hawthorne, born in 1804 in an age that spoke often of inevitable progress, wrote his best fiction about the distant past. Like many other Americans of his time and our own, he sometimes thought of his country as a land of great promise for the hopes of all humanity, as the land of the future, and he sometimes felt embarrassed by her lack of a rich traditional history. Yet he said that he felt haunted by memories of his seventeenth-century ancestors, one of whom had played an important role more than 150 years earlier in condemning twenty people to death for witchcraft, and he studied Puritan history with a persistence that some scholars (along with Hawthorne himself) have considered obsessive.

This mixed attitude toward the present and the past led Hawthorne to confront in his best work some of the most troublesome issues in American society and to use his knowledge of history as a means of speaking to his contemporaries. In discussing *The Scarlet Letter,* I shall try to explain the value of Hawthorne's method, and I shall pay especial attention to the skill with which Hawthorne used allegory to give the English and American novel a new intensity of psychological analysis.

We must remember, first of all, that Hawthorne was not himself a Puritan and that he was probably not a believing Christian. He often expressed an affection for the solid life, for good Madeira wine, and for novels written "on the strength of beef and ale." He admired the realistic novels of the Englishman Anthony Trollope; he enjoyed playing cards; in his early years at Bowdoin College he developed a friendship with the politician Franklin Pierce, for whom he later wrote a campaign biography to help Pierce become President of the United States, and he maintained throughout his life a friendship with several other worldly politicians. He tried repeatedly to gain appointment to political office, and on two or three occasions he succeeded. He wanted to belong to the progressive, gregarious life of the young country that was settling a continent during his lifetime.

But Hawthorne felt and expressed a certain separateness from this community long before he was embittered by losing his political office during a change in presidential administrations. In the twelve lonely years after he graduated from college in 1825 he had lived in virtual solitude in his mother's house in Salem, Massachusetts—writing dozens of his best but gloomiest stories, going out for long walks at night, often taking his meals alone in his room, and reading in great detail not about the present and hopes for the future but about the history of colonial New England. He became friendly with the philosophical anarchist Henry Thoreau. He joined for a time a socialistic community at Brook Farm. And in a story called "The Celestial Railroad" he wrote a sharp satire on the notion of spiritual progress through material invention, a faith cherished by many of his countrymen.

It is in this sort of critique of his contemporaries that we can see Hawthorne's great debt to the Puritanism of his ancestors. He wrote in a time that showed a strong interest in romantic histories, grand epics in which heroic explorers or military leaders moved through sublime scenes. And he, along with thousands of his countrymen, admired the historical romances of Sir Walter Scott and James Fenimore Cooper. He was well aware of the shallow characterization in these works, but he resolved to use the conventional forms as a way of writing a new kind of fiction. Most of the popular writers of romance had been content to treat characters as stereotypes: the dashing, warm-hearted hero who was sympathetic to nature and who obeyed natural laws was pitted against a heartless, intellectual villain who defended the letter of the law. In this scheme the complexity of human character was usually suggested, not within one person, but by contrasts between other groups of simple types, such as the two heroines: the fair lady, whose moderate feelings pointed the way to true values; and the dark lady, who was either too intellectual or too passionate to be a fit mate for the hero. Hawthorne accepted such conventions and transformed them. He called his fiction *psychological romance,* and he declared that he would "burrow into the depths of our common nature." He used the historical romance and its conventions to achieve a deeper psychological intensity than any of his predecessors had accomplished. And, of course, in turning to the past, he turned to the Puritan past.

There are several reasons why this choice was remarkably appropriate. Hawthorne, like his ancestors, was preoccupied with the moral life, with questions of responsibility and motivation, and with the moral and psychological effects of sin or misfortune. He once spoke apologetically of his "inveterate habit of allegory." In writing about the Puritans he was able to bring his readers into a world of people who considered their own lives allegorical. Hawthorne believed that the romance, unlike the novel, did not have to restrict itself to the probable; so long as the romance was true to what he called the truth of the human heart, it had every right to mingle the marvelous and the real. Romances, he said, ought to be written and read by moonlight or by the dim light of the coal fire, in an atmosphere that brings the reader into "a neutral territory, somewhere between the real world and fairyland, where the actual and imaginary may meet and each imbue itself with the nature of the other." Many writers of romance and history in his day found that neutral territory in the distant past, in fifteenth-century Spain or sixteenth-century Mexico and Peru. When Hawthorne chose to write about seventeenth-century Boston, whose people really believed in devils and witches and in a jealous God who intervened in their daily affairs, he chose a community that recognized no clear line between the real world and what we might call fairyland; he chose a community in which it was especially difficult to distinguish between the actual and the imaginary.

The Scarlet Letter is the story of three sinners and the consequences of their acts. The red letter "A" that the heroine is obliged to wear on her bosom represents her adultery, but as the first letter of the alphabet it may also stand for the original sin of Adam, in which Puritans believed all men participated. Children in seventeenth-century Boston had learned their alphabet from a book that printed a little verse for each letter. The first letter was illustrated by this verse:

> In Adam's fall
> We sinned all.

We all sinned with Adam, at the beginning.

Hawthorne's novel begins with a scene on the scaffold, in the market place of Boston, where the heroine stands in disgrace with her infant child held close as if to conceal the letter "A" on her gown. Hester Prynne, a gentlewoman whose husband is thought to be missing at sea, has borne a child fathered by another man, and she stands in disgrace before the entire community. The chief ministers of the community, including the guilty lover, Arthur Dimmesdale, admonish her to reveal the name of her child's father, but she refuses. On this day of her shame, however, her husband (who has been shipwrecked and rescued by Indians) arrives. When he sees his wife on the scaffold, he resolves to conceal his identity and to seek out the child's true father. He assumes the cold name of Roger Chillingworth, and he makes his wife promise to keep his secret.

From these opening scenes the novel moves inexorably to its tragic conclusion. Hawthorne concentrates first on Hester's punishment, her suffering, and her psychological endurance during the next seven years, and then he describes Chillingworth's determined quest for the closely guarded secret. Chillingworth, by instinct or black art, has been attracted to the guilty Dimmesdale, and in the guise of physician and friend he watches for the conclusive evidence. Hawthorne shows us the guilty man's suffering from Chillingworth's point of view, and then we see the minister's full agony from inside his own mind as he struggles unsuccessfully to make a public confession.

When Hester sees how much her former lover is suffering, she resolves to protect him. She tells him of her husband's identity and persuades him to escape with her and her child to another country. But her lover's impulse toward self-destruction and his overwhelming need to confess make this hope impossible. On the day of the planned departure he delivers his last great sermon and then ascends the scaffold, before the whole community; he confesses his guilt, asks Hester's forgiveness, embraces his daughter, and dies. Chillingworth, who has renounced his name in pursuit of revenge, has no life left. Hester leaves the community but returns for penance after her daughter has grown up. The daughter Pearl, we are told by the narrator who has been reconstructing the tale from old records, seems to have married in Europe and led a happy, comfortable life after all.

Hawthorne's great achievement in this simple story is to relate the allegory of sinners and the conflict between intellect and natural emotion so that we see not only his judgment of a historical community but also his clear perception of human psychology and the human predicament in almost any community. All three sinners are isolated from humanity, but each in a different way that is related both to the allegory and to the conflict of intellect and heart. Hester Prynne is the publicly known, partially penitent sinner. Arthur Dimmesdale is the secret sinner. Roger Chillingworth is the unpardonable sinner. Let us consider these characters somewhat more carefully, to discover how Hawthorne gives his allegory the substance and complexity of human reality.

Hester Prynne, though more obviously isolated from society than either of the men, has a closer emotional relationship to humanity than either of them can establish, and she is therefore less seriously damaged. Pearl, her daughter, is the emblem of her sin but also a means of salvation—moral salvation if we accept the Christian terminology of the seventeenth century, psychological rehabilitation if we insist on the secular terminology of a later time. Love and concern for Pearl save Hester from wandering too far in the intellectual and moral wilderness, to which her own pride and her isolation by society tempt her.

Hester's sin, by the standards of Hawthorne's romantic psychology, is excessive passion; because it is a *natural* transgression, an expression of her vital energy, she is stronger than either Dimmesdale or Chillingworth. But she is a complex figure, and Hawthorne sees that her natural vigor must also lead her into further trouble. In being faithful to what he called the truth of the human heart, Hawthorne had to see that the most interesting battle was not between the heart and the intellect but within the heart itself. Hester is not properly penitent. She compounds the sin of passion with the sin of pride. She embroiders the scarlet letter as an elaborate expression of ambiguous defiance and guilt, and she dresses her daughter in equally flamboyant colors. Then, when her daughter asks her about the meaning of the letter, she lies to the child and thus underlines for us the damaging evasiveness of their relationship.

Hester's passion, then, has only been dammed up. Hawthorne has described her as the dark heroine of romantic fiction, with a "rich, voluptuous, Oriental characteristic," and the confinement of her rich, dark hair under a tight cap symbolizes the artificial restraint of her natural passion. Hawthorne sees clearly that, just as her warm generosity leads her to help Dimmesdale by proposing an escape from Boston, it also takes a humanly imperfect form. At the end of her long isolation, she leaps passionately at her last chance for freedom and happiness. Combined inextricably with her natural pity for Dimmesdale is her natural, passionate love for him and her desire for happiness. Their relationship cannot exclude passionate affection. She throws the scarlet letter aside and lets down her dark hair. " 'The past is gone!' " she cries, " '. . . See! With this symbol, I undo it all, and make it as [if] it had never been!' "

But of course the past cannot be undone, and little Pearl, the living result of the past—the emblem also of responsibility to the community for one's past actions—will not come to Hester until her mother puts on the familiar letter again and pins up her hair once more. Hester becomes truly, voluntarily penitent only after her lover has died; only then does she return to New England without a selfish motive.

Dimmesdale, the secret sinner, is also a remarkable study in psychology. His private, partial penitence only becomes a greater punishment, for he shows remarkable cunning in punishing himself by vague hints of confession that work to his public benefit. Throughout the book he denies his natural, human connection with Hester and their child. His awareness of his own guilt keeps his preaching at a level that the most lowly can understand; but the more revered he becomes in his public success, the more painfully he realizes that his every public action violates his cardinal principle of honesty, or truth. The principle he violates is the most important article of Puritan belief and of nineteenth-century romantic individualism: the requirement that a man be a *true* believer, or a *true* confessor, that he reveal to God and to the world what he really is.

Thus it is a mistake to believe that with Dimmesdale, any more than with Hester, Hawthorne concentrates only on the original sin of adultery. Both morally and psychologically, Dimmesdale re-enacts a graver, far more damaging fault every day. His worst punishment is that *all other reality becomes unreal.* Knowing that his penitence is false but unable to think long about other things, he extends his egotism outward into the universe, interpreting a comet and other phenomena as messages sent directly from God to himself. His agony is so severe that the letter "A" which he has secretly seared into his flesh is not too extreme a symbol of his self-torture. His self-punishment is psychological as well as physical, and in portraying him Hawthorne anticipates the dark insights of Dostoevsky.

Roger Chillingworth represents Hawthorne's idea of the unpardonable sinner. Hawthorne, fascinated by the problem of guilt and forgiveness, had once asked in his notebooks what might constitute the unpardonable sin; his answer had come in language that was appropriate to Christian and romantic terminology: the violation of another soul, another heart, simply for the purpose of finding out how it would react. Chillingworth is almost wholly intellectual. From the beginning, he voluntarily isolates himself. Having married a passionate woman much younger than himself, he has sent her alone to the New World; when he discovers her disgrace, he denies his very identity—presumably in order to avoid being known for a cuckold, but also to seek revenge. He thus abandons almost all his human claims on society. He resolves to pursue the secret, *"if only for the art's sake."* With cold science, and a hint of black arts learned from savages in the wilderness, he pries into Dimmesdale's heart for the secret, and he seeks an absolutely perfect revenge: he wants to appear as the best friend to his worst enemy, so that he may torture at will and at last destroy Dimmesdale's soul. His desperate effort in the last scene to prevent Dimmesdale from confessing on the scaffold thus has its allegorical and its psychological validity. Chillingworth's very existence depends on Dimmesdale; curiosity and revenge constitute the obsession that has consumed his life.

Always, then, along with the allegory and the fundamental moral emphasis, Hawthorne is faithful to human psychology, and it is the fusion of these two that gives the book much of its value. In blending them Hawthorne reveals magnificent control of point of view, the position from which the action is seen, for he presents the most important interpretations of individual objects and actions as the interpretations of seventeenth-century characters. Let us consider two kinds of example, the one a character and the other a series of physical phenomena.

Consider first the wildness of little Pearl, the child of the two guilty lovers. To her mother and to all the Puritan characters she is a living emblem of the mother's sin; a major part of Hawthorne's criticism of Puritan thinking is that society's insistence on seeing human beings merely as emblems. In the action of the novel, moreover, Pearl represents the conscience of the community, and evidence that the community is inevitably concerned in the actions of individuals who may wish to escape it. But we must notice that Hawthorne calls little Pearl "a born outcast of the infantile world." He portrays her as an anxious child, what today we would call a hostile child. He takes great care to show us from the opening scene of the book that the infant's mother communicates her own turmoil to the child. With remarkable skill he presents this sort of evidence through the mother's eyes and through the Puritan community's interpretation. The infant, clutched tightly by the mother during the ordeal on the scaffold, "reflects the warfare of Hester's spirit" by breaking into convulsions. Both the mother and other people in the community expect the child to show signs of her sinful origin, and so *they* interpret Pearl's violent temper and some of her wisely perceptive questions as evidence of her bondage to the Devil. What Hawthorne shows us through their interpretations, then, are the natural consequences of a childhood in which the community rejects mother and child, in which an anxious, confused, rebellious mother persists in asking, "Child, what art thou?" and then allows the child to be ruled, not by discipline, but by impulse.

Hawthorne amasses this evidence so skillfully that careless readers are apt to be deceived by the allegorical interpretations into thinking the child preternaturally gifted. What we must remember is that almost every interpretation of Pearl's behavior comes to us through the mind of some seventeenth-century observer and that the child herself has every reason to ask the penetrating questions she asks: Why does her mother wear a scarlet letter? Why does the pale minister who argued so eloquently before the Governor for Hester Prynne's right to retain custody of the child hold the child's hand on the scaffold at midnight, but not in broad daylight? Why does her mother take off the letter and the tight cap in the wild forest, where no child could fail to notice that a new intimacy seems to exist with the minister?

Hawthorne's introduction of symbols is also doubly effective, for he takes excellent advantage of the Puritans' habit of interpreting the smallest signs as expressions of the will of

God. The real Puritans actually interpreted an event such as the killing of a snake in a church as a sign from the divine Providence that governed all human affairs, and Hawthorne had read Puritan journals in which extraordinary phenomena such as the appearance of a comet and more ordinary events such as a mouse's chewing pages from the Book of Common Prayer were seriously interpreted as providential warnings. Throughout *The Scarlet Letter* Hawthorne shows us such phenomena and the Puritan characters' reading of them. One of the most memorably effective is the suit of armor that Pearl and Hester encounter in the hall of the Governor's mansion when Hester comes there to plead for her right to retain the child. In the convex breastplate Pearl sees that the scarlet letter on her mother's breast is reflected in a monstrously magnified form and that the woman herself is almost dwarfed behind it. Through the mother's reaction to this image Hawthorne lets us see (without commenting explicitly himself) how monstrously the society had magnified the importance of one person's sin, and of all sin, so that the individual character and the individual soul and perhaps the individual sin were virtually hidden from view.

The same kind of double relevance gives great value to Hawthorne's exploitation of the natural landscape in this novel. For the seventeenth-century Puritans the city of Boston and the colony of Massachusetts Bay represented the orderly outpost of God's people in the hostile world of the godless, and for them the American wilderness was the realm of disorder, the last stronghold of the Devil. In the romantic world of nineteenth-century American thought, the domain of untouched nature was not far different from this demonic wilderness, for there one's most primitive feelings, the individual will, ungoverned by any notion of divine authority or universal ethics, might find free expression. The wilderness in which Hester Prynne meets Arthur Dimmesdale is thus a bewilderingly ambiguous territory. As we smile at the Puritan's rudimentary effort to read the meaning of natural signs, Hawthorne does not let us forget that the meaning of external nature, like the facts and meaning of human history and the world of human psychology, remains a mystery. Is the forest the domain of evil or the domain of natural love? Does the settlement of the American wilderness bring order and godliness and progress or injustice and misery and crime?

The riddle extends, as I have suggested, to human history itself, not merely to the meaning but even to the facts. In this novel the market place of the new city of Boston is dominated by the gloomy prison, which already seems black with age, and by the scaffold; it is the scaffold that dominates Hawthorne's novel. Yet in spite of all that the narrator can do to reconstruct from a few musty records the life, the unforgettable feelings, of such characters as Hester Prynne, he cannot know and he cannot tell us some of the most important facts. At the end of the novel, Hawthorne is careful to point out, the historian must recognize a certain confusion about what the Reverend Mr. Dimmesdale had done before he died on the scaffold. As we read the dramatic scene itself we have no doubt that Dimmesdale confesses as he embraces Hester and Pearl. But later the honest narrator must tell us that "highly respectable witnesses" denied that the minister had revealed an "A" seared into the flesh over his heart; indeed, they denied that Dimmesdale had ever confessed or even "remotely implied" his complicity in the guilt of Hester Prynne.

I do not believe that Hawthorne means to throw the entire story into confusion at this point. What he does is to remind us that our knowledge of men and their actions is as limited as our knowledge of the meaning of natural phenomena. The little we can be certain of is symbolized by the scraps of evidence that remain, and among them one of the most certain, one of the most universal, is the device on Hester Prynne's tombstone: on a black field, the red letter "A." Just as the characters in the novel interpret phenomena according to their preconceptions, so we may interpret this last symbol in the book according to our own lights. Yet we cannot fail to consider the possibility that this final device might represent two certainties of human fate: the luridness of sin and the blackness of death. The futility of human effort, in the dead certainty of oblivion and the virtual impossibility of knowing truly, hangs like a pall over this magnificently gloomy book.

Hawthorne brought to the American novel an admirable talent for symbolism and a serious interest in historical fidelity, psychological truth, and social order. No English or American novelist before him had been able to represent so convincingly the feelings and thoughts of a passionate woman, and scarcely any American novelist had posed such forcefully critical questions for prevailing nineteenth-century beliefs. It is easy to understand, therefore, why Herman Melville greeted Hawthorne's work with the shock of recognition. In the combination of allegory and historical romance Hawthorne required citizens of the land of progress to consider fundamental questions about human ability and human history. His best book continues to pose these questions for us more than a century later.

3 HERMAN MELVILLE
Moby Dick

Leon Howard

Moby Dick is one of those rare works of literature that have a capacity for growth through some inner vitality which increases with time. Of the nine novels Herman Melville published during his lifetime, it stood midway between his successes and his failures. In fact, it might be counted a failure because it was out of print during the last half of its author's life and remained out of print until the centenary of his birth and the revival of interest in him at that time. Since 1919, however, it has been recognized as a masterpiece—the sort of masterpiece that can serve as a mirror to the changing thoughts and feelings of changing times. It has been examined from many angles by many literary critics and ordinary readers, and it always reflects something new. Some of the reflections associated with it are profound. Some are distorted, superficial, and fleeting. But all have added to our awareness of depths beneath its surface which have not yet been penetrated and which challenge other angles of vision from countries other than America.

What kind of book could have such an exciting effect upon readers of whom its author could not have dreamed? By what complicated act of sensitive perception and creative imagination could it have come into existence? On the surface, it is a mixture of fantasy and realism based upon the South Pacific whaling industry, which was a major commercial activity in mid-nineteenth-century America. The narrator, who calls himself Ishmael to symbolize his position as an outcast wanderer, ships aboard a whaling vessel in New Bedford and finds himself in a real world of hard work and dangerous activity and a strangely unreal world of speculation and mystery. The crew represents most of the races of the world. The captain, in the opinion of the narrator, is mad. The other officers are sane enough, but they are completely dominated by the captain's obsessed determination to pursue, throughout the world, one particular white whale who had previously destroyed the captain's boat and attacked him, leaving him mutilated in body with an artificial leg and injured in mind by the passion for revenge. The story tells of the pursuit and the events incidental to it and of the final epic conflict between man and beast.

Melville names his book after the whale, Moby Dick, and makes the pursuit curiously plausible by emphasizing the notoriety of the easily recognizable, white-humped monster and by using the latest scientific researches into the habits and migrations of the sperm whale. He also gives a factually accurate, though frequently melodramatic, account of the procedures and techniques of whale hunting—the preparation of equipment, the harpooning, the cutting up, and the rendering of the blubber into oil—all of which adds to the verisimilitude of his tale. More than that, he explains the means by which Captain Ahab gains dominance over the mixed crew of savages and civilized men in a way which is psychologically convincing even to modern readers. Yet the book is not naturalistic. Its action is fabulous. Its characters have mythological overtones. Its rhetoric is romantic; its language, suggestive and symbolic. It raises more questions than it answers. No one should read it unless he is willing to risk an extraordinary stimulation to his mind and his emotions.

"What can such a book as Moby Dick mean?" is the question which most often comes to the minds of its readers and the question most eagerly—and variously—answered by literary critics. Its fable has been so often interpreted in so many ways, allegorically and symbolically, that we can now say that Moby Dick "means" almost as many things as it has readers who are deeply involved in the conflicts of life and sensitive enough to become involved in the spirit of conflict expressed in a work of art. To impose any single, literal, orthodox, authoritative meaning upon it would be to destroy the living vitality, the suggestiveness, and the stimulation that are the distinctive qualities of the novel and the essence of Melville's literary art. A more important—because it is perhaps, in the long run, a more illuminating—question concerns the nature of the art: "How was such a book created?"

Like many another work of fiction, *Moby Dick* grew out of its author's experience in living, reading, and reflecting, reconstituted by the imagination under the influence of some new intensity of emotion and purpose at the time of writing. The basic material of the novel came from his own life. He had been a whaler, on three different vessels, in the South Pacific for two and a half years, signing up like Ishmael on a desperate Christmas day in New Bedford and later writing successfully about his experiences, though reserving the technical details of whaling for some special treatment. He had also read every book he could buy or borrow about whaling, and he continued to read while his own book was going through the press, checking his observations and making supplementary ones in footnotes. Furthermore, he had reflected, in private and in one published book review, about the inadequacies of other writers on whaling: none had dealt with what he called the wild and romantic legends of the business —the folklore and tall tales of desperation and courage and of the several almost mythological whales known by such names as Timor Tom and Mocha Dick of whose fierceness every new boatsman was warned to beware.

No one who had not experienced the power of the sea and the excitement of the chase could have written *Moby Dick;* and Melville, we know, was stirred to write the book by a revival of his sea-feeling when he made a voyage to England in the winter of 1849 after having been five years on shore. For when he began his voyage he was planning and making notes in his journal for a historical novel related to the American Revolution. But upon his return, in February 1850, he plunged into something different and wrote so rapidly that within five and one-half months he was able to take a vacation in western Massachusetts and there show one of his friends a manuscript that the friend described as an almost completed "romantic, fanciful and literal and most enjoyable presentment of the whale fishery." But this could not have been the *Moby Dick* we now read, because it was more than a year before that book was ready for the printer and that year (as we know from Melville's letters) was filled with the intense enthusiasm and sometimes the agony of creative excitement. Something happened which stirred him to depths he had never felt before and which caused him gradually to cease referring to his book as a story of "the whale fishery" and to call it his story of "the Whale."

What happened was a simple trigger action which set off a large explosive charge. The action occurred on August 5, 1850, when a number of other literary celebrities were brought together for a country picnic and a dinner party afterward. They formed a mixed group from Boston and New York—the rival literary capitals of the United States at that time—who were different in temperament and who differed in the literary theories to which they subscribed. The New Yorkers were rather naïve and solemn advocates of common nineteenth-century theories concerning the effect of environment on genius. They believed that America was destined to produce a literature as sweeping as its prairies, as mighty as its rivers, and as elevated as its mountains. The New Englanders were skeptical and sardonic, less chauvinistic and more international, more inclined toward satire than toward enthusiasm.

The result was a memorable literary quarrel, which eventually focused on the question whether America could produce a writer of Shakespearean stature. Melville maintained that such a writer, in the nineteenth century, would be a novelist rather than a dramatist, and that he would be more candid than Shakespeare in revealing the black underside of life and speaking the "sane madness of vital truth." Such candor he found, a few days later, in the New England writer Nathaniel Hawthorne, whom he had first met on this occa-

sion and whose stories he had just begun to read with enthusiasm. There is substantial scholarly evidence, in fact, that
Melville began rewriting his book with the challenge of
Shakespearean tragedy in his imagination and the example
of Hawthorne's dark "truth-telling" in his mind.

But what would he dramatize? Shakespeare's mad King
Lear, wildly defying the strongest forces of nature, appealed
strongly to his imagination; so did Hamlet, who, as Coleridge
described him, "looks upon external things as hieroglyphics"
and whose mind is "unseated from its healthy relations" by
his "everlasting broodings." Captain Ahab, the protagonist
of Melville's drama, came to resemble them both as he developed into the type of hero Melville described as "formed for
the noblest tragedies." His proper antagonist became the
white whale, Moby Dick, who was represented in naturalistic
terms as the largest and most powerful animated force in
nature and in symbolic terms as the visible emblem of all
that Ahab considered malignant and evil—"the monomaniac
incarnation," as the narrator put it, "of all those malicious
agencies which some deep men feel eating in them, till they
are left living on with half a heart and half a lung." This
incarnation Ahab was determined to destroy. He would defy
the intangible malignancy of the universe by striking at its
visible emblem. He was mutilated, frustrated, made prisoner
by chance and circumstance, and the white whale had come to
represent the walls of his prison, the "unreasoning mask" of
fate. Sometimes he thought there was naught beyond. But he
had an overwhelming compulsion to "strike through the
mask."

The action, then, is made dramatic by the intensity of
Ahab's purpose, which captures the imagination of his half-
savage crew and subdues the protests of his sane and sensible
first mate. No one can resist the determination which drives
him halfway round the world until he can engage in his final,
magnificent, three-day battle with the whale. But there is
another drama implicit in the long narrative which precedes
this spectacular climax. It can be felt in the very texture of
the narrative—the contrasts between heightened emotional-

ism and factual realism—and in the style of Melville's prose, which ranges from high rhetoric to matter-of-fact description. It is evident in the contrast between Ahab's passionate fury and his shrewd calculation of the course a wandering whale might take. It is symbolized in a description of the ship trying to achieve a balance between two whales' heads, one representing the philosophy of the British empiricist, John Locke, and the other the German transcendentalist Immanuel Kant. It is more plainly revealed in the choice Melville allows the reader to make in interpreting the "fable" of his drama.

If the reader accepts Ahab's view of himself, then the captain of the "Pequod" becomes a hero in the grand tradition, defying fate and all the evil it has to offer until he is destroyed but not defeated. The tradition is basically romantic and especially Byronic, for although Ahab (like his prototype of the same name in the Old Testament) may have "done evil in the sight of the Lord" he possesses the unconquerable pride of Lord Byron's Cain or Manfred. But Melville had a closer model than the Byronic hero. It was the transcendental hero of Thomas Carlyle's *Sartor Resartus*—a book Melville had borrowed shortly before he began the rewriting of *Moby Dick* and read with an enthusiasm which perceptibly influenced his style. Many of Carlyle's mannerisms are reflected in *Moby Dick,* and so are certain characteristics of his humor. And Captain Ahab's view of himself reflects Carlyle's transcendental philosophy: "all visible things are emblems" of some spiritual reality, he had said in *Sartor Resartus,* and they "body it forth." Ahab's similar attitude toward the white whale was expressed in similar language, and his response to it was precisely the response of Carlyle's hero to his conviction that the universe was rolling on to grind him "limb from limb"—a courageous expression of unshakable defiance.

In Carlyle's novel, however, this defiance was a prelude to illumination, faith and an acceptance of the universe. In Melville's it was a prelude to tragedy. Ahab's transcendental notions formed the "tragic flaw" in an otherwise heroic character. The dark fable of Melville's drama is not of man's defeat before the forces of a malignant or indifferent universe. It is of man's defeat within himself.

In order to make this clear we need to go back to that exciting week in early August, 1850, when Melville was being simultaneously stirred by his new conception of a Shakespearean novel and by his discovery of Shakespearean qualities in Hawthorne. It is a certain "blackness in Hawthorne," he wrote at the time, "that so fixes and fascinates me": and he explained his fascination by saying that it was this same blackness of truth, "probings at the very axis of reality" which "make Shakespeare Shakespeare." Melville found this quality explicit in several of Hawthorne's stories. One was called "Earth's Holocaust"; in it all the "vanities and empty theories and forms" of the world were consumed in an allegorical fire but were re-created by "the all-engendering heart of man." Melville found a "profound" and "appalling" moral in Hawthorne's symbolic expression of a belief that evil existed in the heart of man rather than in his external environment. The way this evil affected man was illustrated in another story, "Young Goodman Brown," which Melville found "deep as Dante." In this tale a young man of Puritan New England attends a witches' sabbath and as a result loses his "Faith," allegorically represented by a wife with that name but presented clearly in psychological terms as his confidence that things were what they seemed to be. Whether the experience was a reality or a dream was never made clear nor did it need to be. Hawthorne (and Melville with him) was interested in the psychology of a young man like the Hamlet described by Coleridge who looked upon external things as hieroglyphics and whose mind became unseated from its healthy relations by its everlasting broodings.

Melville's extravagant admiration for these stories by Hawthorne helps explain the narrator Ishmael's view of Ahab, which is altogether that of a man making a psychological diagnosis: Ahab had developed a "frantic morbidness" which caused him to associate with the white whale "not only his bodily woes, but all his intellectual and spiritual exasperations." A sense of self-destructive "intangible malignity," which had existed in the human race from the beginning of time and to which "some deep men" were peculiarly susceptible, had mutilated Ahab's mind until "deliriously transferring its idea to the abhorred white whale, he pitted himself, all mutilated, against it." The fable, then, became that of a noble mind that engendered its own evil and gave birth to tragedy. Or, as Melville put it more explicitly elsewhere in the book: "Be sure of this, O young ambition, all mortal greatness is but disease."

This was not an easy fable for Melville to create or even for him to accept as a means for giving form to his book. His many years as a sailor in the South Seas, among the natives and the missionaries and on board whalers and a man-of-war, had made him a skeptical observer of human illusions and pretensions. But he had a great supply of intellectual energy, ambition, and the will to believe in something. Before he met and read Hawthorne he had been developing a strong interest in transcendental philosophy, listening to Emerson, talking enthusiastically with young transcendentalists, and reading Coleridge as well as Carlyle. The "blackness of truth" he found in Hawthorne brought him back to his earlier attitude of mind and curbed his new enthusiasm for strange ideas. It appealed strongly to the intellectual but not to the emotional side of his nature.

There is one fascinating chapter in *Moby Dick,* called "The Whiteness of the Whale," which in fact shows Melville struggling against his own convictions by trying to find evidence of some sort of knowledge, in man and in beasts, that transcended inductive knowledge based on experience. But the struggle affected the whole of the book. It lies back of the contrasts between fervor and factuality which are observable in his treatment of incident and in his style. It is to be found in the puzzling position of the narrator of the story, who is sometimes a detached observer and commentator but who is often completely consumed in the heat of the action. It leads to all sorts of ambivalences and ambiguities, conflicting implications, and suggestive symbolism which Melville did not bother—and probably would not have been able—to clarify. The tension of an intellectual conflict within Melville himself provides a dramatic texture for the whole narrative.

This conflict, however, was not peculiar to Melville. It was characteristic of the age in which he lived, and the distinctive power of *Moby Dick* is derived from its author's good fortune in being able to incorporate within himself and dramatize in a novel the major intellectual conflict of a century. Later, in the post-Darwinian period, it found a widespread popular expression in a conflict between "religion" and "science." By mid-century, in the more sophisticated literature of England, it had already acquired commonplace symbols as a conflict between "faith" and "doubt." But when the young American sat down in a farmhouse attic, a few days after his thirty-first birthday, to rework his whaling manuscript, nobody was exercised over a conflict between "transcendentalism" and "empiricism" or intuitive as opposed to inductive knowledge. These were philosophical terms used to describe ways of knowing—theories of knowledge which were in active conflict in Melville's day but which had not yet acquired labels that made the conflict obvious. Melville felt the conflict deeply, but he had to invent his own symbols in order to give it meaning.

In doing so, he invented far better than he could have known. Unable to use the abstract words which satisfied his later contemporaries who became involved in the same conflict, he invented a man—a strange, unreal, mythological creature in some respects, but characteristically human in his tendency to evade his perplexities by creating a symbol which gave his life a purpose and his actions meaning. Ahab had the driving purpose of inspiration and the practical shrewdness of a successful man of affairs. He could project part of his personality into the object of his hunt and devote the other part single-mindedly to the details of hunting. He may have been misguided and even mad, but he was never whipped or beaten. He destroyed himself through his own obsession, but he was never conquered.

Melville identified himself with his hero emotionally but disapproved of him intellectually. He admired Ahab for his unshakable heroism, for, as he wrote Hawthorne, he admired all defiant individuals who were prepared to "cross the frontiers into Eternity with nothing but a carpetbag—that is to

33

say, the Ego." But he himself was defying the grandest and noblest illusions of his age when he called Ahab's inspired heroism madness and insisted that all human greatness is but disease. He had written "a wicked book," he said when he had finished, but felt as "spotless as a lamb."

What Melville could not have known was that his later readers would live in a century infinitely more perplexing than his own. It would be a century that offered no simple choice between empirical and transcendental ways of knowing. It would be a century in which the habit of thinking in symbols became commonplace but in which a judgment upon the value of such thinking would become increasingly difficult. We of the twentieth century use the symbols of mathematics to explore the secrets of the atom and those of outer space. We use the symbols of psychiatry to try to cure the frustrations that killed Ahab. The symbols of race, religion, and rival economic systems have become inscrutable monstrosities in the minds of many men. The boundaries between the real and the imaginary have broken down, and we are becoming accustomed to a world that is half naturalistic and half a creation of our own minds. We create symbols to guide our researches, direct our ambitions, and focus our hates— and we have no ready means of distinguishing between those that represent intuitive short cuts to truth and those that represent a neurotic refusal to face the facts of an environment which has become too complex for our inductive faculties. We live in the world of Ahab more completely than Herman Melville or his contemporaries did, and so long as that world continues to exist we will find in *Moby Dick* the stimulating vitality of a story which is partly our own.

4 JOHN W. De FOREST
Miss Ravenel's Conversion

Claude M. Simpson, Jr.

The Civil War which engulfed the United States a century
ago has had a stronger hold on the American imagination
than the two world wars which have recently affected mankind all over the globe. During the present centennial years
the nation's interest has been focused anew on every phase of
the 1861–65 conflict, even to a recent re-enactment of the
fateful battle of Gettysburg for the benefit of curious specta-
tors. Books about the issues underlying the war began to
appear long before fighting erupted. The melodramatic and
sensational *Uncle Tom's Cabin* (1852) was a best seller in
Europe as well as America. There were also many incendiary
tracts such as Hinton R. Helper's *The Impending Crisis of
the South* (1857), which advocated taxing slavery out of existence and sending the Negroes back to Africa. Once the
Civil War became history the flood of books began and has
never stopped; even now some fifty new works are appearing
each year, and the fresh documentation, interpretation, and
reinterpretation seem to find a responsive and dedicated
public.

Among the hundreds of novels about the Civil War
Margaret Mitchell's panoramic *Gone With the Wind* (1936)
is perhaps the most widely known, and Stephen Crane's *Red
Badge of Courage* (1895) is most notable as a pioneering psychological study. Both books enjoyed great public acclaim,
and Crane's small volume is a permanent contribution to the
literature of war as nightmare, impressionistically rendered.

But it is not such books as these that I plan to examine. I propose rather to discuss a neglected novel, one of the very first to appear after the Civil War, written by a man whose reputation has always hovered on the borderline between oblivion and substantial recognition. The novel is called *Miss Ravenel's Conversion from Secession to Loyalty*—a bad title because the main interests of the book are not concerned with ideological affiliations. It was written in 1865, within a few months of the end of the war, but it was not published until 1867. Its author is John W. De Forest, a New Englander who, as a captain in the Union army, saw action in Louisiana and Virginia. His experience determined the structure of the novel. What makes it a notable document, what led Howells to compare De Forest to Tolstoi, what accounts for the continued interest in the book, is its strong vein of realism, its hard look at heroics and heroism, its refusal to idealize war or those who wage it. In these senses De Forest was pointing ahead to the skepticisms of our own century, and we recognize his book as a ground-breaking work even though it contains some trappings of mid-nineteenth-century romance.

De Forest had lived in both the South and the North before the war and thus acquired a perspective shared by few fellow authors. In addition, he had traveled widely in Europe and the Near East during the 1850's, a decade in which Melville traced some of the same routes and Hawthorne immersed himself in England and Italy. De Forest wrote two books on his travels. And before the war determined the direction of his absorbing interests, he tried his hand at fiction with *Witching Times,* a novel concerning the Salem witchcraft hysteria in the seventeenth century, and *Seacliff,* an undistinguished novel of manners. After recruiting a company of Union soldiers in New Haven, Connecticut, he commenced a series of detailed factual letters to his wife (first published in 1946 as *A Volunteer's Adventures*); these, plus certain magazine articles describing his first experience under fire and the siege of Port Hudson,[1] supplied raw material from which he fashioned much of *Miss Ravenel's Conversion.*

[1] *Harper's Monthly*, XXIX (Sept. 1864), 475–482, and XXXV (Aug. 1867), 334–344.

The New York publishing house of Harper purchased the novel for $1250, intending first to serialize it in *Harper's Monthly*. But it seemed too strong for the magazine's family audience and the serialization was dropped in favor of book publication in 1867. Among the reviewers was William Dean Howells, who praised the lifelikeness of De Forest's characters, declaring that "his soldiers are the soldiers we actually know," and calling De Forest "the first to treat the war really and artistically." [2] From this time forward, Howells championed De Forest and did his best to help him gain a public, although he recognized the drawback that De Forest appealed more to men than to the feminine novel-reading audience.

We define De Forest's point of view toward the Civil War when we say that as a Northerner he is strongly dedicated to the preservation of the Union. He has no sympathy for secession or for aristocratic attitudes toward slavery, but he respects the skill of Southern troops. His central consciousness in the novel is Edward Colburne, a modest young lawyer of New Boston (a fictional town modeled on New Haven). Colburne has no military ambition but is commissioned and undertakes to raise a regiment. The task proves to be difficult, once the initial patriotic fervor has passed, and De Forest examines the political problems of recruiting with a certain wry amusement, sharpened by the personal resentment he felt toward party hacks who were given choice military assignments.

As the war progresses, the New England troops are sent by sea to the mouth of the Mississippi for a bold attack on New Orleans. De Forest gives us a series of effective battle scenes, detailing the realities of campaigning with an honest eye to their hardships and crudities. He is often aware of war as a psychological conditioner; here he anticipates themes which Stephen Crane would later develop with great distinction. De Forest recognizes the inevitable emergence of cowardice and fear. He examines closely what he calls the "butchery" of field surgery, with its terrible impact on the psyche of victim and spectator alike. He is especially interesting as he describes

[2] *Atlantic Monthly*, XX (July 1867), 121.

the absolute surprise of a mortal wound. An officer writes his wife:

> I had just finished breakfast, and was lying on my back smoking. A bullet . . . struck with a loud smash in a tree about twenty feet from me. Between me and the tree a soldier with his greatcoat rolled under his head for a pillow lay on his back reading a newspaper which he held in both hands. I remember smiling to myself to see this man start as the bullet passed. . . . [He] remained perfectly still, his eyes fixed on the paper. . . . Presently I noticed that there were a few drops of blood on his neck, and that his face was paling. Calling to the card players [nearby] I said, "See to that man with the paper." They went to him, spoke to him, touched him, and found him perfectly dead. The ball had struck him under the chin, traversed the neck, and cut the spinal column where it joins the brain. . . . It was this man's head and not the tree which had been struck with such a report. There he lay, still holding the New York *Independent*, with his eyes fixed on a sermon by Henry Ward Beecher.[3]

This is underplayed, matter-of-fact reporting, but we notice that De Forest does not stake everything on the ironic detail of the steadily held newspaper, or on the fact that the man is reading a sermon when his life is suddenly quenched. As Gordon Haight has observed, the scene is less theatrical than one to which it has been compared—a famous passage in Crane's *Red Badge of Courage* (Ch. 8) in which the young soldier Henry Fleming, gripped by fear, has run away from his company and stumbles into a cathedral-like clearing in the forest. He comes upon a dead soldier seated with his back to a tree. Crane cannot forbear to tell us that "over the gray skin of the face ran little ants." Henry Fleming shrieks and is unable to move as he stares into the open eyes. The drama here is obviously contrived, and its purpose is not to record a

3 This and all subsequent quotations are from the 1867 text of *Miss Ravenel's Conversion*, as represented by Gordon S. Haight's edition issued as a Rinehart paperback in 1955. A revised text, prepared by De Forest in 1887 when he hoped that a collected edition of his works might be published, was the basis of the 1939 Harper issue, also edited by Professor Haight. It went out of print during World War II and, although superior in some respects, has not been influential.

soldier's death, but to describe an inexperienced youngster's confrontation with macabre details associated with death and to exhibit to us ironies lost on Henry Fleming. Crane's intentions are more complex than De Forest's, partly because Crane is filtering sensation through a more limited mind than the alert intelligence of De Forest's point of view. De Forest's method aims at objective realism, presenting us with fact and leaving us free to draw inferences as we will; to be sure, the author, like a photographer, has arranged his picture and has led our eye by his own selectivity and emphasis. Crane is less interested in fact than in the impression made by certain limited sensory data, and herein lies an important distinction between the two men.

De Forest's glimpses of war include training scenes, boresome inactivity, the occupation of a city, sharp pitched battles (some of which the Union forces do not win), and one extended siege. Where Crane concentrated his action within a few days, De Forest is concerned with the four-year span of the war, and allows us to see how experience toughens and even brutalizes some of his soldiers. Moreover, he looks closely at the phenomenon of military occupation. He describes how the Yankee troops take over New Orleans and run it, how some Southerners are quick to curry favor while others proudly resist any recognition of the conquerors. Rich opportunities for "plunder and low dissipation" await the military officials, whom De Forest pictures as often vulgar and boorish—foreshadowing the post-Civil-War Washington corruption he would later examine in a novel of congressional intrigue, *Honest John Vane* (1875).

Miss Ravenel's Conversion is held together by character rather than plot. The story, reduced to its essentials, contrasts the upright but unexciting Colburne with the dashing, worldly, corrupt Colonel Carter. In New Boston they both meet Dr. Ravenel, a Northerner who has lived much in the South, and his daughter Lillie, whose sympathies are wholly southern. She nevertheless becomes smitten with Colonel Carter. The Ravenels turn up in New Orleans to salvage some of their property from the army of occupation and Lillie

39

marries Colonel Carter. Before the end of the war a distant relative of hers, the fleshly thirty-three-year-old widow Mrs. Larue, compromises Carter. He dies in battle and as the war ends Colburne recovers from his wound and marries Lillie.

This could be a rather mawkish story. What saves it? First of all, a strong antiromantic tone which runs through the book, reinforced by De Forest's Thackeray-like intrusions which deliberately undercut soft sentiment or fond illusion. Although we may dislike the puppeteer's presence, a kind of honesty results when De Forest declares of Lillie Ravenel: "I suppose I ought to state [that she] was very fair," but then he protests against public tastes, adding, "Why then should I strain my conscience by asserting broadly and positively that [she] was a first-class beauty?" On another occasion when he is about to build up a romantic scene between Lillie and a would-be suitor, he deliberately destroys the atmosphere by summarizing the futile scene at once—to spare the reader, he says, "the trouble of turning over a few pages." He apologizes for analyzing Colburne at length, but "the truth is that I take a sympathetic interest in him," and he tells us that Colburne would make Lillie a better husband than the Colonel, "whom she insists upon having."

A second quality of the novel which rescues it from oblivion is its unvarnished view of human character. Although Colburne and Lillie are motivated by respectable moral and ethical principles, De Forest tries not to idealize them. He shows Lillie to be flighty and occasionally shallow, moved by an easy emotionalism; and of course she chooses the wrong man for a husband just because she can be dazzled by an impressive worldliness. De Forest is occasionally severe in respect to Colburne's Puritan stiffness; Colburne is overly serious, and as a male Cinderella is not especially attractive to impressionable females. Much of the life of the book, therefore, resides in the other characters, whose very imperfections make them interesting. Van Zandt, the Colonel's aide, is a resourceful and unprincipled junior officer, drunken and profane. Gazaway is a political appointee, an opportunistic coward and bribetaker. The chief exhibits are Colonel Carter and Mrs. Larue, both of whom are complex enough to deserve our attention and can't be dismissed merely because of some of their obvious personal weaknesses.

Colonel Carter is an amalgam of North and South. He is a Virginian, but has a Connecticut ancestor; he was educated at West Point and is a Union man. (One wonders if De Forest was consciously contrasting Carter with the most notable Confederate officer, General Robert E. Lee, who was also a Virginia West Pointer and was often criticized for turning his back on the federal government which had educated him.) Carter, though not a career Army officer, nevertheless has a professional bearing which sets him off from the greenness of the citizen-soldiers who surround him. Beyond his professional skill, he possesses conflicting personal qualities, admirable and otherwise. He is a hard drinker, a high liver, always in debt for his pleasures, and clearly involved in amorous affairs which, though shadowy, are explicit. He is also gracious, considerate, and fascinating to such an innocent as Lillie Ravenel. His flaws lead him into financial difficulties, and he makes a desperate move to recoup by misappropriating $100,000 of government funds. When his cotton speculation collapses, he concocts an equally dishonest scheme for selling and rebuying government ships so that he may restore the embezzled funds. In this venture the corrupt man succeeds; to cap the irony, within a few days he is promoted to brigadier general, an honor for which he knows he is unfit. Meantime he has let himself be seduced all too easily by Mrs. Larue. The evidence is unmistakable in a letter that falls into Lillie's hands; as De Forest phrases it, "the writer was a guilty woman, and she addressed a guilty man," recalling past assignations and fixing a time "for a future one."

From this point to the end of the book, De Forest alternates between stereotypes of sentimental fiction and subtly accurate insights into human character—compromises resulting from what Edmund Wilson called "an attempt to meet the public halfway." [4] Lillie faints upon reading the incriminating

[4] *Patriotic Gore* (New York: Oxford University Press, 1962), p. 707. Wilson's study of De Forest, pp. 669–742, is detailed and intelligently sympathetic.

41

letter and determines never to see Carter again. She and her father and her young son, Ravvie, leave for the North; all this is cut from the cloth of stage melodrama. But De Forest shrewdly traces Lillie's states of mind as she finds that she does not miss Carter very much, once he has joined the Union army in the field. She probably could have forgiven him, and she can say simply, "I hope he will not be killed," and mean it. Poetic justice seems to demand his end, and he meets it courageously in battle. In a powerful scene De Forest gives him a hero's death without condescension, thus avoiding what might have been stale, didactic manipulation of a character who engages our sympathies despite his flaws.

The equally flawed Mrs. Larue, however, escapes without punishment. The last we see of her she has mended her fortune in a successful (and during wartime, illegal) cotton speculation. De Forest understands her well enough to define her ethical scruples precisely: she didn't mean to cause trouble between husband and wife; why didn't Carter burn her letter—she had burned all of his. Howells felt that there was too much of Mrs. Larue in the novel—and in truth she overshadows the less interesting Lillie. Mrs. Larue is sensual, her Creole morality conveniently elastic (and De Forest suggests a contrast between Catholic license and the Puritan strictness of New Boston). Her fleshliness is implicit in much of her conversation, and when explicit she lapses into French to say things perhaps too strong for De Forest's audience to read in English. If she gave Howells the shudders, we may see in his reaction an unwitting tribute to De Forest's success in so depicting her that her regeneration would be implausible.[5]

Although De Forest's narrative method allows him to intrude at will, his asides instruct us on tangential issues such as the unfairness of the military promotion system or the evils of intemperance. His most important opinions usually come to us through a chorus figure, Dr. Ravenel. Lillie's father was trained in medicine but his present pursuit is min-

[5] Howells' observations on Mrs. Larue are contained in his review of the novel, *Atlantic Monthly*, XX (July 1867), 122, and in his *Heroines of Fiction* (New York: Harper, 1901), II, 157.

eralogy. He has lived in New Orleans and so understands the southern point of view, but he also has New England ties. This combination of commitment and detachment, both in scientific and social realms, serves De Forest well, for Dr. Ravenel can examine questions from all sides without rigid prejudgment. Thus he admires the strength of the New England personality but finds it stiff and "cold as celery"; he admires southern geniality and warmth but regrets the energy spent justifying slavery on highly emotional grounds. As a parent he is wise in indulging Lillie, and avoids alienating her in the cruel manner of Henry James's Dr. Sloper in *Washington Square*.

At the end of the war Dr. Ravenel voices the Unionist position. The North won because it had right on its side: "A just system of labor has produced power, and an unjust system has produced weakness." How should the South be punished? He favors action against the leaders, "the responsible criminals," in the belief that once they are put down, the rank and file will be freed from their unhealthy influence and can get to work again. Here, as Edmund Wilson has observed, speaks the confident North before the difficulties of Reconstruction revealed how dependent was the South on its gentry for leadership, how when they abdicated responsibility carpetbaggers (Northern opportunists) and scalawags (Southern renegades) filled the vacuum. De Forest himself worked for the Freedman's Bureau in South Carolina for almost three years during the Reconstruction and, though he didn't see the worst of the abuses, undoubtedly discovered that patching up the wounds was not so easy as it had seemed in 1865.

Dr. Ravenel's mild and quizzical way of voicing his Union viewpoint also serves dramatic ends, for he is sure to be misunderstood by North and South alike. When the Ravenels have been in New Orleans but a short time after its capture by Union troops, the Doctor is knocked on the head one night by some "ardent Southerner" who called him a "Federal spy." Ravenel is imperturbable: "The finest gentleman of the city would have [treated me thus] under the same temptation," he says; but the incident has its effect on Lillie, who

43

begins to lose her lifelong attachment to the South in which she had grown up. Dr. Ravenel later tries an idealistic experiment of operating a farm on which freed Negroes work for wages. He proposes to produce, he says, "not only a crop of corn and potatoes, but a race of intelligent, industrious, and virtuous laborers." Although his rational approach cannot be very successful, it does allow De Forest some humorous pages in which he can define certain problems concretely. The Negroes are often shiftless and undependable, but Dr. Ravenel is not naïve enough to be surprised. "Don't reproach them for being stupid," he says. "For nearly a century the whole power of the Republic, North and South, has been devoted to keeping them stupid." It will take time to undo such prolonged "selfishness." Lillie must teach them to read (a shocking order to her, for it has been against the law). His arguments, familiar to us today, must have seemed dubious to many of his contemporaries. "Negro children are just as intelligent as white children until they find out that they are black. Now we will never tell them that they are black; we will never hint to them that they are born our inferiors." When Lillie "mischievously" pursues the matter, inquiring, "Are you not going to ask in our colored friends" to the evening meal, the Doctor replies: "Why no. I don't see the logical necessity of it. I always have claimed the right of selecting my own intimates." But he goes on to admit that at some of the "most aristocratic houses of New Orleans" he has sat "with less respectable people." (This general distinction between civil and social equality was one which the native New Orleans writer George Washington Cable would draw in the 1880's, and it would be partially responsible for Cable's having to flee from the South.) Before the Doctor's optimistic theories can be fully tested, the farm is overrun by Confederate troops; De Forest allows him just enough success to justify his principles, while at the same time hinting at difficulties which the Doctor only partially understands.

Apart from the agricultural chapters the novel pays little attention to the Negro. There are, however, traces of situations, such as what to do with the colored families crowding in upon Federal troops and demanding freedom and protection, which Faulkner would invest with tense emotion in his sequence of Civil War stories, *The Unvanquished,* just as he would make one of his central myths out of the white man's responsibility for wronging the Negro. De Forest, intent upon describing what his eyes have seen, seldom holds the focus long enough or steadily enough to make it yield its maximum drama. His purpose is, to be sure, panoramic, and his canvas is broad. His chief shortcoming, as Edmund Wilson has suggested, is that his work fails to "communicate in any convincing way the passions supposed to be felt by the characters." [6] This defect is less important in *Miss Ravenel's Conversion* than in his other novels, but here it may account for De Forest's incomplete success with his avowed favorite, Colburne. Colburne acts with reserve. When De Forest tells us that Colburne has a great laugh, that as a budding lawyer he makes a strong appeal to a jury, we need to see it to believe it. De Forest's powers of observation are remarkable, and his insistence on honesty in reporting makes his work live; perhaps his own critical stance, plus the tempting example of Thackeray, can be blamed for his failure to adopt fully the dramatic, objective narrative method so much admired today.

Miss Ravenel's Conversion remains a noteworthy and rewarding novel, especially when viewed historically. It is noteworthy that anyone writing at the end of the war could achieve such perspective on the conflict and its aftermath. Howells praised the book again and again, saying on one occasion that "it does not shrink to pitiful dimensions even when put by the side of Tolstoi's *War and Peace.*" [7] This comparison is extravagant but not without some justification, for both authors saw the complexity of war and tried to write honestly of it without the heroics of the romancers. They saw war as more than men and matériel, more than merely military activity. De Forest's comment to Howells suggests some of the contemporary difficulties. "Let me tell you," he said,

> that nobody but [Tolstoi] has written the whole truth about war and battle. I tried, and I told all I dared, and perhaps all I could. But there was one thing I did not dare tell. . . . I ac-

[6] *Patriotic Gore, op.cit.,* p. 702.
[7] *Harper's Monthly,* LXXV (Sept. 1887), 639.

45

tually did not dare state the extreme horror of battle, and the anguish with which the bravest soldiers struggle through it. . . . Oddly enough, the truth is not true to the uninformed.[8]

And here he stresses the sense of confusion which Tolstoi so successfully pictured on a vast scale and Stephen Crane was to exploit through the mind of a bewildered Civil War private.

Howells characterized the author of *Miss Ravenel's Conversion* as "a realist before realism was named." And he saw in De Forest's work "strong proof that we are not so much lacking in an American novelist as in a public to recognize him." [9] De Forest was ahead of his time and the novel-reading public of his age never recognized him, despite all that Howells could do. In our own century the strong meat of war novels may make it difficult for us to see how much we owe to De Forest. But the active revaluation of American literature in recent years has led to a substantial critical appreciation of *Miss Ravenel's Conversion*, even though it is a century late.

[8] Quoted by Howells in *Harper's Monthly*, LXXIV (May 1887), 987.
[9] *Harper's Monthly*, LXXIV (Feb. 1887), 484; *Atlantic Monthly*, XXIX (March 1872), 365.

5 HENRY JAMES
The Portrait of a Lady

Richard Poirier

The way in which *The Portrait of a Lady* first appeared is itself evidence that James had reached the end of his apprenticeship as a novelist. Beginning in October 1880, it ran in simultaneous installments in *The Atlantic Monthly* and *Macmillan's Magazine*. Such distinguished international auspices are indicative of the secure reputation that James had achieved, not only in England, where he had decided some five years earlier to settle for life, but also in an America that tended to be critical of its expatriate writers. One might say that James had arrived at a position to which Isabel Archer, the heroine of this novel, aspires: to be released from any provincialities of response, to have access to a number of alternatives from which to choose and on which to base judgments, and to be able to take an abundantly large and imaginative view of human experience.

Isabel comes to the Old World hoping to experience some of the freedom denied her in the New, and it is one of the many complications of James's treatment of the relation of Europe to America that she should endow the English estate where we first see her as a guest of its American owners, the Touchetts, with the promises of a frontier—a frontier less of wealth, though this is profusely available, than of knowledge,

Brief sections of this essay have been rewritten from my book, *The Comic Sense of Henry James*, © Richard Poirier 1960 and used by permission of Oxford University Press, Inc.

appreciation, and taste. "The rich perfection of Garden-court," we are told, "at once revealed a world and gratified a need." Her need is summed up in a word that recurs through-out the novel and which furthers the irony of such a quest's taking place in Europe with a cast nearly wholly American: she wants to be "free." When her charming and ailing cousin, Ralph Touchett, persuades his father to make Isabel rich he does so by saying that "She wishes to be free, and your bequest will make her free." Specifically, he is hoping to prevent her ever having to marry; it is of course marriage and the reality of the life she discovers in Europe as Osmond's wife that deprive her of even the illusion of freedom.

But before the chastening experiences of Volume II Isabel is allowed the self-delighting innocence of Volume I in which, among other assertions of independence, she rejects the proposals of Lord Warburton out of an apparent distaste for the "system" he represents. Marriage to him, she thinks, "failed to support any enlightened prejudice in favour of the free exploration of life." Her ambitions seem to reach beyond Warburton to something undefinable. They cannot ever, therefore, be satisfied by the American suitor who follows her around Europe, Mr. Caspar Goodwood, the very squareness of whose jaw suggests to her "a want of easy consonance with the deeper rhythms of life." She thinks at first that she has discovered such a consonance in Madame Merle. She meets this lady at Gardencourt and is almost immediately impressed by her achievement of what Isabel calls the "aristocratic situation"—of being "in a better position for appreciating people than they are for appreciating you." It is not long, however, before Madame Merle seems to her "to exist only in her relations, direct and indirect, with her fellow mortals," and not until she meets Osmond, little knowing that her marriage to him will be engineered by Madame Merle, does she discover someone who fits her requirements. He has, among other virtues, no visible relationship to anyone except his daughter Pansy, whose mother will turn out to be Madame Merle. In Ralph's phrase he is a "vague, unexplained American of unknown origins who lives in Florence because Rome is too vulgar" and, in Isabel's account, he has been able "to renounce everything but Correggio." She can thus assure Caspar Goodwood that she is "marrying a nonentity," readily agree with Mrs. Touchett that he has "no money, no name, no importance," and tell Ralph that Osmond has "no property, no title, no honours, no houses, nor lands, nor position, nor reputation, nor brilliant belongings of any sort. It is the total absence of these things that pleases me." Her choice is carried out in defiance of everything that can be called society, a choice thus characteristic of a peculiarly American and romantic conception of "freedom." One finds it in *Huckleberry Finn,* in *Walden,* above all in Emerson.

Isabel's choice of Osmond makes it extremely appropriate that Mrs. Touchett first discovers her in Albany, "trudging over the sandy plains of the history of German thought." No history of German thought in the nineteenth century would fail to make Kant as conspicuous to an American reader as Emerson already had. According to Emerson we are indebted to Kant for the very term "transcendentalist" which Emerson was to make famous. Isabel, like many of the heroines of English fiction, is an orphan, a kind of Becky Sharp; but the specifically American quality of this novel is that by virtue of the nature of her ambitions she is better called an Emersonian Becky Sharp. Her situation frees her from allegiance to social hierarchies, but the advantage she sees in her social mobility has nothing to do with the freedom to act indiscriminately in pursuit of wealth and position. Quite the contrary. She wants knowledge, enlightenment, above all a kind of independence of any measure outside her own mind. To Madame Merle's belief that "we are each of us made up of a cluster of appurtenances," Isabel, with all the overstatement of Thoreau and of a young person in a moment of frustrated loyalty to a beloved and wiser adult, grandly responds that:

> I think just the other way. I don't know whether I succeed in expressing myself, but I know that nothing else expresses me. Nothing that belongs to me is any measure of me; on the contrary it's a limit, a barrier, and a perfectly arbitrary one. Certainly the clothes which, as you say, I choose to wear, don't

49

express me; and heaven forbid they should! To begin with it's not my choice that I wear them; they are imposed upon me by society.

Her marriage to Osmond is the event most consistent with her view of reality. She exults in the fact that Osmond is a "specimen apart." With brilliant daring James even allows him to lay claim to the Jamesian (and Emersonian) virtue of renunciation, of giving up practical social ambitions and advantages in the interests of some presumably higher ideal. James thus indicates in yet another way how Isabel's imagination responds to the same possibilities in life to which his own is romantically but altogether more critically, more despairingly attracted. Osmond tells her that his life has affirmed "not only my natural indifference—I had none. But my studied, my wilful renunciation." So great is the appeal of his separateness, of his "originality," by which she means his exclusiveness of any socially observed types, that she cannot heed even his outrageous candor when he tells her before the marriage: "No, I am not conventional. I am convention itself," a prediction of Ralph's terrible remark on his deathbed that Isabel has been "ground in the very mill of the conventional."

James's rendering of the Isabel-Osmond relationship is of historical and literary importance as a comment on the Emersonian way of life. Emerson had come to see James in his crib, had read with great admiration James's letters from Europe to the elder James, and in the year before *The Portrait* he had met James both in Europe and in Concord. Though in his essay on Emerson James praises the Emersonian vision "of what we require and what we are capable of in the way of aspiration and independence," he had a patronizing conception of the narrowness of Emerson's intelligence, especially its lack of social sophistication. And in Osmond one can find, if not a further critique of Emerson, then at least an ironic extension of his ideas into areas where they serve as a "front" for vulgarity and ambition. Osmond is a mock version of the transcendentalist, fitting Emerson's characterization almost perfectly: "It is a sign of the times, conspicuous to the coarsest observer," Emerson writes in his essay, "The Transcenden-talist,"

> that many intelligent and religious persons withdraw from the common labors and competitions of the market and the caucus, and betake themselves to a certain solitary and critical way of living, from which no solid fruit has yet appeared to justify the separation. They hold themselves aloof: they feel the dispro-portion between their faculties and the work offered them, and they prefer to ramble in the country and perish of ennui, to the degradation of such charities and such ambitions as the city can propose to them . . . this part is chosen both from tempera-ment and from principle: with some unwillingness too, and as a choice of the less of two evils. . . . With this passion for what is great and extraordinary, it cannot be wondered at that they are repelled by vulgarity and frivolity in people.

"He has a great dread of vulgarity," Ralph says of Osmond in an early warning to Isabel, "that's his special line; he hasn't any other that I know of." To be aware of Osmond as a cor-rupt transcendentalist makes it less surprising that Isabel, whose mental processes are authentically Emersonian, should see an image of herself in the man she marries.

Isabel is quite obviously an easy object of criticism, which could extend from her to the Emersonian attitudes she ex-pounds. James's skeptical affection for those atttitudes is evi-dent in the way he protects his heroine, even in her most excessive moments. He saves her, in James's own phrase, from the "scientific criticism" of which "she would be an easy vic-tim . . . if she were not to awaken on the reader's part an impulse more tender and more purely expectant." The meth-ods by which James himself awakens in the reader the impulse to be tender and expectant to a heroine who "has a great deal of folly in her wisdom" are a further symptom of James's own dedication to an ideal of freedom. His style is committed to keeping his favorites from being fixed and labeled as, say, the grotesque and charming Henrietta Stackpole fixes and labels them. Henrietta, Isabel's best friend from home, ar-rives at Gardencourt to be both a measure of Isabel's advance from provinciality and a foil for Ralph. Ralph, aptly called by James an "apostle of freedom," regards Henrietta as "the all judging one," the categorizer. Much of the broadest comedy in the first half of the novel derives from the conversations between these two characters and the contrast between his supple and extemporizing mind and her attempts to confine him within her doctrinaire and superficial limits: " 'I don't suppose that you are going to undertake to persuade me that *you* are an American,' she said. 'To please you [he replied], I will be an Englishman, I will be a Turk!' 'Well, if you can change about that way, you are very welcome,' Miss Stackpole rejoined." Ralph's civilized playfulness with Henrietta is an illustration of those qualities that encourage Isabel to a necessary self-assurance when she is dealing with him. With him, indeed with all of the Touchetts, she can express herself without fear of being called to a restricting account of motive or consistency. To *listen* to the way Ralph treats Isabel is to hear the way James also treats her. We catch in Ralph's style James's own intention to allow Isabel the full liberty of self-expression and discovery.

The scene in which this treatment of Isabel is most charmingly dramatized occurs in the first volume, well before her engagement to Osmond, and it indicates two very important things about the quality of literary expression in the novel whenever Isabel is being shown in a critical light. It is noticeable, first of all, that James permits Ralph to exercise a comic inventiveness, a capacity to avoid all obvious pedagogical seriousness, thereby allowing Isabel to come painlessly, even with a kind of pleasurable embarrassment, to a recognition of her own absurdity. What we subsequently recognize is James's ability to take care of his heroine without resorting to any of the blatancies or idealizations that are noticeable in some of the earlier novels, especially *The American*. The smile showing through the style and calling for an answering smile from the reader is like that which James admired in Alphonse Daudet—"the expressive and sympathetic smile . . . of the artist, the skeptic, the man of the world." In the following dialogue and indeed throughout the novel the reader can actually *feel* that "respect for the liberty of the subject,"—in this case, Isabel—which James calls in "The Lesson of Balzac"—"*the* great sign of the painter of the first order."

"Well," said Isabel, smiling, "I'm afraid it is because [Henrietta] is rather vulgar that I like her."

"She would be flattered by your reason!"

"If I should tell her, I would not express it in that way. I should say it is because there is something of the 'people' in her."

"What do you know about the people? and what does she, for that matter?"

"She knows a great deal, and I know enough to feel that she is a kind of emanation of the great democracy—of the continent, the country, the nation. I don't say that she sums it up, that would be too much to ask of her. But she suggests it; she reminds me of it."

"You like her then for patriotic reasons. I am afraid it is on those very grounds that I object to her."

"Ah," said Isabel, with a kind of joyous sigh, "I like so many things! If a thing strikes me in a certain way, I like it. I don't want to boast, but I suppose I am rather versatile. I like people to be totally different from Henrietta—in the style of Lord Warburton's sisters, for instance. So long as I look at the Misses Molyneux, they seem to me to answer a kind of ideal. Then Henrietta presents herself, and I am immensely struck with her; not so much for herself as what stands behind her."

"Ah, you mean the back view of her," Ralph suggested.

"What she says is true," his cousin answered, "you will never be serious. I like the great country stretching away beyond the rivers and across the prairies, blooming and smiling and spreading, till it stops at the blue Pacific! A strong, sweet, fresh odour seems to rise from it, and Henrietta—excuse my simile—has something of that odour in her garments."

Isabel blushed a little as she concluded this speech, and the blush, together with the momentary ardour she had thrown into it, was so becoming to her that Ralph stood smiling at her for a moment after she had ceased speaking.

"I am not sure the Pacific is blue," he said, "but you are a woman of imagination. Henrietta, however, is fragrant—Henrietta is decidedly fragrant."

The sweetness of Ralph's temperament and the tenderness of his pleasure in Isabel's artless enthusiasm is never more ingratiatingly dramatized than here. Such a passage should be remembered when, in Volume II, we see Isabel in Rome as the wife and hostess of Gilbert Osmond: "She was dressed in black velvet; she looked brilliant and noble." In Rome she is reduced to representing her husband; in Gardencourt, with Ralph, she is expressing herself. In this exchange, she recognizes the absurdity of her speech without anyone's needing to remark it. In his revision of the novel for the Collected Edition some years later, however, James made a point of having her description of Henrietta and America carry even more of a comic burden. For the statement that Henrietta "reminds" her of the continent, James substitutes the line "she vividly figures it"; for Isabel's statement that she likes what "stands behind" Henrietta, he later provided the phrase "masses behind." Both changes allow Ralph's remark about the "back view of her" to become funny in the slightly lewd manner that led James to name one of his characters Fanny Assingham. The possibility of a human being representing something or someone else, which bears on what happens eventually to Isabel, is here the object of comic ridicule. Henrietta becomes, in Isabel's description, a grotesquely literal representation of the size and smell of the whole American continent.

The ultimate sadness of Isabel's situation is that while she sees in Ralph a capacity for appreciation not unlike what she discovers also in Osmond, she cannot recognize in Ralph's humor the guarantee that with him her own tastes and predilections will not be insidiously stifled, as they are by Osmond. After three years of marriage she comes to the discovery that Osmond "took himself so seriously, it was something appalling." Repeating to Ralph the erroneous charge often made by Henrietta—"You will never be serious"—Isabel reveals her incapacity to recognize the significance of Ralph's playfulness. No wonder she can mistakenly see in Osmond the virtues that belong only to Ralph. The superficial similarity between the two men is another instance of James's insistence on the complexity of moral choice by showing a correspondence between the admirable and the corrupt. Osmond is made into Ralph Touchett *in extremis,* and Isabel may remark that:

> Ralph had something of this same quality, this appearance of thinking life was a matter of connoisseurship; but in Ralph it was an anomaly, a kind of humorous excrescence, whereas in Mr. Osmond it was the key-note, and everything was in harmony with it.

"Everything was in harmony with it"—in that phrase, carrying implications of a systematic measuring and "placing" of experience, is the secret of the essential difference between Ralph's (and James's) connoisseurship and Osmond's. Ralph is a connoisseur, but in expressing this fact he shows the reverse of a desire, so horribly evident in Osmond, to make everything harmonious with the prejudices of his own taste.

On the other hand, James's phrase in describing Ralph, "his boundless liberty of appreciation," might well describe James's own ideal as a novelist and, as I have suggested, the aspiration which he treasures but must see defeated in Isabel. She is involved in a quest for that personal condition to which all of James's favorites are drawn, the condition, again, of freedom. James is painfully aware that "freedom" can only exist as an incentive. You act *as if* it could in reality be achieved. "Still we have the illusion of freedom," the hero of a much later novel of James's remarks, "therefore don't, like me to-day, be without the memory of that illusion." In stressing the autobiographical elements in *The Portrait* I have dealt with the way in which it comments on James's heritage of Emersonian "self-reliance," the way in which Isabel's vague ambition is represented as an achieved and more subtle condition in Ralph, were she able to see it, and, in James's own style, as a preferred experience to the reader. The term which gathers these autobiographical elements together is again the term "freedom," and what makes us the more aware of James's personal investment in the word is that it recurs not only in his fiction but in his essays, notably, as already mentioned, in "The Lesson of Balzac," a lesson, in part, of Balzac's "joy in [the] communicated and exhibited movement [of his characters], in their standing on their feet and going of themselves and acting out their characters," as contrasted to "the marked jealousy of [Becky Sharp's] freedom that Thackeray exhibits from the first." Thus, "freedom" defines not only an ideal to which James's characters are often dedicated but also the condition within which the great practitioners of his art have labored. When he speaks, in still other places, of the world as the subject of the novelist's attention, his language is often noticeably similar to Isabel's when she is theorizing about her repeated ambition to take "a large human view of her opportunities and obligations."

There is, for example, James's characteristically expansive and kindly letter to the Deerfield Summer School in 1889, replying to an invitation to discuss the art of the novel. His letter is an appeal for freedom of observation as a necessary prerequisite for fiction of a high order. His phrasing might well remind us that Ralph's intention in giving Isabel a fortune is to allow her the freedom to take full advantage of her desire "to begin by getting a general impression of life." James begs the students:

> Oh, do something from your point of view, an ounce of example is worth a ton of generalities; do something with the great art and the great form; do something with life. You each have an impression colored by your individual conditions; make that into a picture, a picture framed by your own personal wisdom, your glimpse of the American world. The field is vast for freedom, for study, for observation, for satire, for truth. . . . I have only two little words for the matter remotely approaching the rule or doctrine; one is life and the other freedom. Tell the ladies and gentlemen, the ingenious inquirers, to consider life directly and closely, and not to be put off with mean and puerile falsities, and be conscientious about it. It is infinitely large, various and comprehensive. Every sort of mind will find what it looks for in it, whereby the novel becomes truly multifarious and illustrative. That is what I mean by liberty; give it its head and let it range. If it is in a bad way, and the English novel is, I

think, nothing but absolute freedom can refresh and restore its self-respect.[1]

Assertions that Isabel has an "immense curiosity about life," or that, as against Osmond, she pleads the "cause of freedom," or other uses of words like "freedom," "liberty," and "knowledge" are so frequent in this novel that there is no need to collect them here. Isabel has faith in exactly those ideals that James wants the novelist to pursue in his writing. When he is talking about fiction his vocabulary is often like Isabel's when she is describing her hopes and ambitions. Isabel's career shows us what happens when an ideal of freedom that is a governing principle in James's art also becomes a defining principle of life. In his relation to Isabel as artist, James is much like Ralph in his relation to her as spectator. She is a refreshment to the imagination of each of them: to Ralph, because she is an original, liberated figure who can gasp when meeting Lord Warburton that "It's just like a novel!" and then proceed to reject his proposal; she is a refreshment to James's imagination because she is a new, if not wholly original, kind of fictional heroine whose ambitions can only be defined by abstractions like "freedom" or "knowledge." She cannot be placed in any of the convenient typologies of earlier fiction. As if to show Isabel's uniqueness James surrounds her in this novel with relatively conventionalized figures like Henrietta, Madame Gemini, Osmond's sister, or like Osmond himself and Madame Merle. By these contrasts to Isabel he ensures that we will not mistakenly apply to her some of the limiting definitions that are relevant to most novels. By the very fact that both Isabel and Henrietta say that they want to investigate the "inner life" of Europe, for instance, the reader is forced into an acceptance of at least the comparative seriousness of Isabel's intention. In this and in other ways James is everywhere protecting Isabel from the kinds of definition a reader is customarily allowed to make of an orphaned heroine suddenly exposed to a world

1 Leon Edel, ed., *Henry James: The Future of the Novel* (New York: Vintage Books, 1956), pp. 28–29.

of wealth and glamour. In the interest of preventing us from placing her in any particular category James even commits what was for him a cardinal sin in earlier writers. Quite early in the book he begins to intrude into the narrative, begging us not to "smile" critically at Isabel and even giving away his plot in the warning that "those who judge her severely may have the satisfaction of finding that, later, she became consistently wise only at the cost of an amount of folly which will constitute almost a direct appeal to charity."

The difficulty of James's task in this novel is that he must allow the reader to respect Isabel's innocent admiration even while making him aware of James's own very educated criticisms of what she admires. Thus, he must show us the extent to which Madame Merle *is* charming at the same time that he hints at her meretriciousness; not to do so would lay him open to the charge of surrendering his point of view to a girl who is "often the victim of meagre knowledge." Similarly, the novel cannot evade the psychological implication of Isabel's marriage to a "sterile dilettante," as Ralph calls Osmond. Is her act not a result of sexual fear of the handsome, bearded Warburton and the Caspar whose kiss near the end of the novel seemed to her like "white lightning," sending her back on the path of duty to Rome and Osmond? And yet James is fully aware that if Isabel's motives become too expressly sexual in the final scenes, then all of her previous acts of high principle might equally be explained as evasions of sexual confrontation. The search for freedom would thereby become little more than a rationalization of Isabel's attempt to escape the "common passions" she so strongly criticizes in the marriage of Bantling and Henrietta. Critics have never been able adequately to adjust the final scenes to the rest of the novel. Most of them work on the principle that if they discover anything covert, especially if it is sexual, they can then forget everything else that the novel has made obvious. Still, the whole literary effort of this novel is designed to keep the reader from finding any merely psychological explanation wholly satisfactory. James strives even at the end to make us see Isabel as a girl genuinely motivated by those ideals which are often his own.

The ending of the novel draws its significance as much from the death of Ralph as from the scene thereafter in the garden between Isabel and Caspar. Ralph's death, seen in the context of his having been in a relation to Isabel which is much like James's relation to her, is an astounding illustration of how the drama in the action of this novel is an imitation of the drama of creative effort that went into the writing. Ralph's death can be taken as a metaphor for the fact that Isabel's freedom can no longer be imagined. It can no longer sustain the life of the imagination—Ralph's or James's. In returning to Osmond she rejoins the living dead, the wholly conventionalized elements of life. She therefore cannot even provide what James found in the actual death of Minny Temple, the girl on whom the character of Isabel is partly modeled. At the time of her death, James wrote to his brother William of the "positive relief in thinking of her removed from her own heroic treatment and placed in kinder hands." Isabel is even denied the "freedom and rest," to use James's words when speaking of Minny, the "eternal freedom" which is given to Minny and, in the novel, to Ralph. With Ralph's death, which is nearly synonymous with the end of the book, Isabel ceases to live in the imagination of freedom. He dies because her life no longer allows him to imagine the possibility that freedom and the life of the world are compatible.

James had a very tenuous sense of the connection between sexual disturbance, on the one hand, and the desire for freedom and death, on the other; the most we can say is that his novel only shows that some such connection was mysteriously at work in his mind. He had a very clear idea, however, about the relationship, which comes through to us in the final chapter, between freedom and death. What Caspar at the end offers Isabel in the garden at Gardencourt is the old call to action and freedom: "The world is all before us." While the intensity of her reaction to Caspar necessarily calls for some psychological speculations, the reasons for her refusal to go away with him are obvious enough. She is simply not in love with him nor has she ever been. But when she hurries away from him she is also escaping his call to leave the "garden" of her dreams now that, like Eden after the fall, it has become the place of desolation. The echo of Milton in Caspar's plea is unmistakably intended. The same line occurs earlier in the novel when Isabel sees her relatives off for America. Having done her duty by these figures out of her past, and in possession of what seems unhampered independence, she walks away from the station into the London fog: "The world lay all before her—she could do whatever she chose." In James's use of the phraseology of *Paradise Lost* ("The world lay all before them where to choose/Their place of rest . . ."), there is a Miltonic sadness that reflects back on all the earlier hopefulness of the book: neither Caspar nor Isabel is free to choose much of anything. His life is in useless bondage to his love for her, while hers is dedicated to its errors. And there is nothing in her act which holds the promise, as does Adam and Eve's, of eventual happiness through suffering, even though Ralph assures her that there is. Her action is absolutely within the logic of her Emersonian idealism, so much so that the logic takes its vengeance. In effect, she tells the reader, to borrow from "The Transcendentalist," that "you think me the child of my circumstances: I make my circumstances"— including, one might add, "my own misery." It is of no importance to her that, in fact, she has been so calculatingly deceived by other people that it is preposterous to assume all the responsibility for her own past. To admit that her destiny has depended on the actions of others, however, would be to subscribe finally to Madame Merle's view that the "self" is determined in part by "an envelope of circumstances" that one does not always create. Isabel's action at the end is fully consistent with everything she does earlier. Now, however, she asserts her idealism of self, not in innocence but in full knowledge of the world. For that reason, freedom, which was the condition of self-creation, becomes a form of indifference to the fact that returning to Rome will, as Caspar admonishes, cost her her life.

6 MARK TWAIN
The Adventures of Huckleberry Finn

Henry Nash Smith

Mark Twain is the most widely read of American authors, living or dead, and *The Adventures of Huckleberry Finn* is by far his most popular book. It was a best seller when it was published in 1885; it has held its audience steadily ever since; and it has been translated into more foreign languages than any other work in our literature. Professor Walter Blair has estimated on the basis of carefully compiled statistics that ten million copies of the book have been printed. For some fifty years after its publication, *Huckleberry Finn* received relatively little attention from the official arbiters of literary taste. But, as Mr. Blair points out, "Beginning in the late 1940's this lack has been remedied with a vengeance. By the end of 1960 critics and scholars [had] published within a fifteen-year period more than a hundred lengthy discussions of the novel." And the critical discussion continues to increase in volume.

How can we account for the unique status of this story told in the language of a fourteen-year-old boy growing up as an outcast in the pre-Civil-War South? Some of the answers to the question are obvious. The book is extremely funny, and its humor seems unfading. Huck's comments that *The Pilgrim's Progress* is "about a man that left his family it didn't say why" and that "The statements was interesting but tough" have a mixture of naïveté and profundity that retains its charm even upon the tenth or the twentieth reading. In addition to its humor, the book has an immense vitality. Mark Twain poured into it his memories of people and places ob-

61

served during his childhood in Hannibal, Missouri, in the 1840's and his years on the Mississippi as a steamboat pilot in the 1850's. Bernard DeVoto called Huck's story "a faring-forth with inexhaustible delight through the variety of America, the heritage of a nation not unjustly symbolized by the river's flow." Furthermore, the narrative is fully accessible. The author does not seem to be trying to get one-up on the reader. It is a book that can be read with pleasure both by scholars and by people who read nothing else but the newspapers.

These qualities point to a less obvious reason for the fascination the book holds for Americans in all walks of life. It bears upon the long-standing and increasingly urgent problem of the identity of this country and its people. Just at the end of the American War of Independence, in 1782, the naturalized Frenchman St. John de Crèvecoeur had asked in his *Letters from an American Farmer,* "What then is the American, this new man?" He proposed an answer that was shrewd and valid for his day, but the question has had to be asked again and again in the history of our literature. James Fenimore Cooper found a different answer from Crèvecoeur's in his backwoodsman Leatherstocking; Emerson stated yet another, much more philosophical, in his address on "The American Scholar"; Walt Whitman devoted most of his *Leaves of Grass* to defining the ideal American type he believed would emerge as the citizen of "these States." And Mark Twain himself had begun his literary career in 1869 by relating the adventures of a rather philistine American Innocent Abroad confronting history and cultural tradition in Europe and the Holy Land.

Fifteen years later Mark Twain arrived at the more definitive answer represented by his ragged orphan boy floating down the Mississippi River with Jim, the runaway Negro slave. At first glance this story of the 1840's may seem to have no connection with the problems of the Cold War in the mid-twentieth century. Recent discussion of the book, however, has made Huck's story seem directly relevant to our present circumstances. Somewhat bewildered by both their power and their responsibilities, Americans have been impelled to seek in art shared images that can help them become aware of their identity as a people. At least, this is a conclusion that has occurred to more than one observer. Let us take it as a hypothesis, and ask what features of Mark Twain's master-piece offer a definition of the American character and the American situation in our day.

We notice at once that the book invites its readers to iden-tify themselves with an adolescent protagonist suddenly ex-posed to novel risks and opportunities. Huck has never before been outside the little river town of St. Petersburg, that is, Hannibal, Missouri; yet now he is launched upon a journey that will take him more than a thousand miles downstream, as the river flows, through a constantly changing panorama of new landscapes, strange characters, unforeseen and unimag-ined dangers. The voyage of discovery that he did not plan in advance and did not want to make has a suggestive similarity to the role of the United States in the mid-twentieth century.

Equally obvious is the fact that Huck's story is a story of movement. He runs away from St. Petersburg in order to es-cape from his father's brutality and the well-meaning at-tempts of the townspeople of St. Petersburg to "sivilize" him. And the outcome of each episode in his story is renewed flight: from Jackson's Island, where he and Jim fear they will be found by slave-hunters; from the wrecked steamboat "Wal-ter Scott" in mid-river on which they encounter a band of robbers and murderers; from the violence and bloodshed of the feud on the Grangerford plantation. This pattern of re-peated movement has characterized American history from the beginning. Frederick Jackson Turner's celebrated "fron-tier hypothesis" maintained that the American character was formed by the experience of advancing westward across the continent. Professor George W. Pierson has included the Turner thesis in a theory which finds Americans ready to move, not only westward, but in every direction. Foreign ob-servers get the impression that Americans are constantly on the road. Certainly no other people has shown such a fondness for the "mobile home" on wheels that can stand for days or months or years in one of the trailer parks lining the high-ways outside every American city, then can be towed by an automobile to a similar location outside another city across the continent. Take an informal census of a group of Americans anywhere by asking them where they were born. You will find not one in five living close to his birthplace. Huck Finn is like that. He is on the move through most of his narrative, and at the end he is about to set out again, for the Indian Territory.

Huck's impulse to run away when he is faced by a problem he cannot solve is closely related to what W. H. Auden has called his habit of "moral improvisation." What he decides in one crisis, points out Mr. Auden, "tells him nothing about what he should do on other occasions, or what other people should do on other occasions. . . ." [1] Since the problem Huck faces is always a new one, he cannot depend on what he has learned from experience as a guide to action. The present does not seem to him continuous with the past, and he therefore has no reason to believe the future will be continuous with the present. Although Mr. Auden does not make the further inference, Huck's moral improvisation might be regarded as one aspect of his indifference to abstract ideas. He sees no basis for regarding a given situation as an illustration of a general principle. Each one must be faced on its own terms.

The disposition to make up policy as one goes along is sometimes called pragmatism, and in a vague sense I suppose Huck must be considered a pragmatist. But this seems too pedantic a term to describe him; he does not really have a philosophy. It is more accurate to say that he relies on intuition rather than reason. His moral improvisation is largely a matter of acting on impulse rather than according to preconceived plan. A good illustration is Huck's behavior when the raft taking him and Jim downstream approaches the mouth of the Ohio River. Jim grows more and more excited because he believes that when he can head up the Ohio he will be out

1 "Huck and Oliver," *The Listener*, L, No. 1283 (October 1, 1953), pp. 540–541.

of slave territory, and therefore be free; and Huck for the first time begins to realize that he is actually helping a slave escape. His conscience, formed by the society in which he has grown up, goads him until he decides he will turn Jim in as a runaway slave. He has actually set out for shore in a canoe, "all in a sweat to tell on" Jim, when he encounters a skiff with two men in it searching for five Negroes who have just escaped from a plantation on the shore. They ask Huck whether the man left on his raft is black or white. "I didn't answer up prompt," Huck says.

> I tried to, but the words wouldn't come. I tried, for a second or two, to brace up and out with it, but I warn't man enough— hadn't the spunk of a rabbit. I see I was weakening, so I just give up trying, and up and says—"He's white."

Then, in order to prevent the men from going to see for themselves, Huck improvises an elaborate story that makes them believe there is smallpox on the raft.

When Huck finds himself unable to carry out his preconceived intention, he falls back on impulse. He acts in this way again and again. Eventually, in fact, he even makes his own generalization about his procedure. As he approaches the Phelps plantation far down in Arkansas, where Jim is held prisoner in a log cabin and where the final sequence of the story takes place, Huck says:

> I went right along, not fixing up any particular plan, but just trusting to Providence to put the right words in my mouth when the time come; for I'd noticed that Providence always did put the right words in my mouth, if I left it alone.

A boy—or a nation—that operates like this will give the impression of having no coherent policy, of behaving in an unpredictable and sometimes even treacherous fashion. Such a boy or nation may seem an unreliable ally because no one can infer from past actions how he, or it, will behave in a future situation. American national policy, both foreign and domestic, has often made such an impression on the rest of the world. But both Huck and the American people are more predictable in the long run than in the short run.

The parallel, however, should not be taken too literally. Mark Twain means to demonstrate that the abstract principles Huck is aware of have been implanted in him by a peculiarly corrupt society—the slaveholding culture of the Old South. He has had no chance to arrive at a rational view of slavery as an institution. Until the time when he runs into Jim hiding on Jackson's Island, he has accepted without question the attitude toward slavery prevalent in St. Petersburg. He considers it divinely ordained and he has never imagined a society in which slavery does not exist. But this slave has been a friend of his for a long time; and when Jim reveals the awful fact that he has run away from his mistress, Huck hesitates hardly a moment. "People would call me a low down Abolitionist and despise me for keeping mum," he says, "—but that don't make no difference. I ain't agoing to tell. . . ."

By enlisting himself in Jim's cause, Huck becomes an outlaw. From this point to almost the end of the story he believes himself to be engaged in a criminal undertaking. He goes through two moral crises in which he is denounced by his conscience, but he finally reaches a clear decision to "go to Hell," that is, to defy what he understands to be the laws of God and of man by remaining loyal to Jim. This appeal from revealed or codified law to an intuitive notion of what is right is a very American trait in Huck. We are notoriously not a law-abiding people. Our crime rate and our divorce rate are high. In this sense there is a pronounced strain of anarchism in our culture. From whatever source it may be derived— from our exposure to frontier conditions or from some other influence—our disrespect for the law and its representatives is the dark aspect of our passionate cult of freedom.

Although Huck does not question the legality of slavery, he does not accept the laws as a guide to action. In fact, all established institutions are alien to him. He has no use for them and by preference no contact with them. He suffers when the Widow Douglas and Miss Watson dress him in conventional clothing, try to teach him table manners and passages from the Bible, and send him to school. The modes of behavior prescribed by custom and tradition seem to him abnormal.

In Huck's unreflecting fashion he illustrates Emerson's aphorism that the American people receive their culture from one continent but their duties from another. From the beginning we have faced a continual need to adapt European traditions and conventions to the new circumstances of this continent. As a consequence, we have had to become accustomed to a more than ordinary discontinuity between theory and practice.

This is the state of affairs that Emerson dealt with in such essays as "The American Scholar" and "Self-Reliance." It is perfectly exemplified in one of the most profound passages of Mark Twain's novel—one in which the dominant figure is, to be sure, not Huck but Tom Sawyer, yet one that defines Huck's own situation very well because Tom is making articulate both the demands of convention and the way Americans have often met these demands. The boys are digging a tunnel under the wall of the cabin where Jim is imprisoned on the Phelps plantation. Tom has insisted that they use only case knives for this purpose because that is the implement used by prisoners escaping from European dungeons in the historical romances he has read. But even Tom has to admit at last that the work is going too slowly. They will have to dig the tunnel with picks. "It ain't right, and it ain't moral," he says with regret. "And I wouldn't like it to get out—but there ain't only just the one way; we got to dig him out with the picks, and *let on* it's case-knives." Calling a spade a spade—or a pick a pick—is not the absolute rule in any society, but Americans have had to make more accommodations of this sort than peoples whose traditional culture grows more directly out of their own experience.

Huck's habit of moral improvisation, his antinomian attitude toward established authorities and institutions, his tolerance of a wide disparity between theory and practice, all derive from the same aspect of his character. In a comment on the book after it was published Mark Twain described Huck as a boy with "a sound heart and a deformed conscience." Although Huck's heart is undisciplined and even the source of subversive impulses, it is nevertheless "sound," that is, not depraved, not wicked, but essentially virtuous. Mark Twain intends for the reader to identify himself with this part of Huck, to feel a thrill of moral exaltation when the ignorant boy decides to go to hell rather than betray his friend. And there can be no doubt of Huck's underlying innocence. He intends harm to no one; he is sickened by the violence of the Kentucky feud and the cynical hypocrisy of the "king" gulling the mourners at Peter Wilks's funeral into taking him for a Christian minister. Huck tries to protect other people from harm, not only his comrade Jim and the orphaned Wilks girls, but even the bloodthirsty bandits on the wrecked "Walter Scott." His deepest emotion is love, most of all of course for Jim. Their comradeship on the raft has been called by one enthusiastic critic, not without some justice, a community of saints; and Mark Twain gives it poetic support by providing for their idyllic moments of solitude a setting of starry sky and quiet water. Nature cherishes them, and the purity of sunrise on the river is an affirmation of both Huck's and Jim's innocence.

Yet this purity is not allowed to endure. The celebrated description of sunrise at the beginning of Chapter XIX ends with a reference to the odor of decaying fish that prepares for the entrance of the rascally "duke" and "king" a page or two later. Huck and Jim can escape only momentarily from the depraved society of the shore. And this society has made an indelible imprint on Huck's character. It has given him the deformed conscience that is at war with his sound heart. His conscience—the voice that condemns him for helping Jim —is the sum total of the fancied obligations, the foolish inhibitions, the perverse constraints imposed on Huck by society. It is thus, by an inevitable extension of meaning, the voice of tradition, of the past, of what Emerson meant by "culture." Huck's innocence is compromised by the only culture he knows, that of the towns along the River, in which slavery has become the focus of moral and legal values, religion is "soul butter and hogwash," honor is expressed in the cowardly ambushes and murders of the feud, and the arts are represented by the comically vulgar ornaments of the Grangerford parlor, or Emmeline Grangerford's doggerel verses, or Tom Sawyer's grotesque "rules" derived from his reading in historical fiction.

The hostile depiction of Huck's conscience is extended further in the story by the characterization of his father and of the women who function as mothers to him. The man who would normally embody for Huck the ideal of wisdom and moral authority is a neurotic drunkard whose beatings actually threaten the boy's life and drive him to flight. The duke and the king, who assume authority over Huck and may therefore be regarded as parodies of the father image, are amusing rascals through the middle section of the narrative, but they are potentially dangerous criminals. As the raft floats farther and farther southward, Huck shows that he understands them fully. He says:

> They took a change, and began to lay their heads together in the wigwam and talk low and confidential two or three hours at a time. . . . Jim and me got uneasy. We didn't like the look of it. We judged they was studying up some kind of worse deviltry than ever.

What they do is to turn Jim in fraudulently, for a reward; and Huck's last encounter with the duke leads to a moment of pure fright. It suddenly occurs to the duke that the boy may represent a danger. " 'Looky here,' he says—'do you think *you'd* venture to blow on us? Blamed if I think I'd trust you. Why, if you *was* to blow on us—.' " Huck adds: "He stopped, but I never see the duke look so ugly out of his eyes before." This orphan has no reason at all to consider his fathers, actual or symbolic, as a source of moral authority; they are quite simply the enemy.

The mother figures seem less menacing. Although Miss Watson is hard and angular, with an ignorant bigotry, the Widow Douglas and Aunt Sally Phelps have traces of motherly warmth. Aunt Sally, the substitute mother who is portrayed at greatest length in the story, is allowed for a moment to awaken remorse in Huck. As she sits all night by the window hoping for Tom's return, he says:

> . . . I wished I could do something for her, but I couldn't, only to swear that I wouldn't never do nothing to grieve her any more.

Nevertheless, most of the time Aunt Sally is a comic victim of the boy's pranks. And like Miss Watson and the Widow Douglas, she is determined to subjugate Huck to the mores of a society that Mark Twain has deprived of all moral authority. The celebrated last lines of the story express a hostility toward her which the reader is expected to share:

> . . . I reckon I got to light out for the Territory ahead of the rest, because Aunt Sally she's going to adopt me and sivilize me and I can't stand it. I been there before.

Most of the women in this fictive world are elderly; they are lawgivers rather than sexual partners, actual or potential. Female custody of the arts is represented by poor dead Emmeline Grangerford. Her two sisters—the proud Charlotte and Sophia, "gentle and sweet, like a dove"—are no more than glimpsed. Huck is perhaps too young to take a romantic interest in girls, although he remembers Mary Jane Wilks vividly enough to declare that "she had more sand in her than any girl I ever see." The fact remains that the adventures of this American protagonist are in effect sexless. Critics have debated the significance of Mark Twain's consistent avoidance of a theme that runs through the literature of the world. Professor Leslie Fiedler has pointed out that two other nineteenth-century American literary masterpieces—Cooper's Leatherstocking series and Melville's *Moby Dick* —also pay virtually no attention to the love of man and woman. This remark could hardly be made about American literature of the twentieth century, and Hawthorne's Hester Prynne stands early in our literary history as a powerful and very womanly heroine. But none of these books can compare with *The Adventures of Huckleberry Finn* in appeal to the American public. The subject is complicated; let us leave it with the remark that the American experience of sexual love may well be markedly different from that of any other people in the world. Maybe American males, like Huck, are afraid of women.

We are on firmer ground when we notice the incomparable rendering in this novel of the American dream of a preindustrial, agrarian Eden. Despite its shadows of violence and terror, Huck's story is remembered by most readers for the pastoral interludes in which the raft drifts down the river in a landscape of breath-taking beauty. Amid the industrial cities and the factories and machines of the twentieth century, American literature has continued to cling to an imagined rural simplicity and innocence as a moral norm. The agrarian tradition in our culture still influences—some critics would say, perverts—public policy. Huck's raft, larger than life and distorted as all images are distorted that pass from the pages of a book into the popular imagination, is one of the principal links between the present and the past in our culture.

Much more complex is the revelation of basic American attitudes in the over-all structure of the book. The narrative begins in the near-farcical mood of *The Adventures of Tom Sawyer,* acquires a rich symbolic meaning as Huck's and Jim's quest for freedom becomes the narrative focus, moves toward the tragic recognition that freedom cannot be attained in this or any world, then suddenly veers back toward farce in Tom Sawyer's arrangements for Jim's "Evasion"— which proves in the end to be merely a gigantic hoax. Is not Mark Twain taking refuge from tragedy in a joke? He probably is, and in doing so he is conforming to a notorious American habit. This trait in our national character is by no means wholly bad. One aspect of it is our irreverence, the attitude that makes the Bronx cheer a familiar response to pretentiousness. Our irreverence protects us against the pompousness of our leaders. But it also insulates us against emotions that we do wrong to avoid; it sometimes makes us frivolous about matters that are truly serious. We should not be flattered to realize that our national identity can achieve so nearly complete expression through our identification with an adolescent boy. We cannot hope to escape all our problems by lighting out for the Territory. And if the time comes when we have to stand and face a crisis instead of passing it off with a joke or running away from it, the image of Huck Finn does not offer us much to go on in the way of techniques for dealing frontally with a world of adult problems and adversaries.

The very mixture of traits in Huck's character, however, makes this book a unique possession of the American people. Its curious blend of humor and satire and incipient tragedy; its apparently arbitrary and improvised structure that nevertheless achieves a coherent over-all effect—these resist placement in any literary tradition, although Huck's vernacular language has been one of the principal influences on American prose in the twentieth century. The book is a literary sport rather than the culmination of a coherent development. Yet the fact that it has in a sense no connections with the past, no history, is perhaps one of the qualities that make it most American. And in the end we can take a good deal of satisfaction in the positive qualities of Huck that seem to reflect a recognizable American identity. His sound heart, his freedom from malice, his loyalty to his friends, his revulsion against cruelty and hypocrisy, are traits that even foreign critics usually credit us with. Huck is also characteristic in his resourcefulness in emergencies. He is not easily flustered and he has an admirable toughness and resilience. If he lacks cultivation, he nevertheless has a keen intelligence: he is shrewd, observant, and clear in his processes of thought. And while he is subject to fits of depression because he perhaps too readily feels guilty, he is essentially stable; he tends to be cheerful in adversity. Yet he has no arrogance at all. Not a bad type, everything considered—rather above average, as national types go.

7 WILLIAM DEAN HOWELLS
The Rise of Silas Lapham

Robert Lee Hough

From the perspective of the mid-twentieth century, it is hard to realize that William Dean Howells was once the most powerful voice in American letters and that his novel *The Rise of Silas Lapham,* on its publication in 1885, was considered daring by some reviewers and "depraved" by others. Today the man that Henry James thought a master and Mark Twain called a stylist "without his peer in the English-writing world" is almost forgotten, and his novels, far from being considered daring or depraved, are criticized for their lack of emotional density. Despite the paperback revolution in the United States and elsewhere, only twelve editions of Howells' novels are in print today (six of these are of *The Rise of Silas Lapham*) while his two best known contemporaries, Mark Twain and Henry James, have some thirty-five and forty editions available respectively. Howells himself was cognizant of his fall from favor. A few years before his death in 1920 he wrote to James, who like Twain was a close personal friend, "I am comparatively a dead cult with my statues cut down and the grass growing over them in the pale moonlight."

Yet though the statues are gone and the honors, the tributes, and the "Howells men" have been swept away with the years, Howells and his ideas have had an important existence. Robert Frost once said that all Americans are eight or ten men and one of them is Howells, and Frost is right. Howells, like Twain, represents what Lincoln, Carnegie, and Edison represent in other areas: the opportunity possible in an egalitarian democracy, the rags-to-riches story, the barefoot boy who becomes a mover of men. Born in semipioneer Ohio in 1837, one of eight children, the son of a small-town printer-journalist who was often on the move, Howells had an up-bringing similar to that of thousands of rural Americans in the nineteenth century. Howells became imbued with certain ideals that he found in the Middle West, one of which was the democratic belief in the value of the life of the common man. When he lived in Ohio, and later in Venice, where he was the American consul during the Civil War, and still later in Boston, Howells began to see literary possibilities in the lives of people around him and in his own life. After all, in a democratic nation, why shouldn't there be a democratic literature? In 1871 he wrote his father from Boston that he hoped to make his way in a new kind of "personalized fiction." This concept of writing, this idea of using as the basis of fiction "the skeleton of actual reality," as Melville called it, grew with Howells during the 1870's and emerged fully developed in his finest work, the novels of the 1880's, *A Modern Instance, The Rise of Silas Lapham,* and *A Hazard of New Fortunes,* all of which have bases in personal experience or observation or knowledge gained through reading and research.

The technique became known as realism; it was physical, factual, pragmatic, and democratic in its biases. It was nothing more or less, Howells said, than a "truthful treatment of material," a "fidelity to experience and probability of motive." It was a combination of method (realism in physical detail and fact) and intent (the authorial effort to present lives as they were really lived). It represented, Howells thought, "the only living movement in imaginative literature" and related the realistic American novels, not to the English, which were still bound up with the romantic, "the passionate and the heroic," but to the French and Russian novels, which were also refusing to look at life through literary glasses.

By 1885 and the publication of *The Rise of Silas Lapham,* Howells was recognized as one of the leaders of American realistic fiction, and the following year he became the unofficial spokesman for the cause when he began his monthly column, the "Editor's Study," in *Harper's* magazine. From this vantage point Howells was able, month after month, to engage in what has come to be known as the "Realism War," the open controversy between realistic and romantic aims in fiction. In 1892, when Howells retired from the "Study," he gathered together his most pertinent comment from the six-year period, added transitional material, and issued the whole as *Criticism and Fiction*, still the central document in nineteenth-century American realism. Because of the close connection, both in time and theory, between *The Rise of Silas Lapham* and *Criticism and Fiction*, it is helpful to consider the latter briefly and to review the conditions which produced both.

It is often difficult today, when the battle for realism seems so assuredly won, to appreciate the position that romantic fiction held in America in the late nineteenth century. One gains some idea of its public favor by looking at the list of best-selling novels for some of the years of the controversy. In 1884 Robert Louis Stevenson's *Treasure Island* was the year's best seller; in 1886 Frances Hodgson Burnett's *Little Lord Fauntleroy* and H. Rider Haggard's *King Solomon's Mines* were the two leading sellers, and Haggard repeated his triumph in 1887 with *She: A History of Adventure*.

Moreover, one gains a real appreciation of the conflict between romance and realism by looking at the periodicals of the time, which were often filled with charge and counter-charge. On one side were the defenders of the older idealistic-romantic tradition—men like Stevenson, Haggard, F. Marion Crawford, and Andrew Lang. Their attack on realism was many-pronged, but basically it came down to a question of purpose. Literature, these men felt, was to entertain, to refresh, and to instruct, and it did this best, not by giving a photographic picture of life, but by taking the reader out of the real world and placing him in an imaginary one where love and adventure and morality could all be intensified. Literature provided escape, and the romantic genre best lifted man out of his workaday world and gave him glimpses of eternal truth.

Howells objected to such a theory because it contaminated

so easily. He agreed with most romantic writers that the finest effect of literature was ethical, not aesthetic, and felt that Hawthorne was one of the finest novelists that America had ever produced. But most romantic writers, Howells found, were not really interested in morality at all; they were interested in effect, in "bouncing" the reader, in "awakening at all cost . . . vivid and violent emotions, which [supposedly] do credit to the invention and originality of the writer." In this way romantic fiction was actually immoral. In *Criticism and Fiction,* Howells wrote:

> Romantic novels hurt because they are not true—not because they are malevolent, but because they are idle lies about human nature and the social fabric, which it behooves us to know and to understand, that we may deal justly with ourselves and with one another.

This concept of literary truth was central to Howells' beliefs. What he wanted literature to become was a kind of artistic mirror by which men saw and understood something about themselves and their environment; this created a more vital, more significant literature than could ever be created by writers who dealt with pirates and princes and "moral pap," as Louisa May Alcott once called romantic novels. What Howells did, in effect, was to expand the concept of what was "moral" to include the true, the probable. This tack, of course, was the one taken by early American authors to combat the Puritan charge that the novel was simply a pack of lies, but Howells buttressed his argument more pragmatically than did Mrs. Rowson. If something was importantly true, it could not be immoral because it informed man on something that he should know. He maintained that:

> We must ask ourselves before we ask anything else, Is it [the novel] true?—true to the motives, the impulses, the principles that shape the life of actual men and women? This truth, which necessarily includes the highest morality and the highest artistry—this truth given, the book cannot be wicked and cannot be weak. . . .

With this statement, with this theory, Howells provided the critical rationale for Stephen Crane's *Maggie: A Girl of the*

Streets, Frank Norris's *McTeague,* and Theodore Dreiser's *Sister Carrie;* he swung open the gates to the twentieth century.

Perhaps the best way to begin a study of *The Rise of Silas Lapham* is to consider it as an antiromance. The story concerns a common man become millionaire, a massive, middle-aged Vermont farmer whose father, forty years before, had discovered a mineral paint mine and thus provided the opportunity which his son's energy and resourcefulness have turned into wealth and a paint company in Boston. The skillful opening chapter, in which Silas is interviewed for the "Solid Men of Boston" series, gives a clear-cut exposition of his qualities: he is vulgar, bragging, and sentimental, yet along with these qualities he has a self-respect, an integrity, and kindness that are endearing. As the chapter ends, Silas sends the reporter's young bride a complete set of his best-grade paint. What an "old fool," the cynical reporter says; "What a good man," the girl exclaims, and this contrast sums up and projects Silas's character in the novel.

His goodness, of course, triumphs, and the book is Howells' supreme eulogy to the integrity of the common man. But Howells was determined that Silas should not be the conventional hero. He wanted a true-to-life, believable American man, and he insisted on Silas' "grayness." In several scenes Lapham is crude and pathetic in his ignorance of the social gap that exists between Lumberville, Vermont, and Boston, Massachusetts. In the scene following the Coreys' dinner party for the Laphams, for example, a party at which Silas becomes drunk and eventually patronizing to Back Bay society, Silas realizes how he must have appeared and compounds his error. "Will you tell your father," he gasps out to young Tom Corey, "I don't want him to notice me if we ever meet [again]?" The same treatment, though subdued, is accorded Silas' wife, Persis, his two daughters, Penelope and Irene, the young lover, Tom Corey, and Tom's parents, Mr. and Mrs. Bromfield Corey. These characters have admirable traits, but they are meant to resemble real people and thus they all have their foibles and weaknesses. Howells does not gild the lily; in fact the most frequent contemporary criticism of the novel was that the Laphams were too common. They were the kind of people, a critic wrote, that one avoided in real life. Howells was always pleased by this kind of recognition of the reality of his characters. He was once told that he seemed interested only in the real and was asked when he was going to create an Ideal Woman. Howells replied happily that he was waiting for the Almighty to begin.

The title of the book suggests the anti-Horatio Alger nature of the main plot. Silas' rise is a moral one and it is this rise that causes his financial ruin. Howells is careful to keep the paradox before the reader: Silas rises as he falls, he is saved morally as he is doomed financially. Actually Silas has three chances to recoup his fortune. He can re-establish himself by selling his now completely devalued Western property either to the rascally Englishmen or to the slippery Rogers, or he can take in the innocent New Yorker who is willing to put money in the paint company without knowing of the ruinous West Virginia competition. Though tempted almost beyond endurance (Silas wrestles with temptation as Jacob wrestled with the angel), he rejects each chance. He has accidentally burned down his new Beacon Street home, the symbol of his social rise; now he deliberately refuses the money which would allow him to maintain his financial position. In a muted variation of the opening scene, Howells closes the book with a conversation between Reverend Sewell and Silas on the farmstead in Vermont, where the Laphams have come back to live. Here Howells makes no romantic concessions; Sewell finds Silas more countrified than ever, even "rather shabby and slovenly in dress." Though quieter, Silas still brags in the old way, but now there is some moral justification for his pride. "One thing he could say: he had been no man's enemy but his own: every dollar, every cent had gone to pay his debts; he had come out with clean hands." Sewell, who realizes what his fortune and pride in being a self-made man have meant to Lapham, asks him if he has any regrets. Silas says, "I don't know as I should always say it paid; but if I done it, and the thing was to do over again, right in the same way, I guess I should have to do it."

It is sad but true, Howells comments in his own person, that the price of civilization is nothing less than that our manners and customs count more in life than our qualities.

Howells' antiromantic feelings are most clearly evident in the secondary strand of action, the Irene-Pen-Tom triangle. Here, in plot and in phrase, Howells re-echoes the dangers of romantic sentiment that he had pointed out in *Criticism and Fiction*. Irene, the younger Lapham girl, falls deeply in love with Tom Corey, and Silas and Persis suppose the affection returned because of Tom's frequent visits to the house. In reality, however, Tom is in love with Penelope, the older sister, and when he reveals this fact, everyone is thunderstruck. Pen, crushed for her sister and guilt-stricken because she feels she may have done something to win him away from Irene, refuses to listen to Tom and sends him away. Up to this point the plot suggests that of a typical romantic novel of the time, one which Howells calls *Tears, Idle Tears* (from Tennyson's poem) and inserts into the conversation at the Coreys' dinner party. There, after Miss Kingsbury has expressed tentative approval of the "wildly satisfying" self-sacrifice of the hero and heroine, the antiromantics take over. Nanny Corey renames the book, *Slop, Silly Slop*, and Reverend Sewell calls such novels "psychical suicide." "The novelists," he explains, "might be the greatest possible help to us if they painted life as it is, and human feelings in their true proportion and relation, but for the most part they have been and are altogether noxious." Later, when the Laphams come to him for advice, the Reverend gets the bit in his teeth:

We are all blinded, we are all weakened by a false ideal of self-sacrifice. . . . I don't know where this false ideal comes from, unless it comes from the novels that befool and debauch almost every intelligence in some degree. . . . Your daughter believes, in spite of her common sense, that she ought to make herself and the man who loves her unhappy, in order to assure the life-long wretchedness of her sister, whom he doesn't love, simply because her sister saw him and fancied him first. And I'm sorry to say that ninety-nine young people out of a hundred . . . would consider that noble and beautiful and heroic; whereas you know at the bottom of your hearts that it would be foolish and cruel and revolting. You know what marriage is! And what it must be without love on both sides.

Howells knew that self-sacrifice proceeded from romantic pride and egomania and was doubly dangerous because its springs were hidden under conviction of nobility. He was fascinated by its emotional hold on people and by its literary possibilities; in *Letters Home, Indian Summer,* and *The Minister's Charge,* as well as in *The Rise of Silas Lapham,* he deals with virtually the same plot: a triangle in which one member considers sacrificing herself. Pen comments on the silliness of *Tears, Idle Tears,* but when faced with the same situation in her own life she is unable to shake off the tenacity of the ideal. Eventually, of course, she accepts Tom, but only because her love proves stronger than her other feelings. Even Mrs. Sewell takes a sentimental view of the situation and feels contempt for Pen because of the misery she has caused Irene, and her shocked husband is able to wring only a partial retraction from her.

The weaknesses of the book too, at least in part, stem from Howells' literary philosophy. The big "bow-wow," he said, anyone can do; all you have to know is the trick of the thing. But the little "bow-wow," that was something different, that required consummate skill, and Howells was forever trying to bring it off. Howells' insistence on the average, the commonplace, the usual gives *The Rise of Silas Lapham* its realism, but it also gives it an evenness that keeps the novel from rising to heights. Howells' dislike of the melodramatic or sensational often undercuts the legitimately dramatic. There is, for example, no highly charged, "big" scene in the novel though Howells had opportunities both in Silas' story and the love plot. The longer scenes all tend to be expository, such as the opening interview, or comic, such as the Coreys' dinner party. The genuinely dramatic moments are rendered in short scenes or in narration. Tom's revelation of his love for Pen, for instance, is given in four pages, and the awful significance of his avowal—the fact that everyone has supposed him in love with Irene—is not explained to him until forty pages later, where in another scene of four pages Pen discloses the reason for her reaction. Narratively, there is no reason that the two events could not go together, and if handled properly, they might form a highly effective emotional scene. But Howells chooses to split them, and it is this kind of fragmenting of sensation which gives the book its levelness and which has caused some later realists to agree with Frank Norris that Howells' brand of realism is generally as exciting as "a cup of tea" or "a walk around the block."

There is no doubt that the last fourth of the book is less successful than the earlier portions, and though on the whole Howells is extremely skillful in his plotting, there is a general slackening of pace in the last six or seven chapters. George Arms, one of Howells' best critics, attributes the letdown to the author's inability to maintain his comic tone. "Howells," he says, "becomes too preoccupied with his characters as potentially tragic figures." This is true, but as Arms suggests without elaborating, the matter is more complex than this. Howells apparently decided, for sound artistic reasons, that the two strands of the plot should end together, but that Lapham's rise-fall should occupy the major part of the last one hundred pages. Accordingly, all the major complications of the love story are unraveled by Chapter 19 and action almost ceases in this part of the story, with Pen unable to make up her mind whether to accept or reject Tom. Thus the stage is clear for Silas, and here the author's low-key realism fails him. Howells decided against building toward a climactic financial collapse which might have been dramatically effective but apparently was not sufficiently probable. Instead Lapham's ruin becomes a slow disintegration with his speculation in stocks, his glutting of the paint market, his dealings with Rogers, the destruction of the Beacon Street house, and the competition from the West Virginia company all combining to bring him down. Though these matters are simplified by Howells, they clog the momentum of the action and the fact that Howells is forced to narrate many of the business involvements and to deal with them so summarily robs the story of its earlier density.

The long delay also undermines the earlier character portrait of Pen, who is forced to wait in the wings so long that the reader begins to wonder about her. Before Tom's proposal, she is shown to be the most perceptive of the Laphams and in some ways the most independent and mature. But after Tom's offer, because Howells needs the stage for the financial story, Pen simply wrings her hands and mopes in her room. Her willy-nilly attitude and her inability to decide in the only rational way possible make her seem like quite another girl. Paradoxically, Howells' realism for Silas results in a kind of unreality for Penelope.

Thus, in both its weaknesses and strengths, *The Rise of Silas Lapham* reveals a moral or literary attack on the romance, but were the book no more than this, it would have long since been relegated to grandmother's trunk in the attic. That it is more is due, in the first place, to Howells' craftsmanship. Though there are lapses, the book, on the whole, is masterfully put together. Signposts lead somewhere; details anticipate situations. Bartley Hubbard's notice of the pretty girl in Lapham's anteroom and his comment that she is the kind of a girl that wives do not like to see in their husbands' offices has significance later in the novel. So does the early mention of Silas' dabbling in stocks, the Persis Brand, and Tom's interest in the foreign distribution of Lapham's paint. The point of view is skillfully handled. Howells is almost always where he should be: in Silas' mind during the comic ordeal of the dinner party, in Tom's mind for the Back Bay judgment on Lapham's behavior, in Mrs. Corey's mind for the Brahmin reaction to Tom and Pen's marriage.

The symbols help to integrate and explain the novel. Persis is explicitly projected as Silas' conscience early in the novel; she is the one who reminds him of his conduct toward Rogers. When at the end she wavers and is unable to help Silas in his crucial decision, the reader can measure both the temptation and the moral rise of her husband. The new house on Beacon Street functions as a symbol for Silas' material and social hopes. It rises as they rise, is destroyed as they are destroyed. These are major symbols and help link various sections of the book, but there are other smaller referents which clarify character or situation. Irene, for example, is constantly associated with ribbons and pins, and when she leaves Tom for the first time in the book, her "blue ribbons [fluttered] backward from her hat, as if they were her clinging thoughts." When Silas is seeking Persis' permission to build on Beacon Street, he takes her to view the lot. She has been holding back because she is reluctant to change their way of life. When she sees the plot, she is impressed. " 'Yes, it's sightly,' " she says, "lifting her hand from the reins, on which she had unconsciously laid it." Immediately after, Lapham announces that *he* has made up his mind to build on the lot. Bromfield Corey declares that the relationship with the Laphams is something that cannot be done by halves; he then cuts his orange and eats it in quarters. With such symbolic action Howells is able to reveal rather than tell; he achieves, to a great degree, what he once called "dramatic demonstration," that is, letting the story tell itself. The symbols turn inward and explicate the action, thus allowing the author, to all appearances, to remain on the sidelines.

Howells' craftsmanship is perhaps best displayed in his handling of scene. One is surprised on examining the novel to find how much of the story is told in dialogue, particularly in the first three-fourths of the book. One chapter after another is simply a series of scenes, occurring usually between two people (Howells felt that all really dramatic encounters occurred between two people) and serving both to explore character and advance the action without the author's narrative intervention. Howells was much impressed by James's "scenic method," partly, perhaps, because it allowed such scope for his own gift of recording conversation. Here Howells combines his own word sense and his ear for dialect to run the range from the blunt Vermont twang of the Laphams to the proper Bostonian accents of Bromfield Corey. As with all good dialogue, one can visualize the characters from it. Silas says:

Well, then, the fellow set down and told me, "You've got a paint here," says he, "that's going to drive every other mineral paint out of the market. Why," says he, "it'll drive 'em right

> into the Back Bay!" . . . Then he went into a lot of particu-
> lars, and I begun to think he was drawing a long-bow . . .
> young chap, and pretty easy; but every word he said was gospel.
> Well, I ain't a-going to brag up my paint. . . .

As befits an author who wrote over twenty light farces in addition to his novels, Howells uses his dialogue to produce
most of the droll, witty humor of the book. Bromfield Corey,
who is a dilettante and an amateur painter, tells his son Tom,
who wishes to join Lapham's paint firm:

> It's a consolation to think that while I've been spending and
> enjoying, I've been preparing the noblest future for you—a
> future of industry and self-reliance. You never could draw, but
> this scheme of going into the mineral-paint business shows that
> you have inherited something of my feeling for color.

Howells' ability in handling scene goes beyond a talent for
dialogue; it has to do with the motivation of character, the
revealing of the right fact at the right time, and the relationship between one scene and another. In many ways the novel
is a story of social gaps, and one can gain some appreciation
of Howells' talent by studying the alternation of scenes that
occur in the Corey and Lapham houses at various times
throughout the novel.

Beyond these aspects of Howells' technical skill, the book
has the *sine qua non* of realistic fiction: the texture of life.
This quality is cumulative; it comes to the reader through
detail, speech, incident, and characterization. At the end
most readers feel that they can accept Howells' characters as
"real" people and that the author is seriously interested in
what happens to real people. Howells may be weak in places,
but he does not cheat. In fact, if Howells, in a few passages,
seems to us overly concerned about the morality of literature,
it reveals that we have lost something of the idealism and
high purpose that he held for fiction. In America, Bromfield
Corey says, all civilization comes through literature:

> A Greek got his civilization by talking and looking, and in some
> measure a Parisian may still do it. But we, who live remote from
> history and monuments, we must read or we must barbarize.

The great tragedy, Howells says in *Criticism and Fiction,* comes when one reads and barbarizes.

In the final accounting, *The Rise of Silas Lapham* has not proven itself a classic. It is not alive today in the same way that *Huckleberry Finn* and *The Red Badge of Courage* are. Nonetheless, in its artistry, its quality of "felt" life, and in its theme, which is nothing less than the Biblical question, "What shall it profit a man, if he shall gain the whole world, and lose his own soul," it is a novel that a writer and a literature can take pride in. And if the book does fall short of total greatness, its failure is partly due to the goal that Howells set for himself. In the book Charles Bellingham calls for the novel of the commonplace. He says:

> The commonplace is just that light, impalpable, aerial essence which [writers] have never got into their confounded books yet. The novelist who could interpret the common feelings of commonplace people would have the answer to "the riddle of the painful earth" on his tongue.

Howells was willing to settle for nothing else.

8 STEPHEN CRANE
The Red Badge of Courage

John Berryman

The wars of men have inspired the production of some of man's chief works of art, but very undemocratically. Napoleon's wars inspired Goya, Stendhal, Beethoven, Tolstoy; a prolonged bicker of 1100 B.C. inspired the poet of the *Iliad*, who celebrated and deplored three centuries later a little piece of it near its end; the Wars of the Roses resulted in Shakespeare's giant effort, again long afterward; the Athenian empire's ruin was adequately dramatized by a participant, the greatest of historians; Picasso made something of the soul-destroying Civil War in his native country. But what came of Cromwell's war? Or of the atrocious conflict between North and South in the United States?

Thirty years after it ended came a small novel by a very young man, called *The Red Badge of Courage*. The immediate literature of the Civil War has been beautifully studied of late in Edmund Wilson's *Patriotic Gore,* but no one would claim for that literature any such eminence as belongs, after almost seventy years, to Stephen Crane's novel. A critic seems to be faced, then, with alternative temptations: to overrate it, as an American, because it chronicles our crucial struggle, or to underrate it, in the grand perspective of the artists just mentioned, because it appears to assert neither the authority of the experienced warrior nor the authority of the historical artist—Tolstoi having both, Thucydides both. Crane was no scholar and had seen no battle. Yet some authority should be allowed him, and identified, for his work has not only brilliantly survived but was recognized instantly abroad—in England—as authentic; professional military men were surprised to learn that he was not one.

It is hard to see how anyone, except a casual reader, could overrate *The Red Badge of Courage* for patriotic reasons, because, though the book does indeed handle parts of the battle of Chancellorsville, it is not really about the Civil War. For instance, it shows no interest in the causes, meaning, or outcome of the war; no interest in politics; no interest in tactics or strategy. In this book, these failures are a merit, in opposition to the supreme fault of *War and Peace,* which is philosophical and programmatic. Here we have only parts of one minor battle, seen from one ignorant point of view, that of a new volunteer. One would never guess that what has been called the first modern war was being studied. All the same, as from the weird diagrams of Samuel Beckett emerges the helpless horror of modern man, we learn, as we learn from few books, about the waiting, the incomprehension, rumor, frustration, anxiety, fatigue, panic, hatred not only of the enemy but of officers; about complaints of "bad luck" and the sense of betrayal by commanders. This is a losing army. Since every intelligent man has to be at some point afraid of proving himself a coward—which is what the ordeal of Crane's protagonist is about—the story presents itself to us initially as making some claim to universality. The claim is strengthened by Crane's reluctance to divulge the name of the hero (it is Henry Fleming) or the names of the only other two people who matter—the tall soldier (Jim) and the loud youth (Wilson)—or the identity of the regiment, or the geography. By *leaving things out* the author makes his general bid for our trust.

But of course he has put in things too, and our problems are where he got them and how he put them. The main things he put in are reflection and action. Much of the book really is battle. Crane had read *Sebastopol,* Tolstoi's short novel, and declared that he learned what war was like from football; after starring in baseball at the two colleges he

briefly attended, he coached a boys' football team in New
Jersey. One of the staff at his military academy, a major-
general, had seen action at Chancellorsville and liked to talk
about it. Crane had played war games as a child, and talked
with veterans, and read (with disappointment and contempt)
magazine articles on the Civil War. Later, after witnessing
substantial parts of the Greco-Turkish War, he said, "*The
Red Badge* is all right." I don't know that we can say precisely how he learned what he knew, except to recognize in
him an acute visual imagination and an inspired instinct for
what happens and what does not happen in conflict. Here is a
short passage:

> He expected a battle scene.
> There were some little fields girted and squeezed by a forest.
> Spread over the grass and in among the tree trunks, he could
> see knots and waving lines of skirmishers who were running
> hither and thither and firing at the landscape. A dark battle
> line lay upon a sunstruck clearing that gleamed orange colour.
> A flag fluttered.
> Other regiments floundered up the bank.

Some of the features of Crane's *style* appear: his convulsive
and also humorous irony ("expected," as if he would not see
it but he saw it, and "firing at the landscape"), its violent
animism ("squeezed"), its descriptive energy ("knots and
waving lines"—like an abstract-expressionist painting). But a
Tolstoyan sense also of futility and incomprehension is
swiftly conveyed, and this is only partly a product of the
style. He is inventing, he is experimenting. Crane himself
goes in for this language—several times he speaks of "experiment" and says of the youth, "He tried to mathematically
prove to himself that he would not run from a battle." In the
action, then, the fantastic and the literal cooperate. The re-
flective aspects of the novel are another matter.

The scene of this extremely simple novel is laid in a single mind. It starts with soldiers speculating loudly about
whether there is going to be a fight or not. Then "a youthful
private" goes off to his hut: "He wished to be alone with

some new thoughts that had lately come to him." This has the effect of understatement, putting so flatly the youth's debate with himself about his honor, but it is literal, besides introducing the theme of intense isolation that dominated Crane's work until a later story, his masterpiece, "The Open Boat," where human cooperation in face of the indifference of nature is the slowly arrived-at subject. In *Red Badge* his youth broods in private, having crawled into his dilemma, or hut, "through an intricate hole that served it as a door"—and the rest of the book provides a workout of the plight. On the first day he does well, and then runs away. A Union soldier clubs him in the panic retreat; Crane's ironic title refers to the "badge" of that wound; the youth is taken for a good soldier. He witnesses the death of his boyhood friend, the tall soldier, a true hero. Returned, by the kindness of a stranger, to his regiment, he is cared for as a combatant by the loud youth, toward whom he is also enabled to feel superior in that, scared earlier, Wilson entrusted him with letters to be sent in the event of his death and has now, shamefacedly, to ask for their return. Next day he fights like a hero or demon. Such is the story. Perhaps many readers take it as a novel of development, a sort of success story, and this view is encouraged by the climactic passage:

> He felt a quiet manhood, non-assertive but of sturdy and strong blood. . . . He had been to touch the great death, and found that, after all, it was but the great death. He was a man. . . .

It is possible to feel very uncomfortable with this way of looking at the book. For one thing, pervasive irony is directed toward the youth—his self-importance, his self-pity, his self-loving war rage. For another, we have only one final semiself-reproach for his cowardice and imposture:

> He saw that he was good. . . . Nevertheless, the ghost of his flight from the first engagement appeared to him and danced. There were small shoutings in his brain about these matters. For a moment he blushed, and the light of his soul flickered with shame.

I find it hard to believe that in this passage Crane is exonerating his hero without irony. Finally, we have very early in the book an indication of his pomposity (his mother's "I know how you are, Henry"), and there is pomposity in his final opinion of himself as a war demon. That would suggest a circular action, in the coward middle of which he appeared to reveal his real nature, or in fact did reveal it, by running. The irony embraces, then, all but the central failure.

It is easy to feel uncomfortable with this view, too—more particularly because the apparent wound of the first day is indeed a real wound, and its silent pretension is later justified. On the other hand, the irony never ends. I do not know what Crane intended. Probably he intended to have his cake and eat it too—irony to the end, but heroism too. Fair enough. How far did he fail?

Again I invoke, as praiseworthy, that which is not done. The youth is frantically afraid of being found out (he never is found out) but except in the passage just quoted he never suffers the remorse one would expect. Intimate as Crane is with his hero psychologically, still the view he takes of him is cold, unsentimental, remote. This certainly preserves him from any full failure (though there have been many reliable readers from the day the book was published to now who have not liked it, because they regarded it as artificial and sensational).

The coldness leads to a certain impersonality, and it is a striking fact that some of Crane's deepest private interests find no place in the novel; in fact, they are deliberately excluded. Three of them are worth singling out. In his earlier novel, or long story, called *Maggie,* laid in New York's Bowery, Crane dramatized a distinct social philosophy—environmentalist, deterministic, and convinced that "the root of slum-life" was "a sort of cowardice." Yet his indifference to society in *The Red Badge* is complete, and it would not do to say "Of course it would be," for an army *is* society.

So with the matter of personal philosophy. We happen to know Crane's views perfectly, because he put them at length in letters to a girl (Nellie Crouse) by whom he was fascinated in 1895–96. He wrote:

For my own part, I am minded to die in my thirty-fifth year [he died at 28, in 1900]. I think that is all I care to stand. I don't like to make wise remarks on the aspect of life but I will say that it doesn't strike me as particularly worth the trouble. The final wall of the wise man's thought however is Human Kindness of course.

Exceptionally for him, Crane capitalized the two words. Now it might have been supposed that, bringing his hero through to maturity in *The Red Badge,* he would have concentrated in this area. But no. It seems impossible not to conclude that the splendid burst of rhetoric with which the novel concludes is just that, *in part*—a burst of rhetoric—and that Crane retained many of his reservations about his hero. As the wisest of modern British novelists, E. M. Forster, once observed, novels almost never end well: character desires to keep on going, whereas remorseless plot requires it to end. I hardly remember a better instance. Yet the last page is confidently and brilliantly done:

> It rained. The procession of weary soldiers became a bedraggled train, despondent and muttering, marching with churning effort in a trough of liquid brown mud under a low, wretched sky. Yet the youth smiled, for he saw that the world was a world for him, though many discovered it to be made of oaths and walking-sticks. He had rid himself of the red sickness of battle.

But *then* comes a sentence in which I simply do not believe. "He turned now with a lover's thirst to images of tranquil skies, fresh meadows, cool brooks—an existence of soft and eternal peace." In short we are left after all with a *fool,* for Crane knew as well as the next man, and much better, that life consists of very little but struggle. He wrote to Miss Crouse of

> . . . a life of labor and sorrow. I do not confront it blithely. I confront it with desperate resolution. There is not even much hope in my attitude. [Perhaps I should mention that at this time Stephen Crane was an international celebrity.] I do not even expect to do good. But I expect to make a sincere, desperate, lonely battle to remain true to my conception of my life and the way it should be lived. . . . It is not a fine prospect.

The shutting out of his hero from his personal thought redeems for me, on the whole, the end of the book.

The absence of interest in religion in *The Red Badge of Courage* is even more surprising than the other indifferences, whether seen in a critical way or in a biographical way. Henry Fleming, orphan of a farm widow, was seminary-trained. What emerges from the training is scanty indeed. "He would die; he would go to some place where he would be understood. It was useless to expect appreciation of his profound and fine senses from such men as the lieutenant." This is a fine and funny passage, not deeply Christian. Then there is the famous passage about the wafer, long quoted as a war cry for modernism in American fictional art. Unutterably wounded, upright, the tall soldier has sought a private ground away from the retreat, in a field mysteriously chosen, followed by the youth and a tattered soldier, for his dance of death:

> As the flap of the blue jacket fell away from the body, he could see that the side looked as if it had been chewed by wolves.
>
> The youth turned, with sudden, livid rage, toward the battle-field. He shook his fist. He seemed about to deliver a philippic.
>
> "Hell—"
>
> The red sun was pasted in the sky like a wafer.

Pasting is a failingly temporary operation (for the pagan god of the sky?) handed us here as an overpowering rebuke to the youth's rebellion. A wafer is thick nourishment, too, is it not? Disdain and fury against the prerogatives of majesty seem to be the subject. Even here it is hard to decide just how far Crane is sympathetic with the youth and how far critical of him. Revolt, in a seminary youth, should have been better prepared: one would welcome a *trace* of his Christian history, pro or con; that Crane never provides. Shortly afterward we hear:

> He searched about in his mind for an adequate malediction for the inadequate cause, the thing upon which men turn the words

of final blame. It—whatever it was—was responsible for him, he said. There lay the fault.

Crane did not here believe in evil. Henry Fleming is not evil, nor is anyone. A strange setup for an ambitious novel. Determinism is in control: "It . . . was responsible for him." Or is it? For the next little words are *"he said"*—which may be a repudiation. Again we are in the seesaw, which is not a bad place to be, so long as one trusts the writer.

Crane's religious history can be treated briefly. He could not help being the son of a clergyman and of a madly missionary woman. He told an interviewer:

> That cooled off and when I was thirteen or about that, my brother Will told me not to believe in Hell after my uncle had been boring me about the lake of fire and the rest of the sideshows.

Another time he said:

> I cannot be shown that God bends upon us any definable stare, and his laughter would be bully to hear out in nothingness.

I think we may conclude that neither this personal opinion nor the fierce scorn of Christianity that flashes in many of Crane's brilliant poems really has anything to do with the purely naturalistic framework—from this point of view—of *The Red Badge of Courage.*

With the word "naturalistic," however, we turn to some consideration of the artistic affiliations of the novel. All the categorical terms that have been applied to Crane's art are slippery, but let me deny at once that he was a naturalist. The naturalists—Frank Norris, say, and Theodore Dreiser— are accumulative and ponderous. Crane's intense selectivity makes him almost utterly unlike them. Crane himself, when hardly more than a boy, allied his creed to the realism preached—in revolt against the slack, contrived, squeamish standards of popular American fiction in the nineties—by his first admirers, William Dean Howells, then the country's leading critic, and a younger writer, Hamlin Garland. But

Crane's work does not resemble theirs, either, and he seems to have meant, in his alliance, only that art should be "sincere" (one of his favorite words) and truthful. Like many another young genius, he regarded most writers as frauds and liars, and in fact perhaps most writers *are* frauds and liars. But epithets so vague as "sincere" and "truthful" tell us very little. The best term is undoubtedly that of his close friend, the far greater novelist, Joseph Conrad (though whether a *better* writer it is probably too soon to say), who observed in a letter to a mutual friend that "He is *the* only impressionist, and *only* an impressionist."

If we can accept this characteristically exaggerated but authoritative judgment, we are in a position to make some reservations. Conrad and Crane, when they met in England in 1897, immediately recognized an affinity for one another; Conrad was soon charged by reviewers with imitating Crane (a charge he denied, to Crane). In truth, parts of *Lord Jim* are much indebted to *The Red Badge;* yet Conrad clearly did not regard himself as an impressionist. Next, there exist in Crane's work obviously realistic and fantastic elements (as in Conrad's and in that of their friend, Henry James, also domiciled in the south of England at this time), two Americans and a Pole re-creating English fiction, which was languishing, so far as form was concerned, in the powerful hands of Thomas Hardy and Rudyard Kipling. The power of experiment came from abroad, as later from Joyce and Hemingway and Kafka, and in poetry from T. S. Eliot and Ezra Pound.

Finally, the use of irony enters so deeply into most of Crane's finest work (all five latter authors are ironists) that the simple term "impressionist" will hardly do, and my uncertain feeling is that Crane is best thought of as a twentieth-century author. Authorities date modern American literature, some from *The Red Badge* in 1895, some from the reissue in the following year of *Maggie*. This critique is not the place for an exposition of the nature of irony in relation to Crane, but perhaps something of that will emerge from a summary study of his style. By way, though, of winding up the impressionist reservations, let me reinforce Conrad's label with a quotation from Crane:

> I understand that a man is born into the world with his own pair of eyes and he is not at all responsible for his vision—he is merely responsible for his quality of personal honesty. To keep close to this personal honesty is my supreme ambition.

Ill, dying indeed, hard-pressed with guests and fame and need for money, working incessantly, he said to a journalist visitor during his last year of life: "I get a little tired of saying, 'Is this true?'" He was an impressionist: he dealt in the way things strike one, but also in the way things are.

This famous style is not easy to describe, combining as it does characteristics commonly antithetical. It is swift, no style in English more so, improvisatorial, manly as Hazlitt; but at the same time it goes in for ritual solemnity and can be highly poetic. For example, as an illustration of the speed of his style:

> For a moment he felt in the face of his great trial like a babe, and the flesh over his heart seemed very thin. He seized time to look about him calculatingly.

Here we are already into something like the poetic tone which is well illustrated in the opening sentence of the novel: "The cold passed reluctantly from the earth, and the retiring fogs revealed an army stretched out on the hills, resting." This is a high case of the animism already referred to. The color of the style is celebrated; maybe he got it from a theory of Goethe's, but the style is also plain, plain. Short as it is, it is also unusually iterative; modern and simple, brazen with medieval imagery; animistic, dehuman, and mechanistic; attentive—brilliantly—to sound:

> As he ran, he became aware that the forest had stopped its music, as if at last becoming capable of hearing the foreign sounds. The trees hushed and stood motionless. Everything seemed to be listening to the crackle and clatter and ear-shaking thunder. The chorus pealed over the still earth.

95

Adverbs are used like verbs, word order deformed: somebody leans on a bar and hears other men "terribly discuss a question that was not plain." But the surest attribute of this style is its reserve, as its most celebrated is its color. Crane guarantees nothing. "Doubtless" is a favorite word. The technique of refusal is brought so far forward that a casual "often" will defeat itself: "What hats and caps were left to them they often slung high in the air." Once more we hear a Shakespearean contempt, as in *Coriolanus*. In a paradoxical way, if he will not vouch for what he tells us, if he does not push us, trying to convince, we feel that he must have things up his sleeve which would persuade us if we only knew them. As for color: "A crimson roar came from the distance" is the mildest example I have been able to find. His employment of it here is not only not naturalistic (what roar was ever red?) but is solely affective, that is, emotional, like his metaphorical use, in the novel, of devils, ghouls, demons, and specters. Crane made use of a spectrum. A final item is his rueful humor: "He threw aside his mental pamphlets on the philosophy of the retreated and rules for the guidance of the damned."

On that note we might end, except for a poem written by Stephen Crane several years after the novel, called "War Is Kind"; it is one of his major poems, and one of the best poems of the period. In the novel there is little of the pathos of which he had already shown himself a master in *Maggie,* and little of the horror informing his best later war stories. These qualities come to life in the poem.

Crane makes a sort of little bridge between Tolstoi—supreme—supreme?—and our very good writer Hemingway. But these superior gentlemen are not competitors. One of the most cogent remarks ever made about the poet of the *Iliad* is that he shared with Tolstoi and with Shakespeare both a virile love of war and a virile horror of it. So in his degree did Crane, and before he had seen it.

9 FRANK NORRIS
McTeague: A Story of San Francisco

Carvel Collins

Frank Norris' *McTeague: A Story of San Francisco,* published in 1899, has been called the "first important Naturalistic novel" in the United States. William Dean Howells thought it brought a new mode into American literature with the "effect of a blizzard." A few leading American critics had accepted European literary naturalism in the 1880's, and a few earlier works of fiction had pointed toward naturalism. Stephen Crane's naturalistic short novel, *Maggie,* had been published six years before *McTeague.* But because of the greater extent to which *McTeague* imported into the United States the attitudes and devices of European naturalism and because of its greater length and force, it outweighs *Maggie* as a pioneering work. Despite numerous weaknesses *McTeague* is the aesthetic superior of *Maggie.*

Naturalism, at its beginning, owed much to the works of Balzac and Stendhal, but the first novels recognized as fully naturalistic were those written after the middle of the nineteenth century by Flaubert, the brothers Goncourt, Daudet, Maupassant, and Zola. These artists wrote their grim and violent fiction partly out of personal hurt and despair in a time of general disillusionment and also partly in reaction against the brighter excesses of romantic literature, but most of them believed that it was to the rapidly expanding science of their time that they owed whatever was naturalistic in their art. They said that they were trying to write "the Truth," and that to do it they were borrowing from science not only its materialism and determinism but its detachment, unmorality, direct observation, and "frank acceptance and depicting of the thing as it is."

In their emphasis on the overwhelming forces which drive mankind, literary naturalists usually depicted life in the lower levels of society. Especially interested in "the brute within," they often chose as central characters people with little intellect but remarkable physical qualities, such as McTeague, or people driven by oversimplified psychological defects, such as Trina McTeague, with her masochism and morbid parsimony. This strong emphasis on incompetents and the forces which cause them to degenerate made grotesques of many characters in naturalistic fiction. Zola, who had faith in future reform despite the depth of his pessimism concerning the present, excused his school's grotesque characters and low settings by saying that naturalists, like scientists, should be willing to stir up "the fetid" in unpleasant places because, as the physiologist Claude Bernard had written, ultimate knowledge is a "superb salon, flooded with light, which you can only reach by passing through a long and nauseating kitchen." [1]

In dealing with this sometimes sordid subject matter, the naturalists incorporated in their method the collection of masses of details, an extension of Balzac's method intensified by their respect for experimental science. After drawing on whatever store of useful technicalities their own experiences furnished, the naturalists depended on research, the accuracy of which they were willing to go to great lengths to ensure. Zola, for example, prepared a careful record of the technical facts of railroading for one novel and of coal mining for another. Norris studied the Harvard Library's copy of *A Textbook of Operative Dentistry* so he could load *McTeague* with the dental minutiae of bud-burs and gutta-percha. Throughout, the naturalists' most characteristic tool was the notebook.

Desiring to be "scientific" and detached, yet motivated in part by outraged moralism, the naturalists made irony an

1 Emile Zola, *"The Experimental Novel" and Other Essays*, trans. Belle M. Sherman (New York: Cassell, n.d.), p. 27.

essential part of their method. Not wanting to enter into their novels as a chorus-speaking commentary, they let their anger and bewilderment find expression through an ironic juxtaposition of events, described with apparent detachment.

In his discussion of the naturalists' method, Zola said that the novelist "should operate on the characters, the passions, on the human and social data, in the same way that the chemist and the physicist operate on inanimate beings." Partly as a result of this "experimental method"—whether or not they ever really achieved it—most naturalists concentrated on man's external rather than his internal world. This concentration did much to encourage the movement of fiction away from naturalism. Gradually, with greater knowledge of psychology, increased familiarity with symbolism, and strong compulsions toward rediscovery of "myth" in the innumerable interpretations of that term, writers came to consider naturalistic fiction not so interesting as fiction less confined to externals. Yet naturalism was influential in helping to bring literature to a closer, freer examination of reality. By writing *McTeague* when this mode was only becoming established in this country, Frank Norris performed a service for literature in the United States.

Norris was born in Chicago in 1870 and at the age of fifteen moved to San Francisco. Since he showed some talent for drawing, his well-to-do family took him to Paris in 1887 to study art. Back in San Francisco after two years in Paris, Norris spent several months writing a long romantic poem and preparing to enter the University of California. In four years at that university he contributed to college publications and sold stories to magazines. His biographer, Franklin Walker, reports that people who knew Norris in the university remember him as often carrying copies of French editions of Zola's novels and giving passionate defenses of that leading literary naturalist. In Zola's sensationalism, love of large canvases, and massing of documentation, Norris found the combination his temperament demanded. In the years to come he would jokingly sign some of his letters "The Boy Zola."

While Norris was in the university his parents were divorced, his father remarried, and Norris found himself no longer the potential heir to a fortune. His biographer feels that this withdrawal of large financial expectations, coupled with the impact of Zola's novels, turned Norris' attention to the life of the underprivileged. In naturalist fashion he began to record details of life in the poorer sections of San Francisco.

When his four years at the University of California ended in 1894, he enrolled at Harvard College to take a writing course. Under the encouragement of his instructor, Lewis E. Gates, to whom he later dedicated the novel, he worked on *McTeague* until he finished the episode of Trina's murder. He then apparently had difficulty in disposing of the murderer and put the manuscript aside.

After one year at Harvard, Norris went to South Africa to write travel letters for a newspaper. When Jameson's Raid interfered with his plan he returned to California, to become assistant editor of the *San Francisco Wave,* for which he wrote sketches, stories, and serials. Late in 1897, granted a few weeks' leave from the *Wave,* Norris completed *McTeague,* which he submitted to publishers without success, meanwhile writing *Moran of the "Lady Letty."* After moving from San Francisco to New York to work for the McClure publishing syndicate and finishing a semiautobiographical novel entitled *Blix,* Norris went to Cuba as a correspondent in the Spanish-American War. Back in New York in 1898 he began work as a manuscript reader for the recently formed house of Doubleday, McClure and Company.

Finally, in February 1899, *McTeague* was published. With its appearance Norris received more attention, favorable and unfavorable, than *Moran of the "Lady Letty"* had brought him. Most encouraging was a long and complimentary review by the influential William Dean Howells, recognizing *McTeague* as an important step in the "expansion of American fiction."

Within a few weeks of the publication of *McTeague,* Norris finished *A Man's Woman,* which even he called "slovenly." With these books off his hands, he immediately formed plans for a trilogy about wheat—the first volume, *The Octopus,* to be set in the San Joaquin Valley of California. He went to California in order to "study the whole thing *on the ground*" in Zola's fashion, complete with notebook. He soon reported that facts about wheat farming were "piling up BIG." After a few months he returned to New York to write the novel. Remembering the inadequacies of *Moran* and of *A Man's Woman,* he decided to go back "*definitely* now to the style of *McTeague*" and make the trilogy "straight naturalism with all the guts I can get into it."

Doubleday, McClure had become Doubleday, Page; in January 1900, the new firm hired Norris as a special manuscript reader. That summer Theodore Dreiser, one year Norris' junior, submitted to Doubleday the manuscript of *Sister Carrie,* his first novel and one superior to Norris' *McTeague.* Norris, recognizing the quality of that work, at once generously and energetically became its defender when the self-imposed censorship of the publishers prevented its regular distribution.

Norris' *The Octopus* came out early in 1901 and was an immediate success despite defects which in recent years have lowered it in critical estimation. Norris then set about the preliminary work for his wheat trilogy's second volume, *The Pit.* He moved to Chicago to study the grain market at firsthand; but the writing was a struggle because he did not feel at home with the new subject, nor was his intention clear enough to make *The Pit* a good book. When he had finished it, he began to plan the third volume, *The Wolf,* and even projected another trilogy—one novel for each day of the Battle of Gettysburg.

Norris had returned to San Francisco. *The Pit* had just started to appear as a serial in the *Saturday Evening Post,* from which it was to go on to be the best-selling novel of the following year. He had completed plans for a voyage across the Pacific to gather material at firsthand for *The Wolf.* Suddenly he died of appendicitis, in October 1902.

Since his death, Frank Norris' fiction has dropped to a

considerably lower position in the American literary canon than it held in the last years of his life. There has also been a re-evaluation of his books in relation to each other; *McTeague* has gained favor until in the opinion of many it is his best.

McTeague is the story of a huge, unintelligent miner from the California mountains who becomes a dentist in the city of San Francisco, where a thin layer of sophistication temporarily covers his primitive nature. Eventually the greed of his city associates tears it away, and the novel records the destruction, by so-called civilization, of this back-country innocent. Though Norris sometimes seems snobbishly contemptuous of McTeague, on the whole he presents him with sympathy as lonely and put-upon. When McTeague was a youth at the Big Dipper Mine he led a menial life for which he was fitted because of his great strength and small intellect. His tendency to violence when drunk—presented as an inheritance from his father, in the oversimplified biology of the early naturalists—he had admirably learned to control by avoiding whiskey entirely. He could have lived on happily at the mine.

But his mother's ambition for her son to "better himself" forced McTeague to leave the mountains and set up his modest dental office in San Francisco. There, in what passed for civilization on Polk Street, he retained some primitive contentment, with huge, cheap meals and steam beer and concertina music on Sundays.

When Trina entered his life and, like his mother, set about improving him, he developed a taste for better clothing and better food, thus taking one more step away from the simple world of the Big Dipper Mine. So far McTeague's life seems by conventional measures to be a progress, and it seems so to him when, his dreams fulfilled, he at last can afford to buy an enormous gilded tooth to hang outside his office as the sign of his profession and of his success.

But the trap has already closed on McTeague, as the mousetrap symbol at the end of the fifth chapter points out too obviously. Ironically, on the day McTeague uncrates the golden tooth, he and Trina's cousin Marcus, who is enraged because he has relinquished Trina's money to McTeague, are irrevocably set at odds and McTeague's destruction becomes inevitable. When Marcus arranges for him to be barred from practice as a dentist, McTeague becomes entirely vulnerable to Trina's avarice. Finally, on a night when he is especially depressed by fatigue and exposure brought on by her morbid refusal to give him carfare, McTeague begins to drink and the latent viciousness inherited from his father starts to dominate his life. Later he steals from Trina and after the money is gone returns to beg. When Trina refuses him help and his last remaining self-control slips away, he kills her.

Escaping from civilization back to the Big Dipper Mine, McTeague regains the contentment of his boyhood. "The life pleased the dentist beyond words. The still, colossal mountains took him back again . . ." But the city pursues him for his crime, and he flees. In the mountains, ironically, he discovers a rich vein of the metal for which Marcus has betrayed him and Trina has driven him to murder. But the pursuit begun in the city forces him on, to final destruction.

Looked at in this oversimplified summary, the novel, like much naturalism, is moralistic. The theme of its moralizing is ancient: civilization is corrupt and its vice destroys a man who could have remained innocent in simpler surroundings. Norris' development of this theme in *McTeague* seems to owe much to an amalgam of the literary naturalism he borrowed from Europe with the ideas he picked up from American social and revolutionary thinkers of his time. Such essays as "The Frontier Gone at Last" and "A Neglected Epic" and his first wheat novel, *The Octopus,* clearly show that Norris held many ideas or prejudices in common with the American historian, Frederick Jackson Turner, whose primitivistic theory of the frontier was first published in 1894 and began its great wave of popularity during the years Norris wrote. Among Turner's ideas—which were to dominate the academic study of American history for decades—was the oversimplification which locates good in the country and evil in town. This idea Norris put to work in *McTeague:*

The dentist, who has come to the city from the mountains, is the only foreground character not ruled by avarice. Though gold, which appears throughout the book in the familiar naturalistic use of a single dominating symbol, causes the downfall of other characters because of their avarice, when it is associated with McTeague it does not suggest that he is avaricious but that he is sensitive and has aspirations. This is a crude type of symbolism, but is meant to be somewhat touching. The gold in his office, which Maria, an avaricious servant, often steals and sells to a gold-mad junk dealer, is to McTeague a dental material which he delights to shape for use in his profession. He takes the money from Trina not so much because he is avaricious as because he is angry for the the depths to which her avarice has brought them and because he wants to spend it—which he promptly does. And he does not kill Trina out of avarice for her golden lottery prize but for revenge. McTeague's downfall seems to come not from avarice or even, perhaps, from his extremely bad physical heritage but from the destruction by the city of his control over that heritage. His self-control has kept him harmless for many years, but surrounding him on Polk Street are the corrupt, for whom gold is a mania. These others are, like McTeague, victims of forces outside themselves. But the author treats them with less sympathy than he treats McTeague. For their avarice he punishes them all by violent death before McTeague is finally destroyed.

"We are, in a word, experimental moralists, showing by experiment in what way a passion acts in a certain social condition." So Zola wrote in *The Experimental Novel,* that handbook which attempted to simplify and rationalize the multifarious practices of literary naturalism. If it is true that Norris had in mind something of this sort, he may have owed to Zola the general intention of *McTeague.* He certainly owed to the French naturalist much else that is in the novel. Most of its general structure is similar to that of Zola's *L'Assommoir,* as Lars Ahnebrink has shown in great detail. In each novel the married couple has a happy period before trouble starts. Then both men become idle and, though they formerly had made a point of avoiding alcohol, take to drink. In their decline both wives become scrubwomen. The account of the passage of people of various types along Polk Street in the first chapter of *McTeague* owes much of its structure to an early scene in *L'Assommoir*. The marriage ceremonies in the two books are closely similar. So are the wedding feasts, which also have a parallel in Zola's *Nana*.

La Bête Humaine was probably the novel of Zola's from which Norris drew most in his study of "the brute within" —though his unintelligent adaptation of this element, especially in the second chapter of *McTeague*, shows in its awkward moral rigor slight relation to its model. *McTeague* is also indebted to *La Bête Humaine* for its subplot: the episodes of Maria and her husband are similar to those in which one of Zola's characters obsessively searches a house in an effort to find his wife's hidden gold and kills her when he does not succeed.

There can be little doubt that in *McTeague* Norris' major literary source was Zola's work, from which he drew these and several other specific motifs and devices in addition to the more general naturalistic elements of low milieu, emphasis on heredity, environment, and degeneration, and the use of such subordinate symbols as the quarreling dogs and the mousetrap as well as a single predominant symbol, gold. But Norris' imitation of Zola was not slavish. He was able to make the book his own, giving much of the action verisimilitude by remarkable observation and selection of significant detail. The novel has monumental faults: the crude symbolism is overworked; the conception of the central character is often unsure because of inadequate social and biological theories which Norris had assimilated incompletely; and in the final chapters there is an excessive increase of melodrama. But these failings are not enough completely to demolish the force of the book or the tenacity with which many of its scenes and episodes remain in the mind of its reader.

10 THEODORE DREISER
Sister Carrie

Claude M. Simpson, Jr.

Sister Carrie is a historical landmark in American fiction. Written in 1900, it represents a point of view of the late nineteenth century, but it was not really available to the public until some years after its appearance, and its publication was tinged with curious scandal. In one of its major plot movements it could be accounted a success story, but in this sense it appears to go counter to one of the great American myths: that hard work and perseverance, even more than natural talent and education, will enable one to rise in the world. This myth was most conspicuously incorporated into late nineteenth-century fiction by Horatio Alger, who wrote a shelfful of immensely popular volumes directed at a juvenile audience. *Luck and Pluck, Ragged Dick, Tom the Bootblack* —the titles suggest some of the ingredients of this fiction: the underprivileged young heroes, the emphasis on ambition, the exploitation of sentiment and melodrama. These novels showed orphan boys struggling against poverty, but through industry and frugality (usually accompanied by luck) working their way to positions of wealth and honor. Alger's books expressed an urban dream of success—success attained without sacrifice of ethical restraints and responsibility.

But Alger's formula for success did not take into account the world as Theodore Dreiser knew it. Dreiser very early became conscious of the disparity between the ethics people professed and those by which they lived. In all his work he tried to describe what he had experienced, including his own bafflement in understanding forces at work. In the Frank Cowperwood trilogy, comprising *The Financier* (1912), *The Titan* (1914), and *The Stoic* (1947), he studied an aggressive and ruthless businessman, whose view of life is largely summed up by his motto "I satisfy myself." *The "Genius"* (1915) explored similar amoral drives in the life of an artist equally disdainful of bourgeois conventions. Dreiser was also concerned with the weak, the victims, those who are oftener acted upon than acting; they occupy the center of the stage in *An American Tragedy* (1925), *Jennie Gerhardt* (1911), and *Sister Carrie.*

In simplest terms, Dreiser's world is propelled by power and chance. He is, as Eliseo Vivas has maintained, an "inconsistent mechanist," but he shares with late nineteenth-century European naturalists the desire to explain scientifically the behavior of his characters, even though he is conscious of what he cannot explain. None of his books is more interesting than *Sister Carrie,* his first novel. It announces most of his major themes; it exhibits his characteristic interest in detailed documentation, set forth in a rough-hewn style which possesses genuine strength except when it aspires to elegance; and it tells a story drawn from his own observation, but not without archetypal significance for modern urban man.

Carrie Meeber, the central figure of the novel, comes to Chicago from a small town when she is eighteen years old. She works at a series of unattractive factory jobs, meanwhile living in a bleak, cheerless apartment with the family of her sister Minnie Hanson. An easygoing, plausible salesman named Drouet rescues Carrie from her frustrations and unhappiness, but before long she deserts him for the superior attractions of Hurstwood, a prosperous saloon manager. Hurstwood, whose own domestic life is falling apart, robs the saloon safe and through a pretext persuades Carrie to flee with him to Montreal and then to New York City. He is discovered, has to return the money, and his career is ruined. The New York half of the novel traces Hurstwood's decline in poignant detail. Meantime Carrie, who has been a singularly passive figure, is finally forced to support herself and turns to the theater. Not through acting ability but through instinct and personality she gradually achieves success on the stage, and the novel ends with Hurstwood's suicide and Carrie's establishment in an apartment in the Waldorf Hotel.

To a twentieth-century reader, *Sister Carrie* may seem rather tame. The book is devoid of obscenity, its language is never lurid, and only one passage could conceivably be termed erotic. Yet, after the publishing firm of Doubleday, Page and Company accepted the novel Page tried to persuade Dreiser to withdraw it; when he refused, the publishers fulfilled the bare letter of their contract by issuing *Sister Carrie* but making no effort to sell it. It literally dropped dead from the press.[1] Why this virtual censorship in 1900? Not merely because Dreiser had written about a roué, a kept woman, and a saloon manager—there were less genteel characters in Frank Norris' *McTeague,* which Doubleday, Page had just published. Frank Doubleday's dislike of *Sister Carrie,* abetted by his wife's reaction when she read the proof sheets, was perhaps a businessman's view that the novel would not be popular with the predominantly feminine reading public because its disturbing problems were not magically resolved at the end. Nor was virtue rewarded and vice punished in accord with conventional views of morality. Drouet, the seducer, rose from traveling salesman to branch manager, as if to suggest that personal integrity is unrelated to business success. Hurstwood's crime was followed by his long steady decline, but the consequences are not viewed as the wages of sin. Dreiser suggests instead a purely behavioristic explanation —Hurstwood's inability to adapt himself to the New York environment. Still more offensive was the treatment of Carrie. She became the mistress of first one man and then the other, yet she is not made to suffer for violating social norms appropriate to the usual fictional heroine. Although Dreiser

[1] The vicissitudes of publication are described in greater detail in my introduction to an edition of *Sister Carrie* (Boston: Houghton Mifflin Company, 1959). All quotations in the present essay are drawn from that edition, which is based on the 1900 text.

denies her happiness, he does award her unmistakable success as an actress, and her wistfulness as she sits musing at the end of the novel is a token of her yearning for the ideal—not contrition for sinful action. Indeed, he offers the general observation: "Not evil, but longing for that which is better, more often directs the steps of the erring."

Dreiser's naturalistic view of human behavior was not original with him. The doctrine had been enunciated by Zola in his *The Experimental Novel* and illustrated, though never with complete consistency, by a number of Continental novelists whom Dreiser had not then read. During the 1890's he did read Herbert Spencer, Thomas Henry Huxley, and John Tyndall—an explosive experience—and he also discovered Balzac and Hardy. But the ideas of social Darwinism and the survival of the fittest gave him less a point of view to imitate than a way of formulating the significance of his own experience.

Born of a narrow, pietistic German Catholic father and a warm, tolerant mother, he saw the large family frequently moving about the Middle West, never settled, always poor. It shook the young Dreiser's faith to discover that his father's religious orthodoxy did not keep the family solvent, that strict paternal teachings seemed powerless to prevent one of the sons from becoming an alcoholic and two of the daughters from losing their virtue. Paul, the one son besides Theodore who succeeded, went to New York, changed his name to Dresser, and achieved saloon and night-club fame as a writer of popular songs. Theodore was always impressed by his brother's flashy opulence and openhandedness, but his own way lay in a different direction. After a year at Indiana University his formal education was over, and his direct contact with life as a newspaper reporter began. In Chicago, St. Louis, Pittsburgh, and New York he observed corruption and vice that left him "stunned." He saw the workings of political influence, the elastic ethics that allowed financial trickery to go unchecked, the conveniences that linked wealth and privilege. The weight of his experience undermined family precepts and left him to take refuge in an amoral, mechanistic view of life. This, at least, was the point to which his thought had moved by the time he was middle-aged. When he wrote *Sister Carrie* he had not gone so far, and the novel is a good reflection of the mixed feelings still warring within him.

Dreiser is sympathetic with the frailties of his characters; he intrudes frequently into the novel, usually to excuse and justify their conduct. One reason for these intrusions and justifications may be that the novel, for all its general tone of objectivity, reflects some very personal identifications with his people and their story. Carrie is Dreiser's own age, and her trepidations in searching for a job plus the fascination of the city's alluring delights reflect his adolescent experience in Chicago. In her languor and dreamy nature he has also portrayed a facet of his emerging self as he has described it in his autobiographical book, *Dawn*. Drouet's interest in fine clothes and pretty women is Dreiser's, even if the insouciance of the salesman was not a prevailing mood of the author. Uncannily some aspects of Hurstwood's deracination were prophetic of an episode in Dreiser's life several years afterward, when his own future seemed clouded, his will paralyzed, and his whole personality shaken by a nervous disorder. The title, *Sister Carrie,* has personal overtones, too, for in some particulars the involvement of the heroine with two men in succession, along with a sudden move from Chicago through Canada to New York, is drawn from immediate family history. Otherwise, after the opening chapters when Carrie is living in her sister Minnie's apartment, the "sister" tag is forgotten. Indeed, considering Carrie's whole career, the title can be justified only if we feel that Dreiser wishes to disabuse us of the customary notion of the kept woman by reminding us that Carrie is, after all, a member of a family, even if she has cut herself off from them.

Dreiser is trying to discover through the novel how a sister's conduct could be viewed sympathetically and could even be justified, yet he cannot wholly ignore problems of right and wrong. The result is a double vision: sometimes he views human behavior as responsible to ethical norms, while at other times his deterministic sense persuades him that ethics are meaningless.

Two examples that concern moral choice will illustrate his dilemma. The first occurs in the episodes centering around Carrie's surrender to Drouet. He takes her to dinner, then to a performance of Gilbert and Sullivan's *The Mikado*. The evening draws toward a close in no particular atmosphere of excitement, and our direct view ends as they are holding hands. What Dreiser gives us instead of a seduction scene is a dream of Carrie's sister Minnie. In it she tries vainly to rescue Carrie from dangers connected with sinking, falling, descent into a pit. When next we see Carrie, her "average little conscience" is debating her changed situation. The mirror shows a prettier Carrie, but in her mind she sees a worse. Her conscience, reflecting "the world, her past environment, habit, convention, in a confused way," tells her that she has failed, but it is "never wholly convincing," and she soon stops worrying. The brief skirmish concludes with flat finality: "The voice of want made answer for her." It is as if Dreiser were reluctant to concede that Carrie has faced a moral problem. Yet the literal content of the dream symbols implies that wrong is an ethical reality which he ultimately cannot deny. He does, of course, blur the moral issue in another respect by saying that Drouet "could not help what he was going to do. . . . He might suffer the least rudimentary twinge of conscience in whatever he did, and in just so far he was evil and sinning." Dreiser is not really willing to place the blame on Drouet for what happens; notice that it is Carrie who has failed, not Drouet.

Carrie faces an equally grave crisis when she leaves Chicago with Hurstwood. This is a step which we are not prepared to see her take, and a good deal of contrivance is necessary—more, in fact, than Dreiser is able to make plausible. Earlier in the evening Hurstwood has found the saloon safe open and has toyed with the $10,000 it contains; while the money is out of the safe, its door clicks shut. In his panic he decides he must take the money and flee; he is strengthened in his resolution because his wife has found out that he is seeing Carrie and has asked for a divorce. Carrie on her part has just learned that Hurstwood is a married man and has broken with him. Nevertheless he seeks her out, tells her that Drouet has had an accident, and prevails on her to go with him to the hospital. Before she understands what is happening, they are on a train bound for Detroit and Montreal. When she discovers she has been duped she insists on getting off the train, but Hurstwood gradually quiets her with promises of marriage and a fine new life. The scene is not well motivated; Dreiser allows most of Carrie's strong reaction to go unspoken, and Hurstwood's line of argument is not convincing. Dreiser means for us to believe that Carrie would not have submitted without the promise of a conventional union, and indeed a marriage ceremony (bogus, it later turns out) is performed in Montreal. Beyond this he relies on merely telling us that Carrie, weak of will, hangs in a quandary, "balancing between decision and helplessness." If Carrie has not faced her problem, neither has Dreiser; his failure here is one of fictional technique. By not making Carrie believable in this scene, he has left an ambiguity which hangs over her subsequent life with Hurstwood.

It is commonly said that Dreiser's fictional method is founded on massive documentation, that he relies on slice-of-life technique to create his illusions of authenticity. It would be truer to say, of *Sister Carrie* at least, that he combines objective views with impressions registered through the sensory mechanism of his characters. This double perspective becomes evident if we examine the novel as a period piece. With Zolaesque thoroughness he builds up a picture of a rapidly expanding American city teeming with physical sensation, and emphasizes its awesomeness as it is viewed by the inexperienced provincial who first sees it wholly as an outsider. Dreiser succeeds admirably in making central Chicago come to life. We see its imposing department stores, then a new phenomenon which Dreiser explains. We see offices and warehouses, factories inside and out, including close-ups of Carrie seeking work, being coldly received, finally getting a meager job, and discovering her ineptness, her lack of stamina, her embarrassment at the bold, irreverent talk of young men and women around her. As the story progresses Drouet serves to introduce us to theaters and restaurants. Carrie's life expands to include glimpses of Lake Shore Drive and she begins to imagine what life is like among the upper class. So far the attractions and repulsions of Chicago have been defined chiefly through Carrie's experience (very close, as we have seen, to Dreiser's own). But beyond this impressionistic view—indeed, often embedded within it—is Dreiser's sense of recording phenomena objectively in the spirit of the behavioral scientist. Thus in the midst of a tense scene, we learn that Hurstwood is calling from "one of the first private telephone booths ever erected"; thus Dreiser, describing a theatrical first night, gives the names of all the boxholders, persons never otherwise mentioned. The effect can be flat when he writes from superficial knowledge. He takes us into Hurstwood's household, for instance, in a substantial district of Chicago; our limits of vision are Dreiser's and they are painfully apparent: the conversation is brittle and unnatural, Mrs. Hurstwood seems impossibly wooden, and the adolescent children are cardboard monsters. Hurstwood is said to be worth about forty thousand dollars and to be spending six or seven thousand a year—figures that seem exaggerated for a salaried saloon manager in the 1890's; nevertheless, Dreiser surrounds the family with the luxuries of a millionaire in some of his least convincing factual paragraphs.

With greater success Dreiser stands now outside, now inside the scene once Carrie and Hurstwood reach New York. Their lives are circumscribed, and although Dreiser evokes the notion of the metropolis as the "walled city" to be challenged and conquered, the metaphor is scarcely translated into the "million-footed manswarm" that Thomas Wolfe would have us visualize, or the "buzz and hum" which for Lionel Trilling gives the illusion of complex social phenomena. Dreiser is, I think, sound in suggesting that the modest apartment becomes the limit of a pallid life for the transplanted pair. Hurstwood's small business connection vanishes and before long he is reduced to seeking any job; in this latter phase he tramps the streets, but the city is essentially featureless; if he stops to rest, it is in increasingly seedy hotel lobbies where he feels himself to be an interloper. The great external world now is devoid of local color. The nature of the documentation has changed; Dreiser's art has deepened as he has narrowed his focus.

For the second half of the novel is in the main a study of Hurstwood's deterioration, and the almost imperceptible gradations are within mind and body and spirit. Our attention is directed to the repeated psychological buffets that reduce him slowly but surely to complete despair. In these later pages what we see of New York is methodically related to its impact on Hurstwood. The most fully developed episode is a midwinter streetcar strike which offers Hurstwood a temporary job. Here Dreiser's interest in process has full play, as he shows us how the unskilled strikebreaker learns to be a motorman, how he is inevitably drawn into violence and is injured as the strikers stop the cars and attack the "scabs" when persuasion fails. A grimmer and more poignant chapter, entitled "Curious Shifts of the Poor," introduces us to the underworld of derelicts, reduced to beggary, sleeping in flophouses or doorways, united by the fraternity of want, hunger, and the utter unconcern of the general public. Dreiser's great friend, the editor H. L. Mencken, thought that so much emphasis on Hurstwood was a blemish in the novel, but it is also possible to see a structural balance between Hurstwood's decline and Carrie's rise. If the contrast is almost too neat, it can be argued that Dreiser, by assigning such different fates to persons who alike are guilty of moral error, is challenging conventional ideas of poetic justice. In any case, he is nowhere more successful than in his sensitive tracing of Hurstwood's gradual disintegration, suicide, and burial in an unmarked grave.

Dreiser classifies Carrie as a woman, not of intellect and reason, but of instinct and feeling. It is true that she is not given to systematic thought, and her preoccupations are with the simple, elemental satisfactions that are little more than animal comforts. Such ideas as she has, she seldom voices with vigor. Because she is not forceful, she herself is less interesting than what happens to her; and it is in adversity that both she and Hurstwood inspire Dreiser to his best pages. Carrie's success story is an amalgam of hard work and good fortune —the old "luck and pluck" formula of the Alger books. Dreiser is probably not being ironical when he bases her rise to stardom on a tiny character part in which she catches the audience's eye by frowning while a principal actor sings. We cannot help feeling that the basis of her success is insubstantial, as was Hurstwood's principal stock in trade—his personal affability and his wide acquaintance.

The novel strongly implies that a prevalent American attitude defines success solely in material terms. Dreiser does not attack this attitude with the vigor he directs against his bêtes noires—conventionality and complacency. True, he does bring Carrie to the point of discovering that success and happiness are not identical, but Carrie probably does not understand even this simple axiom; as the novel ends she merely senses that she is restless for some undefinable inner satisfaction. To give his ideas substance Dreiser introduces the Middle Westerner Ames, a rising young man in the electrical business. He is lightly sketched, but through him Dreiser offers a critique of materialistic standards. Ames deplores waste and ostentatious display at a fashionable restaurant; he tries to interest Carrie in such serious books as *Père Goriot;* and he talks to her of her responsibility in maturing her acting talent. Carrie is impressed with him, finding his ideas stimulating and original. But he never succeeds in rousing her from her relatively stolid state of mind. Given Carrie's limited range of perceptions, Dreiser has handled the Ames scenes with proper restraint, even if he sacrifices the possibilities of Ames as a vibrant human being by giving him the rather stiff role of moral preceptor.

Dreiser will return to American materialism in the Cowperwood trilogy, where it is a central motif, and he will blame its false values for the catastrophes of *An American Tragedy* and *The Bulwark.* In *Sister Carrie* he seems to be somewhat fumblingly discovering that popularly accepted

American goals are not above question. He attacks puritanical mores and social attitudes, but the cult of success he half accepts, half rejects. His opinions have not yet hardened into the rigid cynicism of his middle years. A warm humanity plays over the pages of *Sister Carrie* because he communicates with great success a sense of wonder at the mystery of life. The individual is neither master of his fate nor the pawn of implacable forces. Instead, as Dreiser wrote,

> He is even as a wisp in the wind, moved by every breath of passion, acting now by his will and now by his instincts, erring with one, only to retrieve by the other, falling by one, only to rise by the other—a creature of incalculable variability.

Sister Carrie, the unacceptable and unconventional book of 1900, eventually found its public and became a classic. Its shortcomings have always been conspicuous, but Dreiser's power of evoking sympathy, especially for his weak characters, is accompanied by a dramatic quality that time has not much dimmed. His challenge to the values he found dominant is still pertinent. What his world had to offer, as T. K. Whipple observed, registered fully in Dreiser's fiction, for he established a "fruitful, living contact with the American environment." [2] It is not our world, but we can see ourselves in it, and in this sense *Sister Carrie* endures.

2 *Spokesmen* (New York: D. Appleton and Company, 1928), p. 91.

11 EDITH WHARTON
The House of Mirth

Richard Poirier

Daughter of one of the distinguished families of New York City, where she was born in 1862, a descendant of Rhine-landers and Gallatins who could remark of her fellow expatriate Henry James that "he belonged irrevocably to the old America out of which I also came," Edith Wharton was the author of some forty books of fiction, verse, criticism, and reminiscence, before her death in 1937 in Paris. She had lived in Europe for thirty years, mostly on the rue de Varennes but sometimes in an eighteenth-century château where her servants addressed each other as Monsieur and Madame. *The House of Mirth* appeared in 1905. It was the last of her books written while New York was still her home, and, like the best of her fiction, it is a portrayal of life in that city during the closing years of the nineteenth century. Her social background might explain why this book is so mercilessly critical of the commercial forces that had come to dominate the society of New York, but the novel is equally important in her purely literary biography. She tells us that with the writing of *The House of Mirth* she "was turned from a drifting amateur into a professional."

She found her ideals of literary professionalism less in American than in English literature and in the great European novelists—Balzac, Turgenev, and Flaubert. Although she could say that James was "almost the only novelist who has formulated his ideas about his art," the specific influences of James in her work are altogether less pronounced than they are said to be. As a novel of manners, for example, *The House of Mirth* is indebted less to anything of a similar mode in James, like *The Europeans,* than to the fiction of Jane Austen and George Eliot. Her achievements as a satirist prepare the way for Sinclair Lewis, who dedicated *Babbitt* to her. But her peculiarly American satirical broadness stands out mostly by contrast to those more prevalent moments in *The House of Mirth* where she displays an affinity less with Sinclair Lewis than with the earlier novelists of English manners like Jane Austen and George Eliot. At moments it is as if she turned to them for the support of attitudes no longer articulated within the American society she depicts. The result is a precarious mixture of tones, an evidence of discrepancy in Mrs. Wharton between the subject of her satire, which is uniquely American and contemporary, and her dependence at certain points on two English writers who never, even in extremity, felt that their values went unrepresented among the dominant forces in the world around them. Neither of them uses other writers in the manner of Mrs. Wharton—as if literature might provide her the institutional sanctions she could not receive from her own society.

It is, then, of some historical importance that we can hear the accents of Jane Austen and the rhetoric of George Eliot in the pages of this novel. Jane Austen is most in evidence wherever the wit is most secure and least strident, least in anticipation of the satirical style of Sinclair Lewis. When Miss Stepney brings accusations against the heroine, Lily Bart, to Miss Bart's guardian, there are the recognizable encouragements from Jane Austen in the remark that Miss Stepney

> was not sufficiently familiar with the classic drama to have recalled in advance how bearers of bad tidings are proverbially received, but she now had a rapid vision of forfeited dinners and a reduced wardrobe as a possible consequence of her disinterestedness. To the honour of her sex, however, hatred of Lily prevailed over more personal considerations.

In assessing the similarities between Jane Austen and Edith Wharton it should be said that they are not entirely different in their relationships to society. If Mrs. Wharton felt, as one of her old friends expressed it, that life in America "unconsciously for all of us began to change from simplicity to vulgarity in the late eighties," Jane Austen in the first decades of the same century was aware of a similar process in England. "It is hard indeed," as Armour Craig points out, "not to use the inevitable 'age of transition' in reflecting on the kind of world" Jane Austen presents, a world where it is becoming difficult "even to provide a homogeneous guest list for a ball." [1] But the forces of change in Jane Austen's society had to make their way through a social texture altogether more absorbent and less easily discolored than Mrs. Wharton's. Jane Austen's was a society at once stronger and more flexible than anything the American writer could see or imagine in the society of New York. In her autobiographical *A Backward Glance*, Mrs. Wharton herself describes the overwhelming of the old conservative families by those enriched through the expansion of business in the decades preceding *The House of Mirth*, by which time the struggle was pretty much over. It is no wonder that Jane Austen can speak with a satirical modulation and ease that is only sporadic in Mrs. Wharton and is even then more a stylistic echo of the earlier writer than an expression of confidence that her tone will be sustained by any elements in American society as she knows it.

When she is least "English" and most original in her satire in *The House of Mirth*, Mrs. Wharton sounds like an outsider, someone withdrawn to the periphery of society, carrying with her a detailed knowledge of the targets within it. Her satirical descriptions are very precisely aimed but at the same time panoramic in their effect, as if she feels no obligation to make qualifications or exceptions and chooses to enjoy the excesses permitted by her disinvolvement. Alluding to a bad autumn on Wall Street, she mentions

one of the victims of the crash, who, in the space of twelve short months, had made the same number of millions, built a house

[1] Armour Craig, "Jane Austen's Emma: The Truths and Disguises of Human Disclosure," in Reuben Brower and Richard Poirier, eds., In *Defense of Reading* (New York: Dutton, 1962), p. 238.

on Fifth Avenue, filled a picture-gallery with old masters, entertained all New York in it, and been smuggled out of the country between a trained nurse and a doctor, while his creditors mounted guard over the old masters, and his guests explained to each other that they had dined with him only because they wanted to see the pictures.

Lily Bart's career takes her through the various strata of this society, but in an order the reverse of her wishes: from the Trenors of "Bellomont" who feel some of the restraints of "old habits," to the Dorsets who exploit traditional mores as a disguise for the misconduct eventually paid for by Lily; from the ferociously social-climbing Brys to the uncritically pleasure-seeking Gormers, and from there to the outskirts of social acceptability when Lily becomes the secretary of the latest invader from the Western states, Miss Hatch of the Hotel Emporium. Mrs. Wharton's description of Lily's stay with Miss Hatch includes one of the most incisive pictures in literature of hotel life in America, reminding us that her first book of prose was a study of interior decorating:

> Through this atmosphere of torrid splendor moved wan beings as richly upholstered as the furniture, beings without definite pursuits or permanent relations, who drifted on a languid tide of curiosity, from restaurant to concert-hall, from palm-garden to music room, from "art-exhibit" to dress-maker's opening.

Even while these various elements struggle for power they tend in their essential qualities to blend into one another. As a result in this novel there is actually no dramatized conflict of class or of social values. There are only conflicts of economic and social hierarchy, in which the outcome is largely determined by the power of money. Even the efforts of sexual conquest in the book have money as the primary inducement.

One of Mrs. Wharton's subtly achieved implications is that the members of this society must calculate and invest their emotions with the coldness of financial speculators. The alternative, for anyone as impoverished as Lily, is social ruin. "It was seldom," Mrs. Wharton reports in a metaphor that unites financial with emotional economies, that Lily "could allow herself the luxury of an impulse." She is therefore not being luxurious when we see her in Chapter 2 in a train—one of her frequent trips to the great country houses to which her charm, beauty, and little services win her invitations—"studying her prey through downcast lashes while she organized her method of attack." Her prey is Percy Gryce, limited in all things except prudery, a collection of Americana, and the millions which Lily needs if she is to secure a place in the New York society where her parents went bankrupt maintaining even a foothold. As Mrs. Wharton's style would suggest, Lily can be taken here by the reader as only comically threatful to poor Percy; we have been shown in the opening chapter that she is really not studious enough to be a seductress in so theatrical a vein. She has already acted with the generous impulsiveness that will make her the "prey" of her proposed victims. While waiting for the train, she had met Selden, the one man in the book she truly admires despite his lack of prosperity. She had accepted an invitation to his rooms for tea only to be discovered, as she leaves, by Rosedale, a social-climbing Jewish investor and a gossip who promptly catches her in unnecessary and obvious lies about her reasons for being in the building.

Lily's mistake and the consequences it entails justify Mrs. Wharton's claim that in her works "My last page is always latent in my first." Indeed, at the end of the novel, Lily's final hope of being accepted again by the powers of society rests with Rosedale. Having failed with Gryce because of her impulsively expressed wishes to be with Selden, having thoughtlessly accepted what seemed merely the business advice of Gus Trenor, the husband of her best friend, only to discover herself compromised by him, having slipped then to companionship with the Dorsets, where her kindness to the husband is exploited by the wife as a cover for her own amatory adventures, Lily is faced with Rosedale's proposal. He will marry her and give her financial power over her enemies if she will use some letters of Mrs. Dorset that have come into her possession as a way of forcing Mrs. Dorset to withdraw the lies she has been spreading about Lily. Lily's failure to carry out this blackmail is less a matter of ethical principles than, once again, of the impulses that lead her astray from her goal. On the way to Mrs. Dorset's she simply happens to pass Selden's apartment building and, by the sudden decision to visit him, makes a final grasp for the life of moral refinement which she finds in him and which, by her proposed maneuver, she will never find for herself. While there, again on an impulse of generous and exalted feeling, she contrives secretly to burn the letters with which she could have implicated Mrs. Dorset with Selden. She thereby seals her social obliteration.

"Obliteration" is not too strong a word to describe the way in which, near the end of the novel, Lily seems to disappear into the mass of New York, "the thousands of insignificant figures" who watch with her the parade of fashion, in which she herself once took part, along Fifth Avenue. She pays the price for those tiny acts of independence, those generous promptings which have set her apart from society in this book, even when she was being most assiduous in her efforts to join it. To us, as to Selden, her attractiveness is "the way in which she detached herself, by a hundred indefinable shades, from the persons who most abounded in her own style." Her alertness to the possibilities of life is what defeats her by making her deviate from any settled campaign of success. Though she is unfortunately a spendthrift with money, the society of Trenor and Dorset takes its toll of her because she is also an admirable spendthrift of emotions. She is capable, in Mrs. Wharton's noble phrase, "of those shocks of pity that sometimes decentralize a life." It is thus characteristic that to her drab little friend, Gerty, she should give the liberal fraction of the money she is about to spend on a dressing case and that in her treatment of servants she acts like one "long enough in bondage to other people's pleasure to be considerate of those who depend on hers."

Mrs. Wharton is a remarkably tough-minded writer, but it is not possible to escape the suspicion, as the novel progresses, that she is making a possibly sentimental connection between Lily's freedom of impulse and the fact that she is poor and responsive to the poverty of others. The assumption that the life of impulse is somehow associated with the lower regions of society is common enough in literature, very likely a metaphorical carry-over of beliefs about the geography of the human body. In Mrs. Wharton's case, the assumption, once recognized as operative in her book, seems a logical consequence of her very rigid satirical view of the "high" society wherein Lily's career is given dramatic life. In none of the inhabitants of this society, not even in Selden, who likes to be aloof from it, can Mrs. Wharton locate a sustained expression of uncalculated feeling, anything that might create a countermovement to the system of emotional and financial calculation on which the society is built. Even Lily's exposure to chance is a result less of her inward freedom than of her outward condition: the financial precariousness that lets her see a reflection of her possible destiny in the lives of the poor as well as the rich, and to see it with an intimidated sympathy. One can sense this sympathetic quality in Lily even in the poignant scenes that reveal her incapacity to love Gerty, the person who helps her most unselfishly. Lily recognizes in Gerty's "acquiescence in dinginess" a terrifyingly close approximation of her own situation, were she without the spirit that makes her so attractively full of hope. Gerty has a "moral vision which makes all human suffering so near and insistent that the other aspects of life fade into remoteness." It is not Mrs. Wharton's intention to criticize her heroine for being more open to life, by being less moral about it, than is poor Gerty.

Some of Mrs. Wharton's descriptions of working-class life and of the drabness of Lily's surroundings are nearly as painful in their immediacy as anything comparable in Dreiser, whose *Sister Carrie* appeared five years earlier. Accompanying these descriptions, however, is an increasing emphasis on the way spontaneous sympathy and kinship are assets somehow more available to the impoverished than to anyone else in the book. This sentiment accumulates in the next to the last chapter when Lily, having taken her leave of Selden for what will prove to be the last time, sits in Bryant Park, a deserted and lonely figure. The park is at the relatively unfashionable middle of Fifth Avenue, the most luxurious of the avenues of New York, a kind of gathering place of the unlocated, a passage from the private elegance of the East Side to the public show places and tenements of the West. She is discovered there by Nettie Struther, one of the girls Lily had helped at Gerty's club for young women in distress. She goes to Nettie's apartment, into the warmth of her kitchen, and is there allowed to hold Nettie's newborn baby. In this scene, very nearly at the end of the book, Mrs. Wharton makes an anxious and contrived effort to evoke the kind of human relationship disastrously absent from Lily's life. She is suggesting some positive standard to which the reader and Lily might appeal for an alternative both to the community of dinginess, in which Lily feels condemned, and to the society in which she had hoped to live. It is a society, we now remember with some shock, in which there has been no evidence of children or childbearing. The passage describes Lily holding Nettie's baby, and it is written not only to be poignant but to be emphatically metaphorical:

> The baby, feeling herself detached from her habitual anchorage, made an instinctive motion of resistance; but the soothing influences of digestion prevailed, and Lily felt the soft weight sink trustfully against her breast. The child's confidence in its safety thrilled her with a sense of warmth and returning life, and she bent over, wondering at the rosy blur of the little face, the empty clearness of the eyes, the vague tendrilly motions of the folding and unfolding fingers. At first the burden in her arms seemed as light as a pink cloud or a heap of down, but as she continued to hold it the weight increased, sinking deeper, and penetrating her with a strange sense of weakness, as though the child entered into her and became a part of herself.

The passage is not making any simple-minded suggestion that Lily would have been happier had she been satisfied with poverty and the common destiny of motherhood. Our attention is directed beyond the triviality of such "solutions" by the metaphorical urgency of the passage, its efforts to grasp, like the "folding and unfolding fingers" of the baby, an image of organic unity and natural kinship. The impulse, obvious enough in the last sentence, is implicit in the first: "The baby, feeling herself detached from her habitual anchorage, made an instinctive motion of resistance." The passage is meant to remind us of the factitious social unities throughout the rest of the novel, of alliances held together by the power of money and by the shared hypocrisies that constitute a standard for the exclusion of Lily. She is soon to die alone in her own bed with the drugged illusion that the baby is lying with her,

> a gentle penetrating thrill of warmth and pleasure. She settled herself into an easier position, hollowing her arm to pillow the round downy head, and holding her breath lest a sound should disturb the sleeping child.

Her tenderness, expending itself at the end on thin air, is a final expression of the instinctive compassion that has been her ruin rather than her salvation. In the society in which Lily has been living, no spontaneous enactments of human solidarity can occur like those between Lily, the baby, and Nettie. This contrast is impressed upon us with so little evidence of the author's conscious contrivance that it seems to have come from her most profoundly inward grasp of the material. Thus we discover, looking back, that Lily's response to Mrs. Dorset and her schemes was described in nearly the same terms used in the scene with the child: "But compassion, in a moment, got the better of her instinctive recoil from Mrs. Dorset" just as the baby, after an "instinctive motion of resistance" surrenders to a desire for warmth and unity. And the metaphorical parallels are further evident in Lily's thinking of herself as a motherly source of comfort even to her enemy: "It was on Lily's lips to exclaim: 'You poor soul, don't double and turn—come straight back to me and we'll find a way out!' "

What is particularly interesting about this novel, and about some of the most ambitious works of American fiction, is that the author cannot authenticate her sentiments about compassion and kinship, cannot give them a positive embodiment in dramatic scenes without going outside the areas of society where the central conflicts of her novel occur. Instead she moves into areas tangential to them and occupied by characters nearly anonymous. One implication of the metaphors used to describe such characters is that their sympathy and their recognition of human destinies, other than merely social ones, can be a basis for kinship and community, more binding than the power of money. It is here that Mrs. Wharton's critical admiration for George Eliot seems to have become a determining factor in *The House of Mirth*. In her sacrificial sympathy for Mrs. Dorset, for example, Lily is much like Dorothea Brooke in several comparable scenes, especially with Rosamond, at the end of *Middlemarch*. George Eliot's novel is impassioned by an acknowledgment of the developing social fractures in English society on the eve of the Reform Bill in 1832 and of the possible unities achieved, not by economic or scientific schemes, but through the kind of human relationship defined by Ladislaw in his description of a soul "in which knowledge passes instantaneously into feeling, and feeling flashes back as a new organ of knowledge." It is a measure of the difference between the historical situations of the English novelist in 1870 and of the American in 1905 that Mrs. Wharton cannot imagine a society in which her heroine can do more than carry out the first part of Ladislaw's prescription. She transforms her knowledge into compassion but the expression of compassion then reveals an ignorance of the nature of her surroundings that could only come from a beautiful and uncynical nature. Characters like Mrs. Dorset simply are not motivated by needs and feelings that in George Eliot's moral universe are considered inherently human. To assume such motivation in the people of *The House of Mirth* is to be quite simply a dupe, an innocent. In making Lily what we might call an old-fashioned American who believes that people remain as children in their need of love and sympathy, Mrs. Wharton herself is not in the least an innocent. She knows her heroine well enough to recognize that Lily's unsuspicious nature is

in part an expression of the ego that is the underside of innocence: she has the capacity to think so well of herself that she
cannot easily imagine the gross intentions of others with respect to her. When Trenor demands payment of her debts to
him he needs to instruct her in the fact that he is "not asking
for payment in kind." Her feelings are a proper substitute
for his money. All that saves Lily on this occasion is something remaining in Trenor of the society whose passing
Mrs. Wharton laments in her autobiography and, it would
seem, in the characterization of Lily. Trenor is prevented
from forcing his attentions on Lily, we are told, when "old
habits, old restraints, the hand of inherited order, plucked
back the bewildered mind which passion had jolted from its
ruts." Even so short a quotation will indicate that this moment is one of the weakest in the novel, both in its characterization and in the platitudinous coloration of style, not
uncommon in the ladies' magazines for which Mrs. Wharton
sometimes wrote.

In the scene between Lily and Trenor Mrs. Wharton is
trying, quite unsuccessfully, to unite the central areas of social drama in her novel with the standards by which she is
most anxious to judge it, standards which, she would assert,
are still—if weakly—operative in that society. Her failure at
this moment is what perhaps dissuaded her from any further
efforts of the same kind and made it necessary for her at the
end to locate analogous standards of human decency in elements of life uncontaminated by the social forces dominant
in the book. At the end, Lily Bart's misery is said to have
proceeded from her having been denied an ordering principle for her good impulses that is the benefit of those raised,
like George Eliot's rural family, the Garths, in a community
united by memories and customs.

Just before her accidental suicide, Lily reflects:

It was indeed miserable to be poor, to look forward to a shabby,
anxious middle-age, leading by dreary degrees of economy and
self-denial to gradual absorption in the dingy communal existence of the boarding-house. But there was something more
miserable still—it was the clutch of solitude at her heart, the

sense of being swept like a stray uprooted growth down the heedless current of the years. That was the feeling which possessed her now—the feeling of being something rootless and ephemeral, mere spindrift of the whirling surface of existence, without anything to which the poor little tentacles of self could cling before the awful flood submerged them. And as she looked back she saw that there had never been a time when she had any real relation to life. Her parents too had been rootless, blown hither and thither on every wind of fashion, without any personal existence to shelter them from its shifting gusts. She herself had grown up without any one spot of earth being dearer to her than another: there was no center of early pieties, of grave endearing traditions, to which her heart could revert and from which it could draw strength for itself and tenderness for others. In whatever form a slowly accumulated past lives in the blood—whether in the concrete image of the old house stored with visual memories, or in the conception of the house not built with hands, but made up of inherited passions and loyalties—it has the same power of broadening and deepening the individual existence, of attaching it by mysterious links of kinship to all the mighty sum of human striving.

The assumptions in this paragraph are also George Eliot's, whose conservatism is particularly admired by Mrs. Wharton in her review of Leslie Stephen's *George Eliot:* "A deep reverence for family ties, for the sanctities of tradition, the claims of slowly acquired convictions and slowly formed precedents, is revealed in every page of her books." This particular kind of reverence for sanctities has since developed into the mythology of the antiurban and politically conservative literature of the twentieth century. Familiar to readers of Faulkner or Yeats or of T. S. Eliot's essays on culture, this mythology invests heavily in the vocabulary used by Mrs. Wharton, in such words as "rootless," "one spot of earth," "early pieties," "inherited passions and loyalties," "traditions," and the mystique of "the house not built by hands, but made up of inherited passions and loyalties." Mrs. Wharton's use of this vocabulary has the ring of platitude because it is given no nourishing connections to the dramatic substance of the novel. It has its source mainly in the episode of Lily's quite accidental meeting with Nettie Struther, who has not before had any place in the book. Perhaps for this reason there is an air of extemporization precisely at the point where Mrs. Wharton is trying to give us something other than a helpless sense of pity and revulsion to carry away from the disasters we have witnessed. What she does give us is merely a vocabulary. Sharing George Eliot's attitudes, she is deprived of George Eliot's resources—a society in which there really were "grave and endearing traditions" still in visible and even audible evidence.

Some of the contradictions among the critics of this novel in assessing the elusive role of Selden are a result of not fully grasping the literary significance of Mrs. Wharton's dedication to essentially rural traditionalism. Selden has all the intellectual refinements that allow him "a happy air of viewing the show objectively, of having points of contact outside the great gilt cage." But his "points of contact" are essentially literary and are in many ways exclusively of the kinds of contact said to be fatally missing from Lily's life. His "republic of the spirit" is not Mrs. Wharton's ideal community. He is allowed to catch Lily in situations compromising enough to make most men cautious, though not the kind of man whom Mrs. Wharton characteristically admired. Selden's feelings are often as calculated as those coming from inside the "great gilt cage," even though his intentions are not unworthy. He too judges Lily more often by conventional assumptions of propriety than by knowing and trusting her through his affections. When she is most in need of him, after Mrs. Dorset, in a brilliantly paced scene of social tension, forbids her to return to the yacht, Selden offers her everything but the support of his trust:

> The memory of Mrs. Fisher's hints, and the corroboration of his own impressions, while they deepened his pity, also increased his constraint since whichever way he sought a free outlet for sympathy, it was blocked by the fear of committing a blunder.

He is afraid of precisely those impulses by which Lily herself is continually and sympathetically responding, even to Mrs.

Dorset, with whom Selden has earlier had some assignations. Mrs. Wharton is not, obviously, giving us a portrait of masculine sexual inadequacy. Selden's somewhat murky characterization is a result of her not having found a way, at these early stages of the novel, to make about him the point that we can make retrospectively, looking back from the meeting of Lily and Nettie: that he is deficient in a sense of human solidarity and that he knows people not by loving but only by judging them.

The characterization of Selden is an instance of Mrs. Wharton's difficulty in having her standards emanate from within the conflicts she is dramatizing. He is refined, intelligent, courageously self-consulting about ideas within a rigidly conformist society, but his ways of "knowing" people are essentially cosmopolitan—by the guesswork, the gossip, the categorizing assumptions that substitute for the slowly accumulated intimacy on which Mrs. Wharton places such redeeming value. He is unable, by character and circumstance, to "know" Lily in the way the people of George Eliot's provincial Middlemarch can at their best know one another or the way Faulkner's characters can know, for example, that one of their number did not commit a crime when all the apparent evidence has implicated him. Again, the character in this novel who exercises this kind of knowledge has no place whatever in the major line of action. He belongs instead to Nettie's story, which might be called a pastoral version of Lily's: she became unfortunately involved with a "stylish" man, was deserted by him, and left ill and disgraced until rescued (with the help of some money from Lily) by Gerty, who is also ready now to assist Lily in her distress. But the difference in Nettie's story (and it makes all the difference) is a character named George. He has known her since childhood and thus has an intimate knowledge that can make him compassionate rather than critical of her later behavior. The vocabulary with which Mrs. Wharton invests Nettie confirms the relevance of George Eliot to this novel. George Eliot provides the classic image in fiction of a kind of social communion that she derives, as do later anti-cosmopolitan writers, from "some center of early pieties . . . of grave endearing traditions to which the heart could revert and from which it could draw strength for itself and tenderness for others." Nettie ends her story with the happy news that:

> When I got back home, George came round and asked me to marry him. At first I thought I couldn't, because we'd been brought up together, and I knew he knew about me. But after a while I began to see that that made it easier. I never could have told another man, and I'd never have married without telling; but if George cared enough to have me as I was, I didn't see why I shouldn't begin again—and I did.

"And I knew he knew about me"—knowledge of the kind being exercised here allows us to measure the failure of Selden in his treatment of Lily. He is, we are told earlier, unable to "yield to the growth of an affection which might appeal to pity yet leave the understanding untouched: sympathy would no more delude him than a trick of the eyes, the grace of helplessness than a curve of the cheek." The tone here is partisanly feminine in the suggestion, not sustained by the characterization of Selden in his relationships with women, that he is a sexually unimpassioned man. Here again the basis for some of Mrs. Wharton's attitudes fails to be sufficiently objectified within the fictional world she creates. The trouble with Selden is that he will not allow himself to "know" the heroine through his instincts and spontaneous affections. But who can so know her? Beyond him there is only the rhetoric that praises the conditions within which such a way of knowing might have been fostered by the "grave endearing traditions" not available to anyone except, in some apparently elementary form, to Nettie and her George and to the pitiable Gerty. Mrs. Wharton's difficulty in *The House of Mirth* makes any comparison to the English women novelists with whom she deserves to keep company end with a significant degree of contrast. She is a novelist of manners in a peculiarly American way: she cannot imagine a society in which her values are brought into play at the center of dramatic conflict. Instead of being an aggregate of human relationships, subject to modification in the best interests of its members, society for her becomes an expression of impersonal power, even when it is being manipulated by some of its victims.

12 JACK LONDON
Martin Eden

Franklin Walker

Martin Eden is not only one of Jack London's best books; it is also one of his most puzzling ones. It was published in 1909, when London was thirty-three years old and had phenomenally won a world audience with such novels as *The Call of the Wild, The Sea Wolf,* and *The Iron Heel,* and it appeared at what was to prove to be the very peak of his career. The curious thing is that *Martin Eden* tells the exciting story of how a writer made good, overcoming in a spirited way all sorts of odds, but it also tells of how that writer, having reached heights beyond his fondest hopes, kills himself in despair. Therein lies the puzzle that has baffled readers and critics ever since the book appeared.

Jack London was the sort of writer who constantly turned to his own experiences for the material for his fiction. Even the dog Buck in *The Call of the Wild* is a thinly disguised portrait of London, in conflict with civilization and fleeing to a happier life in the cold North, which London knew so well from his Klondike experiences. Buck finally finds himself alone under the stars, to which London had always aspired. As a matter of fact, "Star-Dust" was London's second choice as a title for the book that became *Martin Eden;* "Success" was his first choice, and "Martin Eden," which proved most satisfactory to his publishers, only the third.

"Star-Dust" may actually have been the best title, for it catches the mood of the young writer during most of the novel, when he is so full of energy and enthusiasm that his story holds the reader spellbound. At the opening, Martin Eden is a twenty-year-old sailor who suddenly grows enthusiastic about learning to write. Though he has little formal education—only six years of elementary school—he becomes convinced that he has a keen mind and a creative talent, being given to translating all ideas and experiences into vivid pictures, "visions" which seem more real than reality. He decides that he needs an education to give meaning and coherence to the pictures.

Aided somewhat by Ruth Morse, the university student with whom he has fallen in love, he sets out to gain an education on a "do-it-yourself" plan, like the jack-of-all-trades son of the frontier which London felt himself to be. With four lending cards constantly in use at the public library, systematic lists of new words to learn and of ungrammatical constructions to avoid, and energy enough to apply himself during most of the minutes of his nineteen-hour day—for he found that he could get by on five hours of sleep—he moves rapidly ahead, discovering that in a surprisingly short time he can discuss Charles Darwin and Herbert Spencer intelligently with soapbox orators and even university professors.

All this would sound a bit preposterous were not Martin Eden's experiences in the reading and writing processes essentially those of Jack London. As he pointed out in *John Barleycorn*:

> Critics have complained about the swift education one of my characters, Martin Eden, achieved. In three years, from a sailor with a common-school education, I made a successful writer of him. The critics say this is impossible. Yet I was Martin Eden.

This is indeed good going for a young writer, although by no means unique. The point about it with London is that he found the experience so very exciting and so extraordinarily surprising. The very naïveté of his approach appeals to almost every young person who has secretly hoped to learn to write but has believed that such success belongs only in a Cinderella story. Jack London, like Martin Eden, set out to become an author as though he were beginning a game or, to suggest a better figure, were taking part in a battle. Each rejection slip was another challenge, and the manuscripts continued on their rounds, provided that there were enough pennies left to buy stamps. Finally, according to legend, the pile of Jack's rejection slips, impaled on a spindle, became five feet high—and then came a flood of acceptances. In the meantime, Martin Eden, like Jack London, tried his hand at every type of writing he could think of, from triolets to a tragedy in ponderous blank verse, from drawing-room sketches to adventure novels. Every new experience was raw material for a story, every encounter with an acquaintance an opportunity to exchange ideas about writing. It did not matter that his credit at the grocery ran out after reaching the vast sum of $3.85, that he had to pawn his overcoat and watch and bicycle, that he had to live on beans and go for forty-eight hours without any food at all. It was all part of the game. Martin Eden had willed to succeed, just as London had, and succeed he did.

Jack London helps to dramatize Martin Eden's quest for knowledge and writing success by creating a number of excellent minor figures who serve as either enemies or supporters in his intellectual battle. Ruth Morse's parents are skeptical and spur him on; their business acquaintances, like the successful Alger boy, Mr. Butler, furnish examples of the kind of prominence which the young writer abhors. His two brothers-in-law, blind in their petty mercantilism, alternately bore and infuriate him. One sister, chained to her washtub, can give him only soapy kisses and an occasional meal, but she has some faith in him, which helps. The other sister agrees that he is a dreamer and a loafer for failing to get a regular job. On the other hand, there is his illiterate, warm-hearted landlady, Marcia Silva, who admires him blindly. And, above all, there is Russ Brissenden, the only fellow-writer he meets, who heartens him greatly with his support and, incidentally, turns out to be one of the most vivid characters in the book.

When Martin met Brissenden at the Morse home, he

thought at first that this new acquaintance—with his fine, aquiline nose; long, aristocratic face; and drooping shoulders—was both a featherbrain and a boor. However, over a Scotch and soda at a bar after the party, he discovered that Brissenden was full of fire and had the flashing insight and perception of a true genius. He was a tubercular who was never without his quart of whiskey; he was a cynic, but at the same time a true lover of life, a frank voluptuary who enjoyed good food and intellectual company. Above all, he was a poet whose poetry was "a mad orgy of the imagination."

Martin Eden and Russ Brissenden talked for hours in Martin's squalid room, mixing toddies to stimulate their thoughts. Brissenden took Martin to meet a group of poverty-ridden intellectuals in San Francisco, and there Martin spent one of his most exciting nights discussing idealism, materialism, realism. It was far more stimulating than anything that could be heard in college or at the Morse dinner table. But Brissenden was succumbing rapidly to the ravages of tuberculosis and soon, after leaving with Martin the manuscript of his magnum opus, entitled *Ephemera,* shot himself in the head. Martin succeeded in getting the marvelous poem published in a popular magazine, only to be sickened by the tawdry publicity and platitudinous reactions which resulted.

On two subjects Martin and Brissenden had differed deeply. One was socialism, for Brissenden considered this creed the only hope for the future and felt that Martin's Nietzschean faith in the superman would soon play him false. Also, Brissenden did not approve of Martin's great love, Ruth Morse, whom he called " 'that pale, shrivelled female thing!' " " 'What under heaven do you want with a daughter of the bourgeoisie?' "

Martin's first impulse was to throttle Brissenden at this attack on his sweetheart, but he was, underneath, coming to many of the conclusions that Brissenden had reached. Ruth was getting more and more discouraged with his insistence on writing and his refusal to get a job; because she loved him, she was willing to resist her family for his sake if only he would show sense and follow some course which would make marriage feasible. Ruth Morse had appeared to Martin as a lovely, refined princess when her brother, grateful that Martin had rescued him from an attack by some hoodlums, introduced the young sailor for the first time into the home of her middle-class family. Before this, Martin had known little but grinding work and cheap living. His parents were dead, and he had earned his living by working in canneries, breaking horses on a ranch, sailing before the mast. Ruth had sensed that he had a powerful mind—and certainly a powerful body —and had been fascinated by his thirst to read books, learn to speak grammatically, and acquire good manners. She went about making him over, even persuading him to give up smoking.

Jack London had conceived of his novel as a portrayal of a member of the proletariat who was attracted to the life of the bourgeoisie, only to find that most of the values of the middle class were false. At first Martin is all eagerness. He soon learns to cope with forks, to walk on the curb side of the sidewalk when he squires his lady, and even to wear a stiff collar and a well-pressed suit. One of the most memorable scenes is the opening one, in which the young sailor with his rolling gait and awkward shoulders makes his way through the furniture of the well-stocked Morse living room. He seems in peril at every moment, yet he is so fascinated by the cultivated life of the family that he is willing to take correction humbly in order to move in those admired circles.

Part of the appeal in this strain of the book lies in London's skill in capturing the awkwardness felt by many adolescents in the face of an adult society. Even more of it lies in London's use of his own experiences in pulling himself up from a loveless, poverty-stricken home life to a world which glittered as surely as it does for the characters in Scott Fitzgerald's novels. But there is more passion in *Martin Eden* —more comprehension of the outsider who craves to join the party—than in any of Fitzgerald's novels. This is because Jack London had *been* a really hungry child, had panhandled for food to feed his belly, had ridden the rods below freight cars and the blind baggage on fast express trains, and had even spent a month in the Erie County Penitentiary after being picked up for vagrancy.

Yet Jack London never craved to return to the proletarian world, as did Martin Eden, who, as he finds bourgeois life more and more artificial, thinks of going back to his "own people." The hopelessness of such a course is vividly presented in an episode of the novel in which Martin takes a job working in a laundry, planning once more to use "his brawn instead of his brains." There he works alongside a marvelous character named Joe, who toils so hard during the week to keep up with his employer's demands that he gets drunk every weekend to be able to keep going. The two are truly work-beasts, without a chance for happiness in life. Martin cannot write, he cannot even read, he is so constantly tired. Finally, both men throw up their jobs, Joe to take to the road as a tramp and Martin to return to Ruth and his writing desk. Martin has clearly become declassed—lost between the workman's world, to London always the world of the unskilled laborer, and that of the bourgeoisie. His one remaining hope is to create a new world of his own—to rise above both classes through his writing and then to tell everyone of his independence.

The last quarter of the novel which was to be titled "Success" is quite changed in tone from the first three-quarters, which dealt with a fighting adventure. Brissenden's death crystallizes in Martin an awareness of the false values of literary adulation. Ruth Morse breaks their engagement, and he sees her at last in her true light. And then, quite without reason, Martin sells all his manuscripts and becomes a sensational success overnight. All the people who have snubbed him earlier now crave his attention and receive his contempt. Why had they not helped him when he needed helping, he cries out? Even Ruth comes to him and offers to be his mistress if he will only forgive her for breaking their engagement. But there is no love of life left in Martin; his enthusiasms are all burned out. He no longer enjoys living. Finally he leaves on the steamship "Mariposa" for the South Seas, which seem to beckon him. He never gets there, however. One night, far from land, Martin Eden climbs through the porthole, and, by one final act of will, swims downward until he drowns. The novel ends with the words:

> And somewhere at the bottom he fell into the darkness. That much he knew. And at the instant he knew, he ceased to know.

Many readers of *Martin Eden* have felt that suicide was not by any means the logical conclusion of a story dealing with the hero's success against odds. The unexpected nature of the denouement was fully indicated by the fact that the *Pacific Monthly*, when it began serial publication of the story in 1908, offered $500 to the reader who would most accurately guess the ultimate fate of Martin Eden. Even Jack London, who wrote the book while cruising on his ketch, "The Snark," in the South Seas, seemed uncertain as to how he would complete his story until he actually neared its end. In the previous November, he had written home that "Success" was to be his longest novel and that he was exceedingly happy while writing it, not even caring if "The Snark" was off course. As he approached the completion of his story, he wrote his publishers that the best part would come when Martin got to the South Seas, a destination which he was never to reach. Even while Jack London sailed from Tahiti to San Francisco on the "Mariposa" on a quick trip to straighten out his tangled finances, he was still without an ending to his book. What was he to do with Martin Eden? Doubtless sometime during that voyage the novel was given its unexpected end. London always insisted that Martin's suicide was the logical outcome of his experiences, and perhaps he was right.

Yet the reason that London gave for that suicide, when a controversy over the matter arose, is not very persuasive. Repeatedly he maintained that Martin killed himself because he discovered that his creed of individualism had failed. In a copy of the book given to a friend, he wrote:

> And not one blessed reviewer has discovered that this book is an attack on individualism, that Martin Eden died because he was so utter an individualist that he was unaware of the needs

of others, and that, therefore, when his illusions vanished, there was nothing for him for which to live.

According to London, Martin's mistake was that he did not become a socialist; socialism would have given him a purpose in life. London even offered to debate a minister in his pulpit, planning to convince the congregation that Martin Eden had failed because he did not take up the socialist cause.

It is true that, at one point in the novel, Russ Brissenden, who is a socialist largely because he cannot stomach capitalism, tells Martin that socialism would remake his life.

> You see, I'd like to see you a socialist before I am gone. It will give you a sanction for your existence. It is the one thing that will save you in the time of disappointment that is coming to you.

Yet there is nothing in the book describing Brissenden's socialistic activities, and his desire to help his fellow man does not keep him from putting a bullet into his brain. Nor is Martin even mildly tempted by socialism; rather, he stoutly defends his Nietzschean position during the one occasion when he visits a local socialist meeting. On the other hand, he does not need socialism to be fully aware of the suffering among his poor friends—his washtub sister, his fertile landlady, his desperate mate from the laundry days—and, when his stories begin to sell, he gives his money lavishly to make them happy, clearing mortgages, buying shoes and ranches, and even purchasing a laundry for Joe. Nor does London write as an advocate of socialism. Never in the novel is the reader in doubt of London's admiration for Martin as an individualist. The spirit of the book lies in Martin's success in "going it alone." He is the Alger boy in just one more guise, and the fun of the reading lies in seeing him win his battle— a battle with ignorance, poverty, and, above all, The Establishment, as we would put it today. Never once is the reader concerned with Martin's attitude toward socialism; it plays so small a part in the book that it goes unnoticed.

Doubtless part of the reason that London made so much

of Martin's failure to become a socialist is that he himself was still widely known as a prominent socialist, an avowed Marxist who signed most of his letters with a rubber stamp reading "Yours for the Revolution, Jack London"; who had been first president of the Intercollegiate Socialist Society, lecturing across the country on the inevitable fall of capitalism; who had run for the school board and the mayorship of Oakland as a socialist candidate and was even considered as a socialist candidate for governor of California. Just the year before *Martin Eden* appeared, he had published *The Iron Heel*, a novel which presents in vivid terms the disintegration of capitalism. It is pertinent that it ends before the proletarian utopia is achieved, with society still in the grip of ruthless dictators, men who would be called Fascists and Nazis in another generation. Perhaps London's failure to make a convincing case for socialism as the hope for Martin Eden lay in London's diminishing faith in the socialist revolution. He was not to resign from the party for seven years, but at the time of writing *Martin Eden* he was sailing on "The Snark," no longer active in the cause nor for that matter much concerned with its underlying ideas.

His own "natural" philosophy had always more nearly resembled that of the predatory Wolf Larsen, strong-handed captain of *The Sea Wolf,* than it did that of Ernest Everhard, hopeful leader of the socialists in *The Iron Heel.* Perhaps Joan London, in her biography of her father, comes fairly close to the point when she insists that, in *Martin Eden,* London wrote his obituary.[1] Not only had he lost his active interest in socialism, but he had found success as a writer increasingly hollow. There was something wrong, and he was searching for the answer.

In the light of Jack London's temperament, it is not difficult to understand the suicide of Martin Eden. The foreshadowing of his final act is, in fact, to be found throughout the entire book, even though London may not have known that it was there. It lies in the very intensity of Martin's bat-

[1] Joan London, *Jack London and His Times* (New York: Doubleday, Doran, 1939), pp. 330–331.

tle despite the uncertainty of his goals. The process of succeeding drives him on with exhilaration; he gains intense pleasure in cutting down on his sleep, husbanding every moment, searching for new ideas, savoring the taste of an effective phrase. The battle is everything; the result, nothing. It is not Brissenden's death, nor the breakup with Ruth Morse, nor the discovery that much of cultural life is shallow that does him in. It is, rather, the discovery that he was going nowhere and the deadly realization that he had lost his interest in life. The frenetic activity was followed, dramatically, by an overpowering inertia. He found that he was interested in nothing; that he had difficulty moving from his chair; that neither food, drink, nor companionship would any longer stimulate him. One is tempted to conclude that he had reached the depressive stage of a manic-depressive existence.

His friend Lizzie Connolly, a working girl who would give him anything to bring him back to himself, had it right when she said: "It ain't your body. It's your head. Something's wrong with your think machine." And Martin recognized his trouble when he said to Ruth Morse: "I am sick, very sick. How sick I did not know till now. Something has gone out of me. I have always been unafraid of life. Life has so filled me that I am empty of any desire for anything."

There is some evidence that, at the time he wrote *Martin Eden*, Jack London was more than usually worried that he would lose his mind. These fits of depression following elation had plagued him frequently during his short life, but now they were growing more intense. How could he, who savored life so much, find all so dull and drab? He was to tell about his problem soon in his *John Barleycorn*, an autobiographical story that vividly portrays the "long sickness" of alcoholism which came upon him only too frequently. At least once before writing *Martin Eden*, he had attempted suicide as a way out—curiously, by attempting to drown himself in the Carquinez Straits, near San Francisco. Only the timely arrival of a fishing boat had saved him from death. Now, perhaps that urge became almost unbearable as he looked out his porthole on the "Mariposa." Death—the

"Noseless One," as he called him—would finally be welcomed at his ranch in Glen Ellen, when he was just forty years old.

Fifty books remain—the product of his fevered spirit and tremendous energy. Of them, none is better than *Martin Eden*. Like all his books, it is uneven in structure, sometimes clumsy in expression, at times mawkish in tone. Yet it possesses great lasting power, having more vitality today than it did the day it issued from the press. It gives a trustworthy picture of urban life in California at the turn of the century. It portrays effectively the feelings of an untrained boy coping with the baffling behavior of an adult society. It presents minor and major characters vividly. It says much about the clash in values between the proletariat and the middle class. It anticipates even more of what our own generation is saying about the faults of The Establishment. It tells more than London realized of the joys and depressions of a neurotic temperament, thus sounding remarkably modern in a world accustomed to the trials of the psychologically troubled. And, above everything else, it breathes energy and creates excitement as Martin Eden discovers the world of intellect and wins the battle to express himself.

13 WILLA CATHER
My Ántonia

Wallace Stegner

If, as is often said, every novelist is born to write one thing,
then the one thing that Willa Cather was born to write was
first fully realized in *My Ántonia* (1918). In that novel the
people are the Bohemian and Swedish immigrants she had
known in her childhood on the Nebraska plains; the prose is
the prose of her maturity—flexible, evocative, already tending
to a fastidious bareness but not yet gone pale and cool; the
novelistic skill is of the highest, the structure at once free
and intricately articulated; the characters stretch into symbolic suggestiveness as naturally as trees cast shadows in the
long light of a prairie evening; the theme is the fully ex-
posed, complexly understood theme of the American orphan
or exile, struggling to find a place between an old world left
behind and a new world not yet created.

But to say that Willa Cather found her subject and her
manner and her theme in *My Ántonia* is not to say that she
found them easily. When *My Ántonia* appeared, Miss Cather
was forty-five years old. She had already had one career as a
teacher and another as an editor, and she had published a
good many short stories and three other novels.

The first of these, *Alexander's Bridge* (1911) was a nearly
total mistake—a novel laid in London and dealing with the
attenuated characters and fragile ethical problems of the
genteel tradition. In writing it, Miss Cather later remarked,
she was trying to sing a song that did not lie in her voice.
Urged by her friend Sarah Orne Jewett to try something

closer to her own experience, she revived her Western memories with a trip to Arizona and New Mexico and, after her return to Pittsburgh,

> began to write a story entirely for myself; a story about some Scandinavians and Bohemians who had been neighbours of ours when I lived on a ranch in Nebraska, when I was eight or nine years old. I found it a much more absorbing occupation than writing *Alexander's Bridge;* a different process altogether. Here there was no arranging or "inventing"; everything was spontaneous and took its own place. . . . This was like taking a ride through familiar country on a horse that knew the way, on a fine morning when you felt like riding.[1]

As she herself instantly recognized, that second book, *O Pioneers!* (1913), came close to being the tune that "lay in her voice." She wrote it spontaneously because she was tapping both memory and affection. She thought of the subject matter as a considerable innovation, because no American writer had yet used Swedish immigrants for any but comic purposes, and nobody had ever written about Nebraska, considered in literary circles the absolute home of the clodhopper. Actually, there was nothing so revolutionary about the subject matter—it was merely one further extension of the local-color curiosity about little-known places and picturesque local types. Hamlin Garland had done German and Norwegian immigrants very like these, on Wisconsin and Iowa farms very like Miss Cather's Nebraska ones, in *Main-Travelled Roads* (1891). *O Pioneers!* was new in its particulars, but not new in type, and it was not Willa Cather's fully trained voice that was heard in it. In its method, the book is orthodox; the heroine, Alexandra Bergson, is a type of earth goddess; the theme is the theme of the conquest of a hard country that had dominated novels of the American settlement ever since James Fenimore Cooper's *The Pioneers* in 1823. Miss Cather's novel, in fact, is considerably slighter and simpler than Cooper's of similar title.

[1] "My First Novels (There Were Two)," *Willa Cather on Writing* (New York: Alfred A. Knopf, 1949), pp. 92–93.

145

In her third book, *The Song of the Lark* (1915), we can see Miss Cather systematically and consciously working for the enlargement and complication of her theme. The locale, at least in the beginning, is again Nebraska, though she calls it Colorado; the chief character is again a local girl of immigrant parentage, great promise, and few advantages. But the antagonist here is not the earth, and triumph is nothing so simple as the hewing of a farm out of a hard country. To the problem of survival has been added the problem of culture. The struggle is involved with the training of Thea Kronborg's fine voice; the effort of the novel is to explore how a talent may find expression even when it appears in a crude little railroad town on the plains, and how a frontier American may lift himself from his traditionless, artless environment to full stature as an artist and an individual.

Here we see developing the dynamism between old world and new that occurs strongly again not only in *My Antonia* but in *One of Ours* (1922), *The Professor's House* (1925), *Death Comes for the Archbishop* (1927), *Shadows on the Rock* (1931), and several of the short stories such as "Neighbor Rosicky." It is as if Miss Cather conceived the settlement of her country as a marriage between a simple, fresh, hopeful young girl and a charming, worldly, but older man. Thea Kronborg's German music teacher, Herr Wunsch, is the first of those cultivated and unhappy Europeans who people Miss Cather's fictions—exiles who, though doomed themselves by the hardships of pioneering, pass on sources of life and art to the eager young of a new land. Thea, like Alexandra Bergson before her and Ántonia Shimerda later, is that best sort of second-generation American who learns or retains some of the intellectual and artistic tradition of Europe without losing the American freshness and without falling into the common trap of a commercial and limited "practicality." These are all success stories of sorts, and all reflect a very American groping toward a secure identity.

But even *The Song of the Lark* was not the precise song that lay in Willa Cather's voice. Or rather, it was the right tune, but she sang it imperfectly. The story of Thea Kronborg's struggle to become an opera singer is told with a realism so detailed that it is exhausting; and it ended by offending its author nearly as much as the pretentiousness of *Alexander's Bridge.* "Too much detail," she concluded later, "is apt, like any form of extravagance, to become slightly vulgar." She never tried a second time the "full-blooded method": When the next book came along, "quite of itself, and with no direction from me, it took the road of *O Pioneers!*—not the road of *The Song of the Lark.*"

The next one was, of course, *My Ántonia.* But the road it took was not quite exactly that of *O Pioneers!* For though the place is still Nebraska and the protagonist is still an immigrant girl contending with the handicaps of a physical and emotional transplanting, *My Ántonia* is a major novel where the earlier ones were trial efforts. *O Pioneers!* was truly simple; *My Ántonia* only looks simple. *The Song of the Lark* was cluttered in its attempt to deal with complexity; *My Ántonia* gives complexity the clean lines and suggestive subtlety of fine architecture.

One technical device which is fundamental to the greater concentration and suggestiveness of *My Ántonia* is the point of view from which it is told. Both of the earlier "Nebraska novels" had been reported over the protagonist's shoulder, with omniscient intrusions by the author. Here the whole story is told by a narrator, Jim Burden, a boyhood friend of Ántonia, later a lawyer representing the railroads. The use of the narrative mask permits Miss Cather to exercise her sensibility without obvious self-indulgence: Burden becomes an instrument of the selectivity that she worked for. He also permits the easy condensation and syncopation of time—an indispensable technical tool in a novel that covers more than thirty years and deals in a complex way with a theme of development. Finally, Jim Burden is used constantly as a suggestive parallel to Ántonia: he is himself an orphan and has been himself transplanted (from the East, from Virginia), and is himself groping for an identity and an affiliation. In the process of understanding and commemorating Ántonia, he locates himself; we see the essential theme from two points, and the space between those points serves as a base line for triangulation.

The parallel is stressed from the beginning, when Jim, an orphan of ten, arrives in Black Hawk, Nebraska, on his way to live with his grandparents, and sees the immigrant Shimerda family huddling in bewilderment on the station platform, speaking their strange lost tongue. As he is driven to the ranch under a great unfamiliar sky, across a land that planes off mysteriously into darkness—"not a country, but the material out of which countries are made"—Jim feels so lost and strange and uprooted that he cannot even say the prayers that have been taught him back in Virginia. "Between that earth and sky I felt erased, blotted out."

For Jim, protected by his relatives, the strangeness soon wears away. For the Shimerdas, who have none of the tools or skills of farmers, no friends, no English, and who discover that the land they have been sold is bad and their house a sod cave, transplanting is a harsher trial, and harder on the old than on the young, and on the sensitive than on the dull. With the help of their neighbors the Burdens, the Shimerdas make a beginning, but before their first Christmas in the new land Papa Shimerda, gentle, helpless, homesick for the old life in Prague, has killed himself with a shotgun. Survival, which Miss Cather presents as a process of inevitable brutalization, is best managed by the grasping Mama Shimerda and her sullen son Ambroz. The fourteen-year-old girl, Ántonia, pretty and intelligent and her father's darling, must put off any hope of schooling and become one of the breadwinners for her miserably poor family. The deprivation is symbolic: this is the deculturation enforced on the frontier. The one thing beautiful in her life, the thing she shares with Jim, is the land itself, the great sea of grass, the wild roses in the fence corners of spring, the mighty weathers, and the tiny things—insects and flowers and little animals—that the eye notices because on the plains there is so little else to take the attention.

Ántonia and Jim as children share a kind of Eden, but they are going toward different futures. At the end of the first long section, which is divided between the presentation of the hardships of an immigrant family and Miss Cather's delicate nostalgic evocation of the freedom and beauty of the untamed land, Jim and Ántonia are lying together on top of the Burdens' chicken house while a great electrical storm comes on and "the felty beat of raindrops" begins in the dust. Why, Jim asks her, can't she always be "nice, like this"? Why must she all the time try to be like her brother Ambroz? "If I live here like you," Ántonia says, "that is different. Things will be easy for you. But they will be hard for us."

There are gradations in the penalties of exile; the most violently uprooted have the least chance. Section Two of the novel reinforces this idea by moving the action from the half-idyllic country to the limited and restricting little town of Black Hawk. In pages that forecast some of the attitudes of Sinclair Lewis' *Main Street* (1920), Miss Cather reveals the pettiness and snobbery, the vulgar commercialism, the cultural starvation, the forming class distinctions, the pathetic pleasures of a typical prairie town just beyond the pioneering stage. Ántonia, Lena Lingard, Tiny Soderball, and other Bohemian, Norwegian, and Swedish immigrant girls work as servants in the houses of the so-called "better families," and though they are snubbed by the town girls they demonstrate in their vitality and health something sturdier and more admirable than the more advantaged can show. Those for whom "things are easy" develop less character than these girls deprived of school, forced to work at menial jobs, dedicating their wages to help their families back on the farm. They do not even know that Black Hawk is a deprived little hole, but throw themselves wholeheartedly into the town dances and into any pleasure and excitement their world affords. Miss Cather sums up both desire and deprivation in a brief winter scene:

> In the winter bleakness a hunger for colour came over people, like the Laplander's craving for fats and sugar. Without knowing why, we used to linger on the sidewalk outside the church when the lamps were lighted early for choir practice or prayer-meeting, shivering and talking until our feet were like lumps

of ice. The crude reds and greens and blues of that coloured glass held us there.

It is Jim Burden speaking, but he speaks even more for the "hired girls" than for himself, for he is not confined within Black Hawk's limitations as they are. For him there is more than crude colored glass; opportunity opens outward to the state university in the city of Lincoln. For Ántonia and the others there is only housework, the amorous advances of people like Wick Cutter, the town money-lender, and the probability that eventually they will marry some farmer of their own immigrant background, who will work them like farm horses.

Part Three of *My Ántonia* has been objected to as a structural mistake, because it turns away from Ántonia and focuses on the university and city life of Jim Burden—on the opening of his mind, the passionate response he makes to books and ideas under the tutelage of a favorite professor, the quiet affair he has with Lena Lingard, who has set up in the city as a dressmaker. But the criticism seems based on too simplistic a view of the novel's intention. Though the title suggests that Ántonia is the focus of the book, the development from the symbolic beginning scene is traced through both Ántonia and Jim, and a good part of that theme of development is concerned with the possible responses to deprivation and to opportunity. We leave Ántonia in Book Three in order to return to her with more understanding later.

A high point of Jim's life in Lincoln is a performance of *Camille* that he and Lena Lingard attend. Like so many of Miss Cather's scenes, it expands effortlessly out of the particular and into the symbolic. The performance is shabby, the actors are broken-down, but to Jim the play is magic. Its bright illusion concentrates for him everything that he hopes for as he starts east to Harvard to continue his studies, going farther from his country, back toward the intellectual and artistic things that his country has left behind or possesses only in second-rate and vulgarized forms. It is worth observing that Jim Burden leaves Nebraska on a note of illusion.

Section Four returns us to Ántonia and to Black Hawk.

Back after two years at Harvard, Jim hears that in his absence Ántonia has eloped with a railroad conductor and that after being deceived and abandoned she has returned to her brother Ambroz's farm to bear her child and work in the fields like a man. The contrast between her pitiful failure and Jim's growing opportunities is deliberate; so is the trick of letting Jim come back to Ántonia little by little, first through the stories told of her by townspeople and only later in person. When he does finally go to the farm to see her, the deliberate structural split that began with Book Three is finally mended. Their lives will continue to run in different channels, but they have rediscovered the "old times" that they have in common, the things that by now Ántonia could not bear to leave. "I like to be where I know every stack and tree, and where all the ground is friendly," she says. Her bond is with the land—she all but *is* the land—while Jim will go on to law school and to occupations and associations unimaginable to her. Again Miss Cather catches a significant moment in a reverberating image, to show both the difference and the intimate relationship between these two:

> As we walked homeward across the fields, the sun dropped and lay like a great golden globe in the low west. While it hung there, the moon rose in the east, as big as a cart-wheel, pale silver and streaked with rose colour, thin as a bubble or a ghost-moon. For five, perhaps ten minutes, the two luminaries confronted each other across the level land, resting on opposite edges of the world.

"I'll come back," Jim says, leaving Ántonia, and she replies, "Perhaps you will. But even if you don't, you're here, like my father." Because we must give scenes like these more than realistic value, we recognize here an insistence, not only on the shared beauty of childhood in the new land, but on the other tradition that is going to go on operating in Ántonia's life, the gift of her father with his gentleness and his taste. In Ántonia, new world and old world, nature and nurture, meet as they meet in Jim, in different proportions and with different emphasis.

That union of two worlds is made explicit in Book Five,

when twenty years later Jim Burden returns again to Nebraska and finds Ántonia married to an amiable, half-successful Bohemian farmer, with a brood of healthy boys. She is no longer an eager girl, but a worn woman. But the same warmth of spirit still glows in her, and her life that had been half-wrecked has been put back together. In most ways, hers is an American family; but within the family they speak only Czech, and thus something of Papa Shimerda, something of Bohemia, is kept—something related to those strangenesses that Jim Burden had noted as a small boy: the dry brown chips he saw the Shimerdas nibbling, that were dried mushrooms picked in some far-off Bohemian forest; and the way Mama Shimerda, given title to a cow by Jim's grandfather, seized his hand in a totally un-American gesture and kissed it. A partly remembered but valued tradition and an empty land have fused and begun to be something new.

As for Jim Burden, we understand at last that the name Willa Cather chose for him was not picked by accident. For Jim not only, as narrator, carries the "burden" or tune of the novel; he carries also the cultural burden that Willa Cather herself carried, the quintessentially American burden of remaking in the terms of a new place everything that makes life graceful and civilized. To become a European or an easterner is only to reverse and double the exile. The education that lured Jim Burden away from Nebraska had divided him against himself, as Willa Cather was divided. Like people, the education that comes from elsewhere must be modified to fit a new environment. In becoming a man of the world, Jim Burden discovers that he has almost forgotten to be a man from Nebraska. It is Ántonia, who now achieves some of the quality of earth goddess that Alexandra Bergson had in *O Pioneers!*, who reminds him that no matter where his mind has been, his heart has always been here.

Jim Burden at the end of the novel is in the same position that Willa Cather was in when she finally found the people and themes and country that she was "born to write." The final paragraph is like the closing of a door, shutting in things that until now have been exposed or scattered. As Jim walks through the country he stumbles upon a stretch of the old pioneer wagon road of his childhood:

> This was the road over which Ántonia and I came on the night when we got off the train at Black Hawk and were bedded down in the straw, wondering children, being taken we knew not whither. I had only to close my eyes to hear the rumbling of the wagons in the dark, and to be again overcome by that obliterating strangeness. The feelings of that night were so near that I could reach out and touch them with my hand. I had the sense of coming home to myself, and of having found out what a little circle man's experience is. For Ántonia and for me, this had been the road of Destiny; had taken us to those early accidents of fortune which predetermined for us all that we can ever be. Now I understand that the same road was to bring us together again. Whatever we had missed, we possessed together the precious, the incommunicable past.

It is difficult not to hear in that passage the voice of Willa Cather, who like Jim left raw Nebraska to become a citizen of the world, and like him was drawn back. Jim Burden is more than a narrative device: he is an essential part of the theme, a demonstration of how such an American may reconcile the two halves of himself. And Ántonia is more than a woman and a character. Jim describes her toward the end as "a rich mine of life, like the founders of early races." Miss Cather, who did not believe in laboring a point any more than she believed in overfurnishing a novel, clearly wanted us to take away that image of Ántonia. A mine of life, the mother of races, a new thing forming itself in hardship and hope, but clinging to fragments of the well-loved old. Hence *My Ántonia*—any American's Ántonia, Willa Cather's Ántonia. No writer ever posed that essential aspect of the American experience more warmly, with more nostalgic lyricism, or with a surer understanding of what it means.

14 SHERWOOD ANDERSON
Winesburg, Ohio

Irving Howe

Sherwood Anderson was a minor but significant—sometimes an incomparably lovely—American writer. His life spanned the decades in the late nineteenth and early twentieth centuries in which America was moving from an agrarian to an industrial society. He grew up in a small Ohio town, and his best work—in the collection of related short stories called *Winesburg, Ohio,* as well as in several other stories—deals with the American small town. Anderson was a master of prose lyricism, the kind of "low fine music" he so admired in Turgenev's *Memoirs of a Sportsman.* He was a poet of tenderness, who in his sketches caught something of the native sweetness of American life in its preindustrial phase, but also something of its constrictedness and provincialism. His finest effects are lyrical, nostalgic, evocative; he had little mastery over the larger narrative forms: in fact, he never wrote a completely successful novel.

There was a time, in the 1920's, when his reputation was large and his influence great—so much so that when a distinguished literary magazine, *The Dial,* began awarding an annual literary prize, it gave the first one to Anderson, and the second to T. S. Eliot. Anderson was then regarded as an important representative of the literary "revolt against the village," that is, he released the resentment many of his contemporaries felt against the narrow-spiritedness and "puritanical" moralism which they associated with small-town American life, and he expressed the vague but powerful yearnings they felt for a life that would be freer, nobler, and more beautiful than they had known.

But Sherwood Anderson did more than capture the imagination of American readers with his haunting little sketches of small-town loneliness. His own life seemed, during the free-spirited and Bohemian 1920's, a kind of model for the artist. Into his middle thirties Anderson had lived a conventional middle-class life, running a small paint business and raising a family. But secretly and at night, he tried to compose novels. At the age of thirty-six he abandoned paint factory, wife, and children to strike out for the Bohemia of Chicago, devote himself to the cult of art, and thereby, as Thoreau once put it, "front only the essential facts of life." His work soon attracted the attention of more sophisticated and better educated writers, who tended to look upon him as an authentic American "primitive"—which in some ways he surely was, though with the proviso that primitives can also be very sly and crafty.

In 1915 and 1916, while working in Chicago as an advertising man, Anderson wrote the sketches he would later collect under the title of *Winesburg, Ohio*. The book is a classic American portrait of human bewilderment, a parable about the loss of love conveying a vision of the native landscape cluttered with dead stumps, twisted oddities, grotesque and pitiful remnants of human creatures. Later cultural historians would sometimes protest that his picture of the American small town was unjust, too harsh in its criticism; but Anderson never pretended to be drawing an objective historical portrait; he was writing, as all writers must, from the depths and the pain of his own experience.

I have repeatedly met people from countries whose cultural style must be very different from that of the late-nineteenth-century, mid-Western America which Anderson portrayed, but who have nevertheless felt extraordinarily moved by, immediately at home with, the world of Winesburg. People from Scandinavia, Turkey, and Italy have told me that Winesburg reminded them of their own village, for villages throughout the world have a great deal in common, both in their beauties and their ugliness. Anderson wrote not merely about a particular moment in American historical development; his stories, for all their fragility, capture something that is universal, a note of nostalgia and loss, a quality of rare tenderness.

It is a quality that takes one back to Turgenev's "low fine music." In Turgenev's *Memoirs of a Sportsman*, Anderson admired most that purity of feeling which comes from the author's strict refusal to violate or impose himself on his characters. Between *Memoirs of a Sportsman*, which Anderson called "the sweetest thing in all literature," and *Winesburg* there are obvious similarities: both are episodic novels containing loosely bound but closely related sketches, both depend for impact less on dramatic action than on a climactic lyrical insight, and in both the individual sketches frequently end with bland understatements that form an ironic coda to the body of the writing. These similarities could certainly be taken as tokens of influence—if only we were certain that Anderson had actually read Turgenev before writing *Winesburg*.

But if Turgenev's influence on *Winesburg* is not quite certain, there can be no doubt about Mark Twain's. Between the America of Anderson's boyhood, which is the setting of his best work, and the America of Huck Finn there are only a few intervening decades, and the nostalgia for a lost moment of American pastoral which saturates *Huckleberry Finn* is also present in *Winesburg*.

Shortly after he came to Chicago Anderson was introduced by his brother Karl to the early writings of Gertrude Stein. Though he laughed at Stein when he first read her, she seems to have stimulated him in a way few other writers could. To Anderson, Stein suggested that, at least in the actual process of composition, words could have an independent value; they could be fresh or stale, firm or gruelly, colored or drab. After reading the fanatically monosyllabic *Three Lives* Anderson would hardly try again, as he had in his first two novels, to write "literary" English. But despite such surface similarities as repetition of key words and an insistently simple syntax, their styles had little in common. Stein's language was opaque, leading back into itself and thereby tending to replace the matter of fiction, while the language of *Winesburg* was translucent, leading quickly to the center of the book's action. Stein was the best kind of influence: she did not bend Anderson to her style, she liberated him for his own.

And that, essentially, was what the Chicago literary milieu did. It persuaded Anderson that American writers needed an indigenous style which, if only they were bold enough, they could then and there construct; it taught him that before language could be used creatively it might have to be crumbled into particles; and it made him conscious of the need for literary consciousness.

Anderson had recalled that during the years immediately preceding *Winesburg* he would often take with him on advertising trips pages torn from Gideon Bibles, which he read over and over again. This recollection tells us most of what needs to be known about the making of *Winesburg*. Its author had not the slightest interest in religion, but his first experience in a literary environment had made him aware of writing as writing and had taught him where to find its greatest English source. He had begun to work as a conscious craftsman.

In its fundamental quality *Winesburg* is nonrealistic; it does not seek to gratify the eye with a verisimilitude to social forms the way a Dreiser or a Lewis novel does. In rather shy, lyrical outbursts the book conveys a vision of American life as a landscape eerie with the cracked echoes of villagers rambling in their lonely eccentricity. Again and again *Winesburg* suggests that beneath the exteriors of our life the deformed exert dominion. And *Winesburg* echoes with American loneliness, that loneliness which could once evoke Mark Twain's chant of praise to the Mississippi pastoral but which has here become fearful and sour.

Winesburg is a book largely set in twilight and darkness, its backgrounds heavily shaded with gloomy blacks and marshy grays—as is proper for a world of withered men who, sheltered by night, reach out for that sentient life they dimly recall as a racial inheritance that has been squandered away. Like most fiction, *Winesburg* is a variation on the theme of reality and appearance. The deformations caused by day (public life) are intensified at night and, in their very extremity, become an entry to reality. From Anderson's instinctively right placement of the book's central actions at twilight and night comes some of its frequently noticed aura of "lostness"—as if the most sustaining and fruitful human activities could no longer be performed in public communion but must be grasped in secret.

The two dozen central figures in *Winesburg* are hardly characters in the usual novelistic sense. They are not shown in depth or breadth, complexity or ambiguity; they are allowed no variations of action or opinion; they do not, with the exception of George Willard, the book's "hero," grow or decline. For Anderson is not trying to represent the immediate surface of human experience; he is rather drawing the abstract and deliberately distorted paradigm of an extreme situation, and for that purpose fully rounded characterizations could only be a complicating blemish.

The figures of *Winesburg* usually personify to fantastic excess a condition of psychic deformity which is the consequence of some crucial failure in their lives, some aborted effort to extend their personalities or proffer their love. Misogyny, inarticulateness, frigidity, God-infatuation, homosexuality, drunkenness—these are symptoms of their recoil from the regularities of human intercourse and sometimes of their substitute gratifications in inanimate objects, as with the unloved Alice Hindman who "because it was her own, could not bear to have anyone touch the furniture of her room." In their compulsive traits these figures find a kind of dulling peace, but as a consequence they are subject to rigid monomanias and are deprived of one of the great blessings of human health: the capacity for a variety of experience. That is why, in a sense, "nothing happens" in *Winesburg*. For most of its figures it is too late for anything to happen, they can only muse over the troubles which have so harshly limited their spontaneity. Stripped of their wholeness and twisted into frozen postures of defense, they are indeed what Anderson has called them: grotesques. And the world of *Winesburg*, populated largely by these back-street grotesques, soon begins to seem like a buried ruin of a once vigorous society, an atrophied remnant of the egalitarian moment of nineteenth-century America.

The conception of the grotesque, as actually developed in the stories, is not merely that it is an unwilled affliction but also that it is a mark of a once sentient striving. In his introductory fantasy, "The Book of the Grotesque," Anderson writes:

> It was the truths that made the people grotesques . . . the moment one of the people took one of the truths to himself, called it his truth, and tried to live his life by it, he became a grotesque and the truth he embraced a falsehood.

These sentences suggest the significant notion that the grotesques are those who *have* sought "the truths" that disfigure them. By contrast the banal creatures who dominate the town's official life, such as Will Henderson, publisher of the paper for which George Willard works, are not even grotesques: they are simply clods. The grotesques are those whose humanity has been outraged and who to survive in Winesburg have had to suppress their wish to love. Grotesqueness is not merely the shield of deformity; it is also a remnant of misshapen feeling, what Dr. Reefy in the sketch "Paper Pills" calls "the sweetness of the twisted apples."

Winesburg may thus be read as a fable of American estrangement, its theme the loss of love. The book's major characters are cut off from the basic sources of emotional sustenance—from the nature in which they live but to which they can no longer have an active relation; from the fertility of the farms that flank them but no longer fulfill their need for creativity; from the community which once bound men together in fraternity but is now merely an institution external to their lives; from the work which once evoked and fulfilled their sense of craft but is now a mere burden; and, most catastrophic of all, from each other. The very extremity of their need for love has itself become a barrier to its realization.

The grotesques rot because they are unused, their energies deprived of outlet, and their instincts curdled in isolation. As Waldo Frank has pointed out in his fine study of *Winesburg,* the first three stories in the book suggest this view in a complete development. The story, "Hands," depicts the loss of creativity in the use of the human body. The second story, "Paper Pills," pictures the progressive ineffectuality of human thought, pocketed in paper pellets that no one reads. And the third story, "Mother," relates these two themes to the inability of Elizabeth Willard, *Winesburg's* mother-figure, to communicate her love to her son. In the rupture of family love and the consequent loss of George Willard's heritage, the theme of the book is completed.

The book's central strand of action, discernible in about half the stories, is the effort of the grotesques to establish intimate relations with George Willard, the young reporter. At night, when they need not fear the mockery of public detection, they hesitantly approach him, almost in supplication, to tell him of their afflictions and perhaps find health in his voice. Instinctively, they sense his moral freshness, finding hope in the fact that he has not yet been calloused by knowledge and time. To some of the grotesques, such as Dr. Reefy and Dr. Parcival, George Willard is the lost son returned, whose apparent innocence and capacity for feeling will redeem Winesburg. To others among the grotesques, such as Tom Foster and Elmer Cowley, he is a reporter-messenger, bringing news of a dispensation which will allow them to re-enter the world of men. But perhaps most fundamentally, he seems to the grotesques almost a young priest who will renew the forgotten communal rites by which they may again be bound together.

As they approach George Willard, the grotesques seek not merely a sudden expressive outburst, but also a relation with each other that may restore them to collective harmony. They are distraught communicants in search of a ceremony, a social value, a manner of living, a lost ritual that may, by some means, re-establish a flow and exchange of emotion. Their estrangement is so extreme that they cannot turn to each other though it is each other they really need and secretly want; they turn instead to George Willard, who will soon be out of the orbit of their life.

In only one story, "Death," do the grotesques seem to meet. Elizabeth Willard and Dr. Reefy embrace in a moment of confession, but their approach to love is interrupted by a stray noise. Elizabeth leaves: "The thing that had come to life in her as she talked to her one friend died suddenly." A few months later, at her deathbed, Dr. Reefy meets George Willard and puts out "his hand as though to greet the young man and then awkwardly [draws] it back again." The hoped-for discovery is aborted; the ritual of communal love remains unrealized.

The burden that the grotesques would impose on George Willard is beyond his strength. He is not yet himself a grotesque mainly because he has not yet experienced very deeply, but for the role to which they would assign him he is too absorbed in his own ambition and restlessness. The grotesques see in his difference from them the possibility of saving themselves, but actually it is the barrier to an ultimate companionship. George Willard's adolescent receptivity to the grotesques can only give him the momentary emotional illumination described in a lovely story, "Sophistication." On the eve of his departure from Winesburg, George Willard reaches the point

> when he for the first time takes the backward view of life. . . . With a little gasp he sees himself as merely a leaf blown by the wind through the streets of his village. He knows that in spite of all the stout talk of his fellows he must live and die in uncertainty, a thing blown by the winds, a thing destined like corn to wilt in the sun. . . . Already he hears death calling. With all his heart he wants to come close to some other human, touch someone with all his hands. . . .

For George this illumination is enough, but it is not for the grotesques. They are a moment in his education; he a confirmation of their doom.

In the story "Queer" these meanings receive their most generalized expression, for its grotesque, Elmer Cowley, has no specific deformity: he is *the* grotesque as such. "He was, he felt, one condemned to go through life without friends and he hated the thought." Elmer Cowley decides to leave Winesburg, but in a last effort at communication he asks George Willard to meet him at the midnight local. He cannot speak.

> Elmer Cowley danced with fury beside the groaning train in the darkness on the station platform. . . . Like one struggling for release from hands that held him he struck, hitting George Willard blow after blow on the breast, the neck, the mouth.

Unable to give Elmer Cowley the love that might dissolve his queerness, George Willard suffers the fate of the rejected priest.

From "Queer" it is possible to abstract the choreography of *Winesburg*. Its typical action is a series of dance maneuvers by figures whose sole distinctive characteristic is an extreme deformity of movement or posture. Each of these grotesques dances, with angular indirection and muted pathos, toward a central figure who seems to them young, fresh, and radiant. For a moment they seem to draw close to him and thereby to abandon their stoops and limps, but this moment quickly dissolves in the play of the dance and perhaps it never even existed: the central figure cannot be reached. Slowly and painfully, the grotesques withdraw while the young man leaves the stage entirely. None of the grotesques is seen full-face for more than a moment, and none of them is individually important to the scheme of the dance. The distances established between the dancers, rather than their personalities, form the essence of the dance. And in the end, its meaning is revealed in the fact that all but the one untouched youth return to precisely their original places and postures.

When Anderson first sent his *Winesburg* stories to the *Masses, Seven Arts,* and the *Little Review,* he intended each of them to be a self-contained unit, as in fact they may still be regarded. But there was clearly a unifying conception behind all the stories: they were set in the same locale, many of the characters appeared in several stories, and there was a remarkable consistency of mood that carried over from story to story. Consequently, when Anderson prepared them for book publication in 1919, he had only to make a few minor changes, mostly insertions of place and character names as connectives, in order to have a unified book. Particularly if approached along the lines that have been suggested here, *Winesburg* seems remarkably of a piece.

Winesburg is an excellently formed piece of fiction, each of its stories following an arc of movement which abstractly graphs the book's meaning. There develops in one of the grotesques a rising lyrical excitement, usually stimulated to intensity by the presence of George Willard. Just before reaching a climax, this excitement is frustrated by a fatal inability at communication and then it rapidly dissolves into its original diffuse base. This structural pattern is sometimes varied by an ironic turn, as in "Nobody Knows" and "A Man of Ideas," but in only one story, "Sophistication," is the emotion allowed to move forward without interruption.

Through a few simple but extremely effective symbols, the stories are both related to the book's larger meaning and defined in their uniqueness. For the former of these purposes, the most important symbol is that of the room, frequently used to suggest isolation and confinement. Kate Swift is alone in her bedroom, Dr. Reefy in his office, the Reverend Curtis Hartman in his church tower, Enoch Robinson in his fantasy-crowded room. The tactful use of this symbol lends *Winesburg* a claustrophobic aura appropriate to its theme.

Most of the stories are further defined by symbols related to their particular meanings. More valid than any abstract statement of theme is the symbolic power of that moment in "The Strength of God" when the Reverend Curtis Hartman, in order to peek into Kate Swift's bedroom, breaks his church window at precisely the place where the figure of a boy stands "motionless and looking with rapt eyes into the face of Christ."

Though *Winesburg* is written in the bland accents of the American storyteller, it has an economy impossible to oral narration because Anderson varies the beat of its accents by occasionally whipping them into formal rhetorical patterns. In the book's best stretches there is a tension between its underlying loose oral cadences and the stiffened, superimposed beat of a prose almost Biblical in its regularity. Anderson's prose is neither "natural" nor primitive; it is rather a hushed bardic chant, low-toned and elegiacally awkward, deeply related to native speech rhythms yet very much the result of literary cultivation.

But the final effectiveness of this prose is in its prevalent tone of tender inclusiveness. Between writer and materials there is an admirable equity of relationship. None of the characters is violated, none of the stories, even the failures, leaves the reader with the bitter sense of having been tricked by cleverness or cheapness or toughness. The ultimate unity of the book is a unity of feeling, a sureness of warmth, and a readiness to accept Winesburg's lost grotesques with the embrace of humility. Many American writers have taken as their theme the loss of love in the modern world, but few, if any at all, have so thoroughly realized it in the accents of love.

Read for moral explication, as a guide to life, Anderson's work must seem unsatisfactory; it simply does not tell us enough. But there is another, more fruitful way of reading his work: as the expression of a sensitive witness to the national experience and as the achievement of a storyteller who created a small body of fiction unique in American writing for the lyrical purity of its feeling. No other American writer has so thoroughly communicated the sense of that historical moment when the native sweetness had not yet been lost to our life, when the nation began to stir from provinciality but had not yet toughened into imperial assurance. In the shabby crevices of this world Anderson discovered the lonely and deformed souls who would never be noticed by official society; he found concealed reserves of feeling, of muted torment and love.

There is in all this something of the quality of adolescence. It is precisely this quality of adolescence which has caused most of the uncertainties and difficulties in our response to Anderson's work. When we say—this is the favorite gambit of hostile critics—that Anderson's work deals not with reality but with adolescent gropings, we ignore the reality of those very gropings; we ignore, as well, the fact that from these gropings none of us is or should be exempt. Alfred Kazin has put this matter well:

> When we think of the many who have written more sharply than [Anderson], who have not been content to rest on the expression of dismay, the air of grief, we tend to grow dubious about his significance. What has he done but prepare isolated histories of the puzzled and the bewildered? Perhaps they are not enough, but it is also true that there has always been something of ourselves that we have seen in them, some moment in our lives that was illuminated by theirs.[1]

In that more durable part of his work, *Winesburg* and some of the short stories, adolescence comes through in a radiant comeliness, a sweet surge of feeling. His faults, his failures, and his defeats can hardly be ignored: he was almost always limited in moral sensibility and social perspective. Yet there were a few moments when he spoke, as almost no one else among American writers, with the voice of love.

[1] *On Native Grounds* (New York: Harcourt, Brace, 1942).

15 SINCLAIR LEWIS
Main Street

Daniel Aaron

Main Street may or may not be Sinclair Lewis' best novel (many readers would rank it below *Babbitt*), but it is one of those symptomatic books that literary historians find so convenient as milestones or turning points. It belongs to the special category of book—there is no name for it—which is at once a valid literary work and an explosive cultural event. Greater novelists than Lewis have had to wait decades or longer for a responsive audience, but the publication of *Main Street* in October 1920 (I say this on the authority of Prof. Mark Schorer, Lewis' most searching biographer), turned out to be "the most sensational event in twentieth-century American publishing history." [1]

The immediate success of *Main Street* was not one of those rare and happy literary accidents that overnight transforms some unknown amateur into a celebrity. Lewis had already displayed an uncanny talent for choosing themes or subjects of consuming interest to the public, or likely to become so. He had served a tasking apprenticeship as a short-story writer; he had published five novels and drawn attention to himself as a realist "capable of hitting hard at American faults." Between 1914, when his first novel appeared, and 1920, he had catalogued the sights and sounds of the American scene, listened carefully to the rhythms of Middle-Western talk, and familiarized himself with colloquialisms, slang,

[1] *Sinclair Lewis, "An American Life"* (New York: McGraw-Hill, 1961), p. 268.

and advertising jargon. Although he was not then, or ever, a sensitive literary craftsman, he had learned to write swiftly and competently. Finally, he had acquired a knowledge of the literary market place and of advertising and selling possessed by few of his contemporaries; like Mark Twain he was almost as much interested in the technique of promoting his books as he was in the art of writing them.

It may seem odd, in retrospect, that a novel without any strikingly original characters, without suspense, without any remarkable stylistic merits, should have aroused such a clamor. The plot is ambling and unspectacular. It is merely the story of a romantic half-educated Middle-Western girl, tinged with vague longings, who marries a small-town doctor, rebels against the monotony and drabness of her life, and grudgingly—after a brief flurry of nonconformity—accommodates herself to her husband and her destiny. And yet the day-to-day experiences of Lewis' heroine, Carol Kennicott, devoid of tragedy and often trivial, proved absorbing to hundreds of thousands of readers who vicariously shared them.

Some readers, it must be said, were shocked and angered. Lewis, they felt, had indulged in cheap fun at the expense of the American institutions and at men and women who had made the nation great. He had depicted the small town, that microcosm of Eden, without love or understanding. Sherwood Anderson, for one, never forgave Lewis for reducing American small towns to hot dusty places peopled by boasters and liars, "never tender about anything or anybody, never human." [2] But there were others who rejoiced in his iconoclasm. They saw him as the articulator of their own case against what was mean and dispiriting in North American life.

In choosing Gopher Prairie, "a Minnesota wheat-prairie town of something over three thousand people," as his untidy subject, Lewis was following in the wake of such predecessors as Mark Twain, Hamlin Garland, Harold Frederic, and Edgar Lee Masters. The so-called "revolt against the vil-

2 "Cotton Mill," *Scribner's Magazine*, LXXXVIII (July 1930), 8.

lage" was by no means a new movement in 1920, as Lewis well knew. His contemporaries, Theodore Dreiser and Sherwood Anderson, had thrown a few bombs of their own, but the image of the ideal small town, according to an earlier observer, still lay unclouded in "the mind's eye" of the great American public:

> neat, compact, organized, traditional: the white church with tapering spire, the sober school house, the smithy of the ringing anvil, the corner grocery, the cluster of friendly houses, the venerable parson, the wise physician, the canny squire, the grasping landlord softened or outwitted in the end; the village belle, gossip, atheist, idiot, jovial fathers, gentle mothers, merry children; cool parlors, shining kitchens, spacious barns, lavish gardens, fragrant summer dawns, and comfortable winter evenings.[3]

One has only to contrast this picture-card village with the Gopher Prairie Carol Kennicott surveyed on her arrival to see how systematically Lewis shattered this pretty invention. Gopher Prairie is neither neat nor organized. It is the "planlessness" that overwhelms Carol,

> the flimsy temporariness of the buildings, their faded unpleasant colors. . . . Each man had built with the most valiant disregard of all the others.

The schoolhouse is ugly and overcrowded. Cement garages have supplanted the smithy; the corner grocery is a depressing vision of overripe bananas and lettuce warmed by a sleeping cat. There is still gossip, of course, but it is of a savage and defiling variety. The fathers are artificially jovial; the mothers are not gentle; the young people are mostly loutish. Gopher Prairie, in short, is "slavery self-sought and self-defended. It is dullness made God."

So Carol Kennicott saw it; yet it would be a mistake to leave it at that. Lewis' portrait of the small town is not unrelievedly dismal nor are all of its inhabitants drooling Yahoos. Some have private heroisms. He had modeled Gopher Prairie

---

[3] Quoted in Carl Van Doren, *Sinclair Lewis*, "A Biographical Sketch" (New York: Viking, 1933), p. 22.

on Sauk Center, Minnesota, where he was born and where he spent a not very enjoyable adolescence; his home town was not without the kind of brave beauty Carol conceded to Gopher Prairie. In moments of nostalgia, Lewis would recall the friendliness of Sauk Center, the swimming and the fishing, the ten-mile tramp with a shotgun in October,

> sliding on Hoboken Hill, stealing melons, or listening to the wonders of an elocutionist at the G.A.R. Hall. It was a good time, a good place, a good preparation for life.

Such a confession would seem to moderate Sherwood Anderson's complaint that Lewis missed the poetry of rural life; still, such mellow evocations are not characteristic. If he sometimes remembered boyish pleasures, his biographer has shown us that Lewis was more deeply touched by his humiliations. One of the reasons he wrote *Main Street,* Lewis said later, was to puncture humbug notions about the alleged neighborliness of small towns; and he described how irritated he was, after returning from Yale University during the summer of his sophomore year, by the comments of his father's friends:

> Why don't Doc Lewis make Harry get a job on the farm instead of letting him sit around readin' a lot of fool histories and God knows what all?

Some of these early frustrations undoubtedly went into the making of *Main Street,* but the novel must have owed a great deal to what Lewis once called his "extraordinarily discrepant" literary ancestors—Dickens, Swinburne, H. G. Wells, Housman, Hardy, Hamlin Garland, H. L. Mencken—as well as some unacknowledged ones.

On more than one occasion Lewis honored his debt to Mencken, a brilliant literary and social critic who had begun his derisive commentary on the American bourgeoisie (or "booboisie," to use his own coinage) long before *Main Street* was even an idea in Lewis' head. I have sometimes thought it was Mencken's jovial satire—especially as it applied to that area of the United States he called the "Bible Belt"—that prepared the way for his younger follower and partially accounted for the enthusiastic reception of his work. Mencken's raucousness and exaggeration, his violent social antipathies, find their analogies in Lewis' pages. Both men, moreover, based their virulent and sardonic portraits of persons and places on facts, and yet neither, strictly speaking, was a realist. Perhaps their willful distortions of an America filled with boobs and Philistines and blustering bigots was the most effective answer to the brayings of the "Boosters," the 100 per cent he-men, the "Regular Guys" who spoke for the America of Harding and Coolidge.

Another subversive voice echoing in *Main Street* belongs to Thorstein Veblen, an economist, sociologist, and critic of the business ethos who had become the darling of the literary radicals after the publication of *The Theory of the Leisure Class* in 1899. On the one occasion I met Lewis, he told me that he had never read Veblen. If so, it is still interesting that Miles Bjorstam, Gopher Prairie's handyman and radical, has a book of Veblen in his library; and it is certainly a coincidence, if nothing more, that the town's banker, merchants, real estate men, lawyers, and clergymen are very much as Veblen described them in 1915. Local patriotism and civic pride, Veblen observed at that time, provided the rationale for real estate speculators:

> Pecuniary interest in local land values involves an interest in the continued growth of the town. Hence any creditable misrepresentation of the town's volume of business traffic, population, tributary farming community, or natural resources, is rated as serviceable to the common good. And any member of this businesslike community will be rated as a meritorious citizen in proportion as he is serviceable to this joint pecuniary interest of these "influential citizens." [4]

Main Street dramatizes these Veblenian reflections, and Carol Kennicott seems to be paraphrasing Veblen when she comments:

[4] *Imperial Germany and the Industrial Revolution* [1915] (New York: Kelley, 1946), pp. 334–335.

that the prairie towns no more exist to serve the farmers who are their reason for existence than do the great capitals; they exist to fatten on the farmers, to provide for the townsmen large motors and social preferment; and, unlike the capitals, they do not give to the district in return for usury a stately and permanent center, but only this ragged camp. It is "parasitic Greek civilization"—minus the civilization.

A third less obvious influence but the key to the blurred thesis of *Main Street* was another disturber of the peace, Henry David Thoreau. Lewis repeatedly named Thoreau as the pervasive influence on all of his work—a paradoxical admission considering Lewis' unwillingness or inability to lead the simple life. But the burden of Lewis' message to his fellow Americans was indeed Thoreauvian. Mark Schorer has rightly said that the basis of his plots was "the individual impulse to freedom and the social impulse to restrict it." *Main Street*, at bottom, is a variation on a theme of *Walden*.

The best way to illustrate this Thoreauvian link is to consider more closely Lewis' heroine, Carol Kennicott, that controversial figure maligned and betrayed by her creator. Many of the admirers of the novel—Mencken, to name only one—refused to take her seriously. She was a romantic ninny, after all, dreaming of medieval castles, bearded Frenchmen, nymphs and satyrs, jeweled elephants. Her vision of a remodeled Gopher Prairie as a New England village nestling in a Swinburnian landscape was as pathetic as it was ridiculous. And yet Lewis allows this same woman, whose artistic and literary notions were not so vastly superior to those of the bluestockings in the Gopher Prairie Thanatopsis Club, to preach his satirical sermon to his sheeplike contemporaries and to assail the institutions that enslaved them.

Apparently, in 1920 Lewis was as unabashed a romantic as Carol (in fact he never stopped hankering for a bookish fairyland inhabited by amorous sylphs) and he held his heroine in much higher esteem than did his more sophisticated and cynical friends. Even in the earlier versions of the novel, where she appeared as a character named Fern, Lewis had expressed a faith in her "lucidity of mind" if not in the effectiveness of her efforts, and there is little to indicate that he disagreed with her indictment of the "brisk, spectacled, motor-driving businessmen" of Main Street. To be sure, then and later, he never entirely approved of her nor did he minimize her deficiencies, but he certainly shared her distaste for Gopher Prairie's complacency and hypocrisy, and he encouraged her attempts to stave off what Lewis calls in *Main Street,* the "village virus."

The principal sufferer of that disease is the lawyer, Guy Pollock, a dim and appealing figure who in the early draft of the novel was probably intended to play a larger role than he does in the final version. As he explains it to Carol, the village virus is an infection to which ambitious people in small towns are peculiarly susceptible. Gradually, imperceptibly, it saps them of their hope and energy, narcotizes rebelliousness, reduces the victim to the same dead level of the lifeless majority residing in "a respectable form of hell." Carol finally discontinues her one-woman revolt (it is hard to say whether or not she actually contracts the disease), but she protests, with Lewis' approval, until the end.

In a retrospective look at *Main Street,* Lewis maintained that he was not indebted to Masters' *Spoon River Anthology* nor did he have in mind a corn-fed Emma Bovary, two assertions I accept unhesitatingly, but his claim that he had carefully implanted the idea that "Carol wasn't of as good stuff as her husband," although true enough, is still a little disingenuous. She lacked the stability and perseverance of Dr. Will Kennicott, perhaps even his humanity and quiet courage, but her crusade was Lewis' as well, and it was Carol who conveyed his subversive ideas, not her husband.

Dr. Will is a good physician and surgeon, but he is quite at home with the 100 per cent boosters. He laughs at their jokes. He believes in their primitive politics, and declares:

> Tell you, Carrie, there's just three classes of people: folks that haven't got any ideas at all; and cranks that kick about everything; and Regular Guys, the fellows with sticktuitiveness, that boost and get the world's work done.

Carol, who presumably fits into the second category, cannot swallow this nonsense, and although she loves her husband, she will not sacrifice her individuality to become like him, as he unconsciously desires her to. In one of her frank moments, she says she is a crank not because she is trying to "reform" the town but in order to save her own soul; and here is the real thesis of *Main Street*. The Carol who speaks in this vein is the daughter of Emerson and Thoreau and not the American sister of Emma Bovary.

Then why does Lewis turn against her and later side with her bumbling husband? Why did he write an article in 1924 (a visit by the author of *Main Street* to the office of Dr. Will Kennicott) the point of which is to debunk his former alter ego? He hardly recognizes Carol, he says, when he meets her in the doctor's consulting room. He sees:

> a woman, perhaps forty, a smallish woman with horn-rimmed spectacles which made her little face seem childish, though it was a childishness dubious and tired and almost timid. She must once, I noted, have been slender and pretty, but she was growing dumpy and static, and about her was an air of having lost her bloom.

What is worst, Carol has lost her old spunk. She is cowed and dominated by her powerful confident husband about whom Lewis now speaks in much warmer terms than he did in 1920. The cruel resurrection of Carol suggests a reversal of the author's attitude until we remember that Lewis had never agreed to her *comprehensive* indictment of Gopher Prairie. The Dr. Kennicott part of him exhibited a sneaking fondness for the "boobs" and "slobs" that the Carol Kennicott part of him refused to tolerate.

By 1924 and increasingly afterward, Lewis, the apologist or celebrator of the middle class, is more assertive than the Lewis who assails it. He prefers the company of the doctor to that of his querulous wife with whom he had never openly identified himself. He had even composed a misleading publisher's blurb for *Main Street:* an "eager girl" living the "fish-bowl" existence of a doctor's wife in a small town

173

finally learns "the great secret of life in being content with a real world in which it's never possible to create an ideal setting." This rather silly description, which Dr. Will might have written, belies the novel, but it helps to correct the mistaken view of Lewis as a consistently angry critic of American materialism. America had not produced the kind of civilization that satisfied the Carol Kennicott in him, but then neither had Europe. Like Dr. Will, like Babbitt, he respected the men responsible for reliable automobiles and tiled bathrooms, as a glance at any of his novels will show. Among his portraits of business and professional men, Babbitt is presented sardonically but without rancor, Dodsworth almost reverently, Cass Timberlane romantically. One of the most admirable specimens (to Lewis, at any rate) was Fred Cornplow, an automobile salesman from Sachem, New York, and the hero of one of the weaker novels, *The Prodigal Parents.* He is the remarkable descendant of remarkable progenitors:

> From Fred Cornplow's family, between B.C. 1937 and A.D. 1937, there came, despite an occasional aristocratic Byron or an infrequent proletarian, John Bunyan, nearly all the medical researchers, the discoverers of better varieties of wheat, the poets, the builders, the singers, the captains of great ships. Sometimes his name has been pronounced Babbitt; sometimes it has been pronounced Ben Franklin; and once, if Eugene O'Neill may be trusted, he went by the style of Marco Polo. . . . He is the eternal bourgeois, the bourjoyce, the burgher, the Middle Class, whom the Bolsheviks hate and imitate, whom the British love and deprecate, and who is most of the population worth considering in France and Germany and these United States.

Lewis remained as loyally committed to the best representatives of the middle class as William Dean Howells, a writer he dismissed as a "pious old maid" but to whom he was more closely linked than he perhaps realized.

The panegyric to Fred Cornplow, published in the radical thirties, irritated a number of critics for whom "middle class" was almost a term of abuse. They contrasted the sharpness and pungency of *Main Street, Babbitt,* and *Elmer Gantry* with the increasingly mellow novels that ducked, they thought, the real issues of the day. Lewis, one of them complained, "drew a revolutionary picture of American middle-class life without coming to revolutionary conclusions about it." [5]

Remarks of this sort betrayed an ignorance of Lewis and his position. He had always written as an "insider" even though he seemed to be peering at his society from without. If he rebuked the Babbitts and the whole "crowd" of Dr. Kennicott's friends with their "coarse voices, large damp hands, tooth-brush mustaches, bald spots, and Masonic watch-charms," it was for failing to measure up to their capacities, and the fault lay less with them than with their society. His radicalism had never been deep or abiding—a short exposure to Upton Sinclair's socialism, a quick look at the happy anarchists in Greenwich Village before World War I; it never went beyond a kind of outraged humanitarianism. He preferred lowbrows or middlebrows to highbrows, but he was apparently unaware or uninterested in the niceties of class distinction. The language of the people he admires hardly differs from the language of the people he debunks. Professional men, businessmen, social workers, teachers, laborers, technicians all "bumble" or "chirp" or "warble" or "boom" or "gurgle." His serious discussions on science or religion, as Rebecca West noted, were likely to sound like "Babbittry in reverse."

No reader of *Main Street* can forget the speech of the "Booster and Hustler," Jim Blausser, invited by the Commercial Club to inaugurate their campaign to bring industry to Gopher Prairie and incidentally boost real estate values. Jim Blausser talks in a subliterate, squalid Americanese as remote from standard English as Chinese:

> I want to tell you good people, and it's just as sure as God made little apples, the thing that distinguishes our American commonwealth from the pikers and tin-horns in other Countries is our Punch. You take a genuwine, honest-to-God homo Americanibus and there ain't anything he's afraid to tackle.

[5] Robert Cantwell, "Sinclair Lewis," *The New Republic*, LXXXVIII (October 21, 1936), 299.

Snap and speed are his middle name! He'll put her across if he has to ride from hell to breakfast, and believe me, I'm mighty good and sorry for the boob that's so unlucky as to get in his way, because that poor slob is going to wonder where he was at when Old Mr. Cyclone hit town!

Or again:

Fellow citizens, there's a lot of folks, even right here in this fair state, fairest and richest of all the glorious union, that stand up on their hind legs and claim that the East and Europe put it all over the golden Northwestland. Now let me nail that lie right here and now. "Ah-ha," says they, "so Jim Blausser is claiming that Gopher Prairie is as good a place to live in as London and Rome and—and all the rest of the Big Burgs, is he? How does the poor fish know?" says they. Well, I'll tell you how I know! I've seen 'em! I've done Europe from soup to nuts! They can't spring that stuff on Jim Blausser and get away with it! . . . London—I spent three days, sixteen straight hours a day, giving London the once-over, and let me tell you that it's nothing but a bunch of fog and out-of-date buildings that no live American burg would stand for one minute. You may not believe it, but there ain't one first-class skyscraper in the whole works.

This is dated talk, and many young readers in America today would find these sentences almost as outlandish as foreign listeners do; it is pure parody. But it is parody, nonetheless, of deeply cherished beliefs. Constance Rourke, our wisest and most subtle student of American humor, has written that "American audiences enjoyed their own deflation," and Lewis (whose humor is very much in the American vein) knew his audience well. He shared their sentimentality, their cynicism, their Philistinism, their cheerful irreverence, their dislike of pomposity. Like Jim Blausser, he also exulted in the superiority of his countrymen and relished the pure *Homo americanibus* unspoiled by what he called "the hard, varnished, cosmopolitan cleverness." Toward the end of his life, Lewis would be saying (although not in the accents of Jim Blausser):

Well, I'll tell you I know. I've seen 'em. I've done Europe from soup to nuts. They can't spring that stuff on Sinclair Lewis and get away with it.

Main Street is a work of historical importance, then, not merely as a reflection, partly unconscious, of popular American tastes and assumptions, but also because it helped Americans to understand themselves. T. K. Whipple, one of Lewis' best critics, once described him as a Red Indian "stalking through the land of his enemies." The metaphor is apt, suggesting as it does that Lewis was at once a part of his society and detached from it. On the other hand, is it quite precise? If Red Lewis stalked his enemies, was he not also prowling his tribal land? Were his enemies not fellow Indians who had abandoned the faith in their gods? He was too much a part of his nation, too deeply involved with its hopes, too impatient with its failures, to treat it simply in a tender or simply in a clinical way. Yet somehow, he managed to make his prosaic materials appear fabulous (for America, he said, was as strange to him as Russia and as complex as China) and in a few books to translate his commonplace boobs into archetypes.

Lewis' reputation has steadily fallen since the 1920's for reasons that are fairly obvious. At the outset of his career, he possessed an astonishing vitality, an inexhaustible capacity for work. His curiosity, his sense of the ludicrous, his sharp eye and sensitive ear, made him an excellent reporter of North American banalities and barbarities, equaled, perhaps, only by the more embittered humorist, Ring Lardner. He thoroughly enjoyed his life, and he had an audience with whom he was in close rapport. But his writing, his style, his ideas did not develop. He kept repeating himself, turning out novels on medical research, social work, race relations, and the like without sufficiently engaging himself with the materials he mechanically collected. In a self-portrait written as early as 1927, Lewis presented himself as a master of talk "in certain of its minor and more flippant and hysterical phases," but he confessed that when his audience knew him well, they found him repeating these parlor tricks over and over again, as childishly as the village clowns described in his own *Main Street.* He may have been judging himself too harshly, but his diagnosis was prophetic: Lewis the parodist ended by parodying himself.

Main Street, Babbitt, and *Elmer Gantry*—his three best novels, in my opinion—are marred by the faults that disfigure the books that followed them, but they are the works of the Red Indian, fiercely alert and stalking his quarry. Lewis justly prided himself on his "real, fiery, almost reckless hatred of hypocrisy" even while suspecting himself at the same time of ignoring the virtues of his victims "and picking out the few vices into which they have been betrayed by custom and economic necessity." In *Main Street,* Lewis' anger and good nature, his rancor and his magnanimity are blended; the "harmless jackasses," to borrow the words of Mencken, have not yet gradually converted themselves "into loathsome scoundrels," as they occasionally do in his later books. He castigates his beloved middle class unmercifully, exaggerates its unlovely features, but he does not withhold his confidence in its better instincts. *Babbitt,* as Edith Wharton wrote to him, has "more life and glow and abundance," than *Main Street* but Babbitt himself is an unreflective caricature, so immersed in Zenith that Lewis was "obliged to do the seeing and comparing for him." Whereas *Main Street,* she felt, produced

> a sense of unity and depth by reflecting Main Street in the consciousness of a woman who suffered from it because she had points of comparison, and was detached enough to situate it in the universe.[6]

If American readers no longer pay much attention to Sinclair Lewis, it is not because his arraignment of national failings is completely out of date. Most Americans have long passed beyond the parochialism of Dr. Kennicott's Auntie and Uncle Whittier. They are no longer staggered to learn:

[6] Quoted in Schorer, *op. cit.,* p. 346.

that illegitimate children do not bear any special and guaranteed form of curse; that there are ethical authorities outside the Hebrew Bible; that men have drunk wine yet not died in the gutter; that the capitalistic system of distribution and the Baptist wedding-ceremony were not known in the Garden of Eden . . . that some persons of apparent intelligence and business ability do not always vote the Republican ticket straight.

But the traps and pitfalls that Carol Kennicott tried vainly to circumvent are as abundant as ever, if more cleverly concealed. *Main Street* is more than a period piece on the American small town. It is a reminder, very much in the classic American tradition, that living is not the same thing as existing, that social timidity, ethnic and racial prejudice, complacency, the terror of change, and the fear of freedom can paralyze and kill.

16 F. SCOTT FITZGERALD
The Great Gatsby

Arthur Mizener

A few short years before he died—in 1936, to be exact—Scott Fitzgerald remarked that he had at last given up the idea by which he had lived his life. I think he had not really given it up, for if he had, he would have literally died then, as did Jay Gatsby in the same circumstances. But he believed he had. He described this idea as

> the old dream of being an entire man in the Goethe-Byron-Shaw tradition, with an opulent American touch, a sort of combination of J. P. Morgan, Topham Beauclerk and St. Francis of Assisi.

Feeling this way, he inevitably looked for a *realization* of his inner vision of the possibilities of life; and it seemed self-evident to him that only the rich and successful people in any society have the means and therefore the opportunity to make of life what it is possible for Topham Beauclerk and St. Francis of Assisi to imagine its being.

As a result of looking at the life he knew—American life, that is—in this way, he gradually developed a subtle and fascinating perception of the immensely complex relations between the ability that makes it possible for a man to get to the top in a competitive society and the ability that equips a man to conceive the "Good Life," between the talent for accumulation and the gift of imagination. The gift of imagination was, he knew, vital; no man could visualize the Good Life without it. But wealth, he saw, was important, too—not for itself, but because wealth alone makes it possible for a man actually to live the life the imagination conceives.

The most famous of all anecdotes about Fitzgerald concerns wealth. According to this anecdote, Fitzgerald once said to Hemingway, "The rich are different from you and me," and Hemingway replied, "Yes, they have more money." This exchange never actually took place; Hemingway invented it for a story called "The Snows of Kilimanjaro." But the remark Hemingway ascribes to Fitzgerald is a sentence from one of Fitzgerald's short stories called "The Rich Boy," a brilliant study of the special character of the very wealthy in America. Of Fitzgerald's sentence Lionel Trilling has said, in contrast to Hemingway, that "for this remark alone Fitzgerald is in Balzac's bosom in the heaven of all novelists."

For the rich who made the most of their unique opportunity to live the life of virtue with the maximum imaginative intensity, Fitzgerald felt something like hero worship. For the merely rich, those who did not use their wealth as a means to such a life, he felt the utmost contempt, what he once referred to as "the smouldering hatred of the peasant." He was convinced that the most important moral choice a man could face existed in its most fully developed form among the rich—the real, achievable choice between fineness of perception and of moral discrimination on the one hand, and the brutality of unimaginative, irresponsible power on the other. That is why he thought the rich are different from you and me and why he thought any failure on their part to use their wealth well constituted a crime that you and I are never given an opportunity to commit. It was this crime for which he condemned Daisy and Tom Buchanan in *The Great Gatsby*. Nick Carroway says:

> They were careless people, Tom and Daisy—they smashed up things and creatures and then retreated back into their money or their vast carelessness, or whatever it was that kept them together, and let other people clean up the mess they had made.

It is a great tribute to Fitzgerald's imagination that, despite his disapproval of such people, he understood them. In the end, he makes us see, Tom Buchanan is wistful and pathetic. At their final meeting, Nick Carroway shakes hands with Tom, feeling "suddenly as though I were talking to a child," as indeed he is, for with Tom's passion for what he child-ishly imagines to be "scientific stuff" about white supremacy, his ludicrous and sincere sentimentality about "nice girls" like his wife and his string of coarse, energetic mistresses, he is a fully conceived case of the undeveloped imagination. Daisy is even sadder, a girl who had caught a glimpse of the great life but who lacked the courage to live it, someone who chose in the end to live the sophisticated life rather than the loving life.

This, then, is the real subject of *The Great Gatsby*—the opportunity wealth provides for the realization of the Good Life and the necessity for what Fitzgerald calls "a heightened sensitivity to the promises of life" if people are to imagine the Good Life clearly enough to understand what they have the opportunity to achieve. This subject Fitzgerald visualized with great intensity in *The Great Gatsby;* it governs every detail in the book. Henry James once remarked that the his-tory of the English novel up to his time had been a paradise of the loose end. There are no loose ends in *The Great Gatsby*. This is not just a matter of structure, though the plot of Gatsby is managed with great skill and economy. The complicated series of misunderstandings that lead up to the death of Myrtle Wilson is handled with amazing ease; the parallel between Gatsby's love of Daisy and Nick Carroway's love of Jordan Baker is precise and unobtrusive; the facts of Gatsby's business career are so quietly worked in that we scarcely remember how we learned them. But the really con-vincing evidence of the imaginative pressure under which the novel was created is the way the smallest details reinforce its meaning.

For example, in the book's first scene, when Nick is at the Buchanans' for dinner, Daisy invents one of her character-istic fantastic jokes about the butler who, she says, had to leave his previous position because he was required to polish silver all day and the polish affected his nose. Eighty odd pages later, when Daisy arrives at Nick's to have tea with Gatsby, Nick alludes to this joke. "Does the gasoline affect his nose?" he asks Daisy of the chauffeur, and Daisy says solemnly, "I don't think so. Why?"

Or, when Gatsby is giving Nick his cheap-magazine account of his life, he says that he has

> lived like a young rajah in all the capitals of Europe [and then gets the names wrong]—Paris, Venice, Rome—collecting jewels, chiefly rubies, hunting big game, painting a little.

Nick is disgusted by this patent lie, this picture of what he calls "a turbaned 'character' leaking sawdust at every pore as he pursues a tiger through the Bois de Boulogne." But fifty pages later he sees in Gatsby's bedroom a photograph of Gatsby standing beside Dan Cody on Cody's yacht, and finds himself on the verge of "ask[ing] Gatsby to see the rubies."

Or, when Nick has his last meeting with Tom Buchanan on Fifth Avenue, Tom leaves him to go "into a jewelry store to buy a pearl necklace—or perhaps only a pair of cuff buttons—rid of my provincial squeamishness forever." These particulars are not fortuitous. Tom's engagement present to Daisy had been "a string of pearls valued at three hundred and fifty thousand dollars," and when Daisy, after her brief rebellion, finally appeared for the bridal dinner, "the pearls were around her neck"—like a chain. As for the cuff buttons, Meyer Wolfsheim, the novel's other brutal sentimentalist, is inordinately proud of his cuff buttons. He insists on Nick's examining them carefully, and explains to him that they are the "finest specimens of human molars." Tom's pearls may be, conventionally speaking, in better taste, but their purpose is to demonstrate his ownership of Daisy—the only kind of possession he can really understand—an ownership quite as gruesome in its politer way as Wolfsheim's ownership of men.

This imaginative use of realistic detail is one of the clearest signs that an author's imagination is working with full intensity. Another is fineness of design, and the design of *The Great Gatsby* is skilfully made, too. At its center is Nick Carroway, the narrator. Nick comes from a small, provincial, stable city in the Middle West. He has gone to Yale and there becomes to some extent an Easterner, so that after the war he chooses to live in the charming, rootless, power-hungry society of Long Island, though he is far from understanding fully its character. "Everybody I knew [from Yale] was in the bond business," he says with a glimpse of what is wrong, "so I supposed it could support one more single man."

Nick is thus, in manner and in superficial feeling, an Easterner, but his moral roots, though he does not fully realize it until the end of the novel, are in the Middle West. In the book's first scene we see him responding without doubt to the charm of the Buchanan house and of Daisy, adrift like some informal Fragonard goddess in the "bright rosy-colored space" of its drawing room. It is a very hot evening, too hot for Daisy to struggle up off the sofa when Nick comes in, and Daisy makes one of her charming jokes by way of apology: "I'm p-p-paralyzed with happiness," she says to him.

Yet by dinner time Nick begins to sense something he is not quite comfortable with in the Buchanans, though he is Daisy's cousin and Tom's college friend. "You make me feel uncivilized, Daisy," he says at the dinner table. "Can't we talk about crops or something?"—which is what they would have done at home, in the Middle West. After dinner, when Daisy is telling him about Tom's mistress and about how sophisticated and disillusioned she is, this feeling becomes more serious,

> as though the entire evening had been a trick of some sort to extract a contributory emotion from me. I waited, and sure enough in a moment she looked at me with an absolute smirk on her lovely face, as if she had asserted her membership in a rather distinguished secret society to which she and Tom belonged.

This reference to a secret society is no doubt Fitzgerald's joke at Yale's expense, perfectly natural in the context, since Nick and Tom had belonged to the same secret senior society at Yale. But it is something more, too. What Tom and Daisy have in common with one another and with all the people like them in the book is their membership in the snobbish secret society of the rich who are incapable of living the fully imagined life. Out of ignorance or cowardice they substitute for that life a childish game in which superficial good taste takes the place of genuine responsiveness, "what all the most advanced people think" takes the place of responsible intelligence, and being in fashion takes the place of a seriously imagined purpose. In the end these bonds between Tom and Daisy are stronger than Daisy's love for Gatsby.

Thus the life of Daisy and Tom and their friends is made the image of a life exquisitely graceful on the surface, with a moral defect at its heart that is only slowly revealed to Nick. The Buchanans stand on one side of Nick, at first appealing strongly to his sense of the glamour of Eastern life and, as the book progresses, disturbing more and more seriously his Middle-Western sense of decency. So far as they are concerned, *The Great Gatsby* is a history of the slow but steady decline of Nick's admiration for them, as the full evil of their moral irresponsibility is revealed to him and he loses interest in their glamour. Finally, he can no more accept Daisy's continuing to live with Tom than he can accept Wolfsheim's fixing the World Series of 1919. Daisy says of Tom's philandering, "You see I think everything's terrible anyhow. Everybody thinks so—the most advanced people." But on the whole she is rather proud of being a part of that everything. Nick's instinct, as he says, is to call for the police, just as that was his instinct when he learned that Wolfsheim had played "with the faith of fifty million people—with the single-mindedness of a burglar blowing a safe."

On the other side of Nick stands Gatsby, the son of a poor Minnesota farmer named James Gatz. Having fallen in love with Daisy when he was in training camp near Louisville, he sets out after the war to become as rich and gentlemanly as Tom so that he will be worthy to ask Daisy to leave Tom and marry him. In the simplest and most naïve way possible, with no awareness of the corruption that underlies them but rather taking them as models of the cultivated and civilized life, he sets out to imitate the ways of wealthy people like the

Buchanans. He buys expensive cars; he imports his clothes from England; he seeks out "interesting" people. He even purchases what Nick ironically calls an "ancestral home" just across the bay from the Buchanans'.

Here again we can see the wonderful, unobtrusive skill with which Fitzgerald uses realistic detail symbolically. Houses in *The Great Gatsby* are much richer in meaning than the book's more obvious symbols; this is perhaps most evident in the way the house in Louisville where Gatsby woos Daisy is charged for us with Gatsby's feelings. Houses are especially significant in the book for the way they emphasize the meanings inherent in its central design, which places Nick in the middle with Gatsby on one side of him and the Buchanans on the other.

Nick has grown up in the Middle West, in the "Carroway house in a city where dwellings are still called through decades by a family's name." The Carroway house was no doubt ugly and dull by the fashionable standards of Long Island, but it was genuinely "ancestral." Nick was at home there; but he is so little at home in his West Egg bungalow that he says he has become "an original settler" when someone asks him the way into the village. In contrast to the Carroway house, Gatsby's house next door to Nick's bungalow, "a colossal affair by any standards," is as innocently awful in its ostentation as his clothes and his car—a freshly constructed "factual imitation of some Hotel de Ville in Normandy." In this Cecil de Mille set Gatsby tries to realize his dream.

The Buchanans' "cheerful red-and-white Georgian Colonial mansion," though much more sophisticated in taste, is quite as fake in its own way as Gatsby's mansion, and its owners are quite as temporary occupants: Tom Buchanan has just bought it from "Demaine, the oil man," and at the end of the story he and Daisy, departing, leave no address. Indeed, the only place in which Tom seems ever to have felt enough at home to grieve over its loss is the apartment in New York where he spent odd moments with Myrtle Wilson, a dwelling even more temporary than the house at East Egg.

The Buchanans' house, like their life, is not evidently

ridiculous, as is Gatsby's, but both are essentially dead, as Gatsby's are not. The Buchanans hardly pretend not to drift "here and there unrestfully wherever people played polo and were rich together"; but Gatsby's house and his life, for all their bad taste, are given purpose and meaning by his Platonic concept of himself, by his dreams—at least until the end, when Daisy's betrayal destroys his dream and "perhaps he no longer cared." Even Daisy can see that the innocently tasteless appurtenances of wealth with which Gatsby surrounds himself are expressions of his heroic idealism; Gatsby climaxes the all-important tour of his house on which he takes Daisy by pouring out before her an endless profusion of very showy, though imported shirts; and suddenly Daisy bows her head on the pile and weeps.

What Nick discovers at the end—as perhaps Gatsby finally did, too—is that, however lacking it may be in glamour, the life lived in the "bored, sprawling, swollen towns beyond the Ohio" is the only real one he has ever known. Compared to that, the Long Island life that Gatsby lived in the service of his dream, that the Buchanans lived in the service of their restless sophistication, that even Nick, in his ignorance, lived for a while, is a fantasy. "I see it," Nick says at the end,

> as a night scene by El Greco: a hundred houses, at once conventional and grotesque, crouching under a sullen, overhanging sky and a lustreless moon. In the foreground four solemn men in dress suits are walking along the sidewalk with a stretcher on which lies a drunken woman in a white evening dress. Her hand, which dangles over the side, sparkles cold with jewels. Gravely the men turn in at a house—the wrong house. But no one knows the woman's name, and no one cares.

Because of the importance of the idealism behind Gatsby's apparently meretricious life, Fitzgerald twice has Nick make it explicit. Once he says:

> There was something gorgeous about [Gatsby], some heightened sensitivity to the promises of life. . . . This responsiveness . . . was an extraordinary gift for hope, a romantic readiness such as I have never found in any other person.

And again he says:

> The truth is that Jay Gatsby of West Egg, Long Island, sprang
> from his Platonic conception of himself. . . . [He found him-
> self in a world] of a vast, vulgar, meretricious beauty. So he
> invented just the sort of Jay Gatsby that a seventeen-year-old
> [American] boy would be likely to invent, and to this concep-
> tion he was faithful to the end.

The stress here is on two remarkable characteristics of
Gatsby's life. The first is the purity and intensity of Gatsby's
desire to make real, in the actual world, an ideal mode of
existence. The second is the way he is forced by the conditions of American society to use shoddy materials, to actualize
his dream in the "vast, vulgar, meretricious beauty" which is
all his world makes available to him.

In a few short years after the war, Gatsby becomes as rich
as Tom Buchanan by buying a chain of drugstores and using
them as outlets for bootleg liquor and by organizing a large
and efficient business for the disposal of stolen Liberty bonds.
It is one of the fine incidental ironies of the novel that
Gatsby has a first-rate executive talent and organizes large,
profitable business enterprises with great skill, whereas Tom
Buchanan inherits a huge fortune and never works at all. It
is thus Gatsby, not Tom, who fulfills the conventional American ideal of conduct. It is true that Gatsby's businesses are
illegal, and in the Plaza scene Tom attacks Gatsby with ostentatious piety as "a common swindler." But it is perfectly clear
that Fitzgerald believes there is no important moral distinction between Gatsby's kind of business and any other. At
one extreme of Fitzgerald's business community we have
Wolfsheim and the West Egg people who attend Gatsby's
parties; they are mostly in the movies, in politics, in gam-
bling; they are able to grant the police commissioner frequent favors and have a good deal of influence; they are
surrounded by an air of underworld notoriety. At the other
extreme we have Tom Buchanan and the East Egg people;
they play polo and watch their investments; they have a habit
of authoritative arrogance to which everyone except their

wives yields; they are socially prominent. But despite these superficial differences, these two worlds are fundamentally alike and are in fact interrelated. Both are morally and imaginatively infantile, and some of Tom's friends have invested in Gatsby's businesses. East Egg's manners are more refined than West Egg's, and less honest; that is the only real difference.

But the distinction that matters in *The Great Gatsby* does not depend on how people acquire their money: on that score Fitzgerald has serious doubts about everyone. It depends on how people use their wealth, and of all these people, only Gatsby, despite his bad taste, uses his money really well. In itself, for mere power or possession or self-indulgence, wealth means nothing to Gatsby; he is perfectly ready to throw it away—along with his life—when Daisy destroys his faith in her as the incarnation of his dream. Though Gatsby is, according to the law and Emily Post, a criminal and a fake, beneath his conventionally deplorable surface there is a purity of heart that gives every act of his life remarkable integrity. "No—Gatsby turned out all right at the end." So far as Gatsby is concerned, then, *The Great Gatsby* is a history of the rise of Nick's admiration for him, as the full, imaginative splendor of his purpose is slowly revealed to Nick and he ceases to care about Gatsby's superficial absurdity.

This is the essential design of *The Great Gatsby,* with Nick in the middle, torn between the superficial social grace and the unimaginative brutality of the wealthy and the imaginative intensity and moral idealism of the socially absurd and legally culpable self-made man. At the beginning of the book, Nick is charmed by Daisy and disgusted by Gatsby, who is, as an Eastern gentleman, so obviously a fake. At the end of the book he knows, as he calls out to Gatsby when he leaves him for the last time, that "They're a rotten crowd. You're worth the whole damned bunch put together."

His gorgeous pink rag of a suit made a bright spot of color against the white steps, and I thought of the night when I first came to his ancestral home, three months before. The lawn and drive had been crowded with the faces of those who guessed at his corruption—and he had stood on those steps, concealing his incorruptible dream, as he waved them good-bye.

Gatsby is Fitzgerald's most brilliant image of his deepest conviction, the conviction that life untouched by imagination is brutal and intolerable and that the imagined life must be made actual in the world if a man is to become anything more than a self-indulgent daydreamer. It is, I believe, a peculiarly American attitude. Americans are no doubt proud of their wealth and of the enterprise that is at least in part responsible for it. But they are seldom content with a merely material life; that kind of life seems to them, as Gatsby's life seemed to him after he lost faith in Daisy, material without being real. Only when it is animated by an ideal purpose does it seem real to them. This is, in fact, what we mean by "The American Dream," insofar as that dream is something possessed by each of us individually.

Fitzgerald was perfectly aware that Gatsby is representative in this way, and in the last page of the novel he firmly relates Gatsby's personal dream to the dream that has haunted American history from its beginning. Nick Carroway is sitting on the shore of Long Island back of Gatsby's now deserted house,

And as the moon rose higher, the inessential houses began to melt away until gradually I became aware of the old island here that flowered once for Dutch sailors' eyes—a fresh, green breast of the new world. Its vanished trees, the trees that had made way for Gatsby's house, had once pandered in whispers to the last and greatest of all human dreams; for a transitory, enchanted moment man must have held his breath in the presence of this continent, compelled into an aesthetic contemplation he neither understood nor desired, face to face for the last time in history with something commensurate with his capacity for wonder.

And as I sat there brooding on the old, unknown world, I thought of Gatsby. . . .

T. S. Eliot once called *The Great Gatsby* "the first step in American fiction since Henry James," for in it Fitzgerald realized, for the first time in twentieth-century terms, James's understanding of the dramatic conflict between good and evil that is inherent in American life.

17 ERNEST HEMINGWAY
A Farewell to Arms

Carlos Baker

Since his death in the summer of 1961, a school of critics has arisen which holds that the novel we are about to discuss was really the last, rather than the second, of Hemingway's major works, and that his path as an artist from 1929 to 1959 was a gradual but steady descent. I do not hold with the opinions of this school, for it is my belief that though Hemingway's career as a writer was not without its ups and downs, he made as many triumphs in fiction during the last thirty years of his life as he had in the first thirty. This is not to say, however, that our critical brethren are necessarily wrong in preferring *A Farewell to Arms* over such later works as *For Whom the Bell Tolls* or *The Old Man and the Sea*. It is only to maintain that Hemingway continued to be a very able practitioner of the art of fiction for many years after the publication of *A Farewell,* and that we are not obliged to disparage the later work in order to admire the earlier.

Among the American novels which deal with the First World War of 1914–18, *A Farewell to Arms* has stood up under the weathering of the years as well as any and far better than most. A number of his eminent contemporaries also wrote novels relating to that war. To name only two for purposes of comparison, *Soldiers' Pay* by William Faulkner and *Three Soldiers* by John Dos Passos have long since begun to show signs of literary senility. No reader who works his way consecutively through these three novels could possibly doubt that the honors for continuing freshness, romantic derring-do, and simple reader-interest must be awarded to Hemingway's book. It manages to remain singularly undated at the same time that it perfectly embodies the *Zeitgeist,* the governing moral essence of that far-away time.

Survival power in fiction may at first appear to be a most curious and chancy business. But perhaps it is not so curious, after all. For Hemingway managed to catch and hold in his novel a set of attitudes toward war and human love which are essentially ageless. Moreover, the prose style in which he says his say about the people he knew in that now-ancient war has remained for the most part singularly invulnerable to the assaults of time. When he was writing the book in 1928–29, he worked extremely hard, pruned out excess verbiage with loving care, and rewrote extensively in a considered attempt to fashion a kind of prose that would really last. Malcolm Cowley once remarked that an astonishingly small amount of Hemingway's prose has gone bad over the years. In the same vein, Ford Madox Ford observed that Hemingway's words strike us,

> each one, as if they were pebbles fetched fresh from a brook. They live and shine, each in its place. So one of his pages has the effect of a brook-bottom into which you look down through flowing water. The words form a tessellation, each in order beside the other. It is a very great quality. . . . The aim—the achievement—of the great prose writer is to use words so that they shall seem new and alive because of their juxtaposition with other words. This gift Hemingway has supremely.[1]

Hemingway's posthumous reward for his long labors, which were often carried on under conditions of extreme domestic duress, is that we can still read with pleasure what was first set down in typescript nearly forty years ago. Another part of our pleasure comes from his ability to give us that sense of vicarious participation in events long gone, which is one of the best reasons for reading that anyone has yet been able to discover. None of the histories of the war as it was fought on the Italian-Austrian front can possibly re-

[1] Ford, Introduction to *A Farewell to Arms* (New York: Modern Library, 1932), p. xvi.

produce so exactly how it felt to be under fire, to hear the whump of descending shells during the horrendous bombardments, to carry the wounded to safety unless they hemorrhaged and died along the way, to share wine and rough talk with Italian officers in the regimental messrooms, or to experience the acute physical discomforts of rain and cold and mud and hunger and fear during an inglorious military retreat. Far better than factual history, fiction can seize and hold such experiences as these. Hemingway caught the accents and attitudes of that far-off time so exactly that they have stayed preserved for us in perfect condition, like the honeybee embalmed forever inside the burnished lump of amber.

The literary history of *A Farewell to Arms* is of more than common interest. Except for an accident, it might have been Hemingway's first novel rather than his second. As early as 1922, more than four years before the publication of *The Sun Also Rises,* he had begun to write a story about a young American ambulance driver on the Italian-Austrian front during the First World War. It seems to have been highly romantic in manner and conception. It was also written in a prose style considerably more elaborate and adjectival than the one we customarily associate with the young Hemingway. But this early version of the novel, such as it was, has been missing these forty years. The probabilities are that it long ago dissolved in the waters of a Parisian sewer or went up in flames to kindle someone's kitchen fire in the slums of the capital. For the valise in which it was being carried to Hemingway by his young wife was stolen by a petty thief in the Gare de Lyon in Paris one winter afternoon late in 1922. With it went the typescripts and longhand copies of several other early stories of Hemingway's—virtually all that he had written up to that time. Dismayed and disheartened by his loss, Hemingway did not again try to tell the Italian story until 1928, nearly ten years after the events on which the narrative is based had actually taken place.

Hemingway's own account of his second major attempt to write the novel is also rather dramatic, both geographically and domestically. Few books have been set down in such a variety of places. It was begun in Paris, and continued in Key West, Florida; Piggott, Arkansas; Kansas City, Missouri; and Sheridan, Wyoming. He finished the first draft while living on a ranch near Big Horn, Wyoming. During this period, his second wife, Pauline, was delivered of a son by Caesarean section in Kansas City, and while he was revising his first draft, his father committed suicide by shooting himself in Oak Park, Illinois. Hemingway said:

> I remember all these things happening and all the places we lived in and the fine times and the bad times we had in that year. But much more vividly I remember living in the book and making up what happened in it every day. Making the country and the people and the things that happened, I was happier than I had ever been.

This creative happiness in constructing a narrative of doom bears a curious resemblance to an event which took place only a few years before Hemingway began to write. A visitor to Thomas Hardy's house near Dorchester in England was turned away firmly by the writer's wife. Mr. Hardy, she explained, was busily composing an extremely gloomy poem, and he was enjoying himself so much that he must not under any circumstances be disturbed.

The special pleasure that Hemingway took in his work arose no doubt from his recognition of how much better this fresh new version of the novel was turning out than the one he had lost to the petty Parisian thief a half-dozen years before. Now, with the experience of a first novel behind him, and with more than twenty-five published short stories to his credit, he was at last in a position to do justice to his romantic subject. For in the meantime he had grown up to his task.

He was also succeeding in following a piece of advice he had once offered to his friend and fellow novelist, F. Scott Fitzgerald. If something has hurt you badly, he argued, you must find a way to use it in your writing. You had better not moan and complain about past or present difficulties or personal misadventures. Instead you must use your misfortunes as materials for fiction. If you can write them out, get them stated, it is possible to rid yourself of the soreness in your soul. Although Hemingway on occasion spoke scornfully about William Wordsworth, there is a passage in the poet's great ode which precisely sums up Hemingway's position. "To me alone there came a thought of grief," said Wordsworth. "A timely utterance gave that thought relief, and I again am strong." Or, as Hemingway himself put it in a more modern idiom, "The fact that the book was a tragic one did not make me unhappy since I believed that life was a tragedy and knew it could only have one end." But the business of creativity was the great business. Now, in the late 1920's, setting down a romanticized fictional version of some of the things that had happened to him personally ten years before, Hemingway discovered in the process a greater pleasure than any he had previously known. "Beside it," he said, "nothing else mattered."

The pain and sorrow which he was now using in his novel were based on a double actuality: a pair of traumatic events from 1918–19, neither of which he had been able to forget, even had he wished to do so. The earlier of the two was his severe wounding during the night of July 8, 1918. The boy was not yet nineteen when he joined an American Red Cross ambulance group stationed near Schio in northern Italy. This was early in June. For nearly a month he drove ambulances carrying wounded men to base hospitals. But this was too tame an occupation; he was spoiling for closer contact with the enemy. Early in July he volunteered to go across to the Piave Front where the Italians faced the Austrians from trenches and dugouts so close to the lines that they could hear one another talking. This would mean action, the boy thought, even though his job was only the rather unspectacular one of handing out cigarettes and bars of chocolate to the troops. When he arrived the front seemed quiet, but he soon got more action than he had bargained for. An Austrian *Minenwerfer*, loaded with metal slugs and scrap iron, made a direct hit on the advanced listening post where Hemingway was practicing his very limited Italian with some of the soldiers. Several men were killed outright; one had his legs severed. Although his own extremities were terribly wounded, Hemingway managed to carry the dying soldier back to the main trench, though as he did so Austrian flares lit the scene and a heavy machine gun opened up at knee level on the staggering boy with his bloody burden. Before his heroic journey was done, he had taken two more slugs in the legs. This was the first of the two soul-shaking experiences which he could never forget, and which he had been trying for ten years to embody in prose fiction.

The second of his memorable experiences was a love affair with an American Red Cross nurse in Milan. Her name was Agnes von Kurowsky. Besides being an excellent and experienced nurse, she was young, pretty, kind, and gay. When the boy was brought at last to the comparative quiet and luxury of the base hospital, Miss von Kurowsky was one of those assigned to his case. It was Hemingway's first adult love affair and he hurled himself into it without caution. He seems to have been wholly unaware of the banality of the situation in which the young war hero falls in love with his nurse. Even if he had thought of it in these terms, he would not have cared in the least. For he had managed to convince himself that he was finally and irrevocably in love.

In spite of the fact that they were often separated for varying intervals during the summer and fall of his recuperation, Hemingway saw as much of his nurse as regulations (and competition from his fellow-Americans) would allow. When he sailed for New York in January 1919, his head was full of plans to get a newspaper job, save some money, bring his girl back to the United States, and be married. The traumatic aspect of this experience was that his plans were smashed. After some soul-searching of her own, Agnes decided that it would be a mistake to let a wartime romance try to attain the settled actuality of a peacetime marriage. She was older than he, she was an excellent and dedicated nurse, and she was not at all sure that she wanted to give up so important a profession in order to become another American housewife. Hemingway had not been home very long when he received the letter in which she set forth her conclusions.

It was a severe blow to his pride. He reacted explosively. All her protestations availed nothing. He turned against her with masculine rage and rankling sorrow, even as he had turned toward her while he lay recuperating in the hospital. But he was never able or willing to forget her. Though he subsequently married four times, he kept Agnes' letters all his life. Among the many he had loved and won, she was a perennial reminder of one woman he had loved and lost. She took on the not very enviable status of the goddess who is worshiped while remaining unattainable. As the first love of his young manhood, she remained enshrined in an alcove of his consciousness until the day he died.

To leave the impression that it is merely fictionized autobiography would be unfair to Hemingway's novel. It is far more artfully imagined and put together, for example, than *The Sun Also Rises,* the first novel, which was built directly upon his remembrance of the people he knew and the events he was witness to during the summertime visit to Pamplona in 1925.

One distinguishing mark of *A Farewell to Arms,* as against *The Sun Also Rises,* is that Hemingway's powers of invention were called much more intensively into play. To take one example, the time segment covered in the action of the novel runs from the summer of 1916 to the spring of 1918—many months before Hemingway himself arrived upon the scene. The famous account of the retreat from Caporetto, which the author himself always insisted upon calling the retreat from the Isonzo, was never part of his own experience. It had to be invented ex post facto from a study of contemporaneous newspaper stories and the few military histories then available, supplemented and highlighted by Hemingway's own adventures in a very different section of the world when he was a foreign correspondent covering the retreat of Greek soldiers and civilians in Thrace and Anatolia during the fall of 1922.

Another typical instance of Hemingway's inventiveness is the figure of Catherine Barkley, the English nurse who serves as tragic heroine of the story. The character of Catherine is based, not only on the nurse, Agnes von Kurowsky, but is also a composite portrait of Hemingway's first two wives. He seeks to disguise this fact by changing his heroine's nationality and by causing her to speak in an imitation of British upper-class idiom. But when the nurse and her lover go to live far away from the black tides of war in a Swiss chalet high above the city of Lausanne, Hemingway is clearly recalling his visits to the same region with his first wife, Hadley Richardson, as well as the skiing trips he made with her to the mountain village of Schruns in the Austrian Vorarlberg during three winters in the middle 1920's. Finally, it is at least an educated surmise that the idea of having Catherine Barkley die in childbirth following an unsuccessful Caesarean section was suggested to Hemingway by the fact that his second wife, Pauline Pfeiffer, had a difficult time from the same cause in 1928, just when Hemingway was composing the final chapters of the first draft of his novel.

None of this is very surprising. Any novelist must write from what he knows, taking advantage of the hints and suggestions that fall into his lap by chance. Hemingway's real artistic triumph in *A Farewell to Arms* was the way in which he developed various kinds of natural symbolism to sustain and enrich the story over which he had been brooding for ten years. In moving now to the symbolic aspects of the book, I am fully aware that to many readers the very idea of symbolism is anathema. Such readers will tell you that they like their stories straight, and that we are dealing here with a simple naturalistic tale about a pair of young people, thrown together by chance in the midst of a war they never made. They meet, fall in love, and are separated by vast events beyond their control. When they reunite and run away together, they manage to live for a time in circumstances that are certainly pleasurable and apparently ideal. But the fist of fate is poised to crush them. In the end the girl dies and her lover is left to carry on alone.

Hemingway once called his novel a version of the Romeo and Juliet story. There are of course a thousand points of

difference between Shakespeare's drama of civil warfare between the Montagues and the Capulets and Hemingway's
account of the good and ill fortunes of another pair of star-
crossed lovers. What links the two stories is the carefully
wrought sense of foreboding—our constantly growing awareness of a looming fatefulness at work behind the scenes. Our
skeptical reader may well argue that such a literary paral-
lelism is enough: we need no supplementary symbolism to
convince us of the drama and the pathos of the story. Hemingway felt otherwise. For the symbolism is there, and it got
there only through the most careful planning and the most
extensive rewriting. Let us turn to three phases of the symbolism to see what Hemingway did with them.

Symbolic effects in this novel are achieved through a subtle
process of reiterated suggestion. Among the many which
might be mentioned, we shall be concerned with only three:
the weather, the emblematic people, and the landscapes. The
best known of these is the first: the almost poetic care with
which Hemingway slowly builds up in his readers a mental
association between rain and disaster. This was an association
which came naturally enough to Hemingway himself. His
letters throughout his life are full of complaints against rain
and damp weather. He always took it personally, partly because he was susceptible to the common cold, partly because
damp dark weather induced in his spirit a comparable gloom.
Moreover, in his second experience of war and its effects, he
had personally watched the pitiful stream of refugees plod-
ding through mud and sodden with rain during the memorable evacuation of the civilian population from the city of
Adrianople. Anyone who reads *A Farewell to Arms* with one
eye on the weather will eventually marvel as he watches the
author playing with falling rain as a symbol of imminent
doom. Near the close of the book, when Catherine is ap-
proaching her time of confinement, the weather warms and
the rains arrive. For a whole miraculous winter the lovers
have gloried in their isolation, living happily in their high
mountain fastness, surrounded by healthy cold air and clean
snow, far from the mud and muck of war. Now at last the

rains come, the time for the lying-in draws near, some great change lurks just beyond the lovers' limited horizon, and we begin to sense that Catherine is in mortal danger, as indeed she is.

A second aspect of the symbolism is the way in which Hemingway endows two of Lieutenant Henry's friends with special moral attributes. One is the young Italian surgeon, Rinaldi, a merry comrade and a capable doctor, enthusiastic about his work with the wounded, boasting of his attainments at the operating table, delighted to be of service to humanity. But Hemingway is at pains to present Rinaldi as the victim of his own virtues. The sadness and fatigue of war soon affect him. As we watch, he becomes the homeless man, without visible antecedents, cut off from saving domesticity, driven to desperate expedients in order to keep his sanity in the vast and gloomy theatre of the war. Trying to relax from the rigors of his duties, he contracts syphilis in an army brothel. The man of science is eventually victimized by the filth and disease which surround him.

The second close friend is a nameless Italian priest, a gentle little nut-brown man who seeks as well as he can to exemplify the Christian virtues in a situation where almost everything seems to conspire against them. It is he who tries to persuade Henry to visit the Abruzzi during one of his military leaves. The priest paints an idyllic picture of this mountainous region, with its clear cool air, its plump game birds, its vineyards and orchards, its flute music, its peasant population living simply and amicably as they have done for a thousand years. It is a region close to heaven—or at any rate closer than the Veneto would seem to be. "There," says the priest, "a man may love God without being satirized for his beliefs."

After the first half of the novel, Rinaldi and the priest disappear from the scene. But the qualities they stand for continue to affect the action of the story. When Henry and Catherine reach Switzerland and begin the only approximation of married life that they will ever know, it is the spirit of the priest which dominates their lives. When, on the other hand, they are compelled to leave their lofty station and descend to Lausanne, where Catherine will die, we are forcibly reminded of the world of Rinaldi—the world of doctors and hospitals and imminent death.

The third and last manifestation of symbolic intent in the novel is the subtle way in which the author plays off two levels of landscape against each other. Without following it slavishly, he carefully establishes a pattern in which plains or lowlands are associated in the reader's mind with war, death, pain, sadness, or gloom, while the high mountain regions, whether in the Abruzzi where the priest originated, or in Switzerland, high above Lausanne, where the lovers establish their temporary heartland, are just as carefully associated with pleasure and the good life, joy and health, or whatever stands opposed to the plains of the Veneto where the war is being fought and the great retreat has been made. This poetic association of the heights with pleasure and the depths with pain is Hemingway's version of the *paysage moralisé,* the moralized landscape which he was teaching himself to use as a backdrop for his narratives of action.

In sum, we are suggesting that *A Farewell to Arms* is not at all the naturalistic report which we might at first take it for. One of the major reasons for its continuing freshness, its proven power of survival, is the care which Hemingway lavished on its structure and texture by the symbolic use of weather and character and moralized landscape.

As we approach the end of this demonstration, there is just time to consider one more point about *A Farewell to Arms.* This is the famous conclusion where Catherine dies and her lover says a silent farewell before he walks back to the hotel alone in the falling rain. For years it has been rumored that Hemingway rewrote the closing pages of the novel some thirty-seven times. The figure is very likely exaggerated. But whatever it was, there can be no doubt that Hemingway spent considerable effort on the conclusion, and that the final version, familiar to readers since 1929, is almost infinitely superior to the penultimate version, which has only recently come to light.

In the accepted and familiar version, Hemingway's hero stays with Catherine until her death. Then he goes out to speak to the surgeon: "Is there anything I can do tonight?" The doctor replies that there is nothing to be done and offers Henry a ride back to his hotel. Henry says that he will stay for a while at the hospital. "It was the only thing to do," says the surgeon, apologetically, speaking of the fatal Caesarean section. "The operation proved—"

"I do not want to talk about it," says Henry. The doctor goes away down the corridor and Henry opens the door to the room where Catherine's body lies.

"You can't come in now," says one of the nurses in charge.

"Yes, I can."

"You can't come in yet."

"You get out," says Henry. "The other one, too."

But after he has got them out and closed the door and turned off the light, he discovers that it is no good. It is like saying goodbye to a statue. After a while he goes out and leaves the hospital, and walks back to the hotel in the rain.

This is where the novel ends. Much has been made of this justly famous and tight-lipped conclusion. To many readers it has seemed to be one of the high points of lonely bereavement in modern fiction, a peak of tragic lostness from a generation which suffered thousands of similar deprivations during and after World War I. It has also been seen as the epitome of stoic acceptance of the inevitable. There can be no doubt that this was precisely the effect Hemingway sought to achieve during all his rewritings of the conclusion.

The penultimate version is another matter entirely, and it is very revealing. In place of the laconic interchange between Henry and the attending surgeon, the visit to the room to say goodbye, and the lonely walk back to the hotel in the rain, we have three quite different paragraphs. Henry talks about the difficulty of making funeral arrangements in a foreign country, then of the postwar destinies of the priest and Rinaldi and one or two more, and finally of the return to the hotel, where he falls asleep to awake in the morning to his sense of loss. All the sharp poignancy of the final version is here blunted and destroyed. What is worse, the words themselves seem moist with self-pity.

Hemingway wrote, in the simulated character of Frederick Henry:

> There a great many more details, starting with my first meeting with the undertaker, and all the business of burial in a foreign country, and going on with the rest of my life—which has gone on and seems likely to go on for a long time. . . . I could tell how Rinaldi was cured of the syphilis and lived to find that the technic learned in wartime surgery is not of much practical use in peace. I could tell how the priest in our mess lived to be a priest in Italy under Fascism. I could tell how Ettore became a Fascist and the part he took in that organization. I could tell how Piani got to be a taxi-driver in New York and what sort of a singer Simmons became. Many things have happened. Everything blunts and the world keeps on. It never stops. It only stops for you. Some of it stops while you are still alive. The rest goes on and you go on with it. . . . I could tell you what I have done since March, 1918, when I walked that night in the rain back to the hotel where Catherine and I had lived and went upstairs to our room and undressed and slept finally, because I was so tired—to wake in the morning with the sun shining in the window; then suddenly to realize what had happened. I could tell what has happened since then, but that is the end of the story.

The difficulty with this conclusion is that it drowns us with words and moisture. The rather garrulous self-pity, so visible here, when we juxtapose it with the far more objective stoicism of the final version, offers us a hint that may be worth developing. It suggests what I believe to be true, that the stoicism of the last version was only a mask, adopted and assumed for dramatic show, while under it Hemingway's still wounded feelings were bleeding and suppurating almost as intensively as they had been doing ten years before. Within the short space of seven months, he had been badly smashed up in both war and love. Now, much later, his double wound of body and soul rose to the surface of his memory, and manifested itself in the trial conclusion which we have just examined.

There is no time to expand further upon the matter here. Yet the idea of the stoic mask, assumed as a façade to conceal the psychic warfare which is going on beneath, may help us to explain and to understand much of the braggadoccio which struck his detractors as all too apparent in Hemingway's later life. It may also explain his espousal of the stoic code as a standard of behavior—a standard to which he required all his later heroes to conform. But these are hypotheses better suited to the biographer than to the literary critic. If the next-to-last conclusion of *A Farewell to Arms* betrays a kind of psychological quicksand just below the surface, the final version does not. It is still as firm and fresh as the brook pebbles which Ford Madox Ford so much admired. Whatever Hemingway's future reputation, *A Farewell to Arms* will surely stand for at least another forty years as the best novel written by an American about the First World War.

18 THOMAS WOLFE
Look Homeward, Angel

Thomas C. Moser

It is difficult to speak of Thomas Wolfe except in extreme terms, in superlatives. Even in his lifetime he was a legend; friends, reviewers, and the public referred to him with Hollywood adjectives—stupendous, gigantic, immense. Clearly Wolfe did think of himself in this way and, in a certain sense, these absurd American words are appropriate. He really was a huge man: six and a half feet tall, weighing about two hundred and fifty pounds at his death in 1938, and he looked even larger. His friends report that he walked in long, aggressive strides and threw his arms about in extravagant gestures. He had a gargantuan appetite, not only because he was so big but because he often took time for only one real meal a day. He was as hungry for experience as for food; he wanted, as he said, to explore life "with an encyclopedic thoroughness." Still a student at Harvard and not yet a novelist, he wrote to his mother:

> I know this now: I am inevitable. I sincerely believe that the only thing that can stop me now is insanity, disease, or death. . . . I will go everywhere and see everything. I will meet all the people I can. I will think all the thoughts, feel all the emotion I am able, and will write, write, write.

Write he did. He proved appallingly that he was not simply a giant sponge, inertly absorbing the world. He often wrote for fifteen hours out of twenty-four. Early one morning in New York City, a friend heard a distant chant and looked out the window:

There was Tom, in his battered black fedora and long dark-blue raincoat, swinging along at his tremendous stride and chanting over and over, "I wrote ten thousand words today. I wrote ten thousand words today." [1]

In his hopeless attempt to get everything down on paper, he could not bear to cut out anything:

The business of selection and revision is simply hell for me—my efforts to cut out 50,000 words may sometimes result in my adding 75,000.

When he died, Wolfe had published two very long novels and had left behind a pile of manuscript eight feet high.

But how good was it? *Look Homeward, Angel* has continued to be popular, more popular perhaps than any serious novel by a contemporary. Yet, except for Malcolm Cowley, leading literary critics, most of whom are academics, give it little recognition. But if academics have been cold toward Wolfe, a great writer was not. In 1951, William Faulkner surprisingly ranked Wolfe first among contemporary American writers, himself second, Dos Passos third, and Hemingway fourth. Faulkner explained the ranking this way:

I rated Wolfe first because we had all failed but Wolfe had made the best failure because he had tried the hardest to say the most. . . . My admiration for Wolfe is that he tried his best to get it all said; he was willing to throw away style, coherence, all the rules of preciseness, to try to put all the experience of the human heart on the head of a pin, as it were.[2]

Readers over thirty find Thomas Wolfe difficult to appreciate—not to understand but to appreciate. He often writes very badly, even in *Look Homeward, Angel,* the most finished of his novels. As Faulkner said, Wolfe throws away style and coherence. One recalls that embarrassing passage early in the novel where the infant hero, Eugene Gant, in his crib, thinks of

[1] Nancy Hale, quoted in Elizabeth Nowell, *Thomas Wolfe,* "A Biography" (Garden City, N.Y.: Doubleday, 1960), p. 14.
[2] Quoted in Richard Walser, ed., *The Enigma of Thomas Wolfe* (Cambridge, Mass.: Harvard University Press, 1953), p. vii.

the discomfort, weakness, dumbness, the infinite misunderstanding he would have to endure. . . . He grew sick as he thought of the weary distance before him, the lack of co-ordination of the centres of control, the undisciplined and rowdy bladder, the helpless exhibition he was forced to give in the company of his sniggering, pawing brothers and sisters, dried, cleaned, revolved before them. . . .

He understood that "no one ever comes really to know anyone," that "caught in that insoluble prison of being, we escape it never. . . . Never, never, never, never, never." As he looked at the "huge leering heads that bent hideously into his crib, . . . his brain went black with terror." This passage has been called the "silliest" in serious fiction, not merely because of the gross violation of probability, but because of the sentimentality, the unmotivated hysteria, and, simply, the ineptitude: inserting the five famous "nevers" from *King Lear*, using such a melodramatic cliché as "his brain went black with terror."

Although *Look Homeward, Angel* is his most unified novel, much of the unity is superficial, imposed gratuitously by the subject matter. A middle-class boy, growing up in a small American city, follows an almost predictable series of experiences. Despite Wolfe's frequent assertions of connections, one feels very little sense of growth in the main character, of relations between characters, or of the impact of event upon character. Although the dramatized incidents are often utterly persuasive, even very moving, their effects upon the characters are not realized. Wolfe is a perfect example of Hemingway's famous statement: "You'll lose it if you talk about it." When Eugene argues with his mother, when he loses his girl friend, when his roommate dies—in each case Wolfe talks about the painful effects, and each time he loses much of the feeling created by the dramatized scene. The dialogue and the gestures are just right; the hero's thoughts and the author's comments are often wrong.

Failing so radically in the two crucial artistic requirements of style and coherence, surely Wolfe deserves our indifference. But he does not always fail in these matters, and he succeeds brilliantly in other ways. If we let his weaknesses obscure his strengths, the fault may lie, after all, with ourselves. According to the publisher,

> Each new generation as it comes along rediscovers and claims this book for its own. For Wolfe wrote about youth, and he spoke to youth more convincingly than any American writer has ever done.

To appreciate Wolfe older readers must be willing to recall their own youth sympathetically and to look again at the world with youthful eyes—eyes that, despite the distortions of sentimentality, may see in some ways more clearly than those of age.

Why do academic critics disapprove of Wolfe? Partly, at least, because Wolfe did not write the kind of book an American novelist of the 1920's *ought* to have written. Somehow, Wolfe ought to have written in the tradition of Flaubert and James and Conrad, the tradition of exquisite craftsmanship. Hemingway and Fitzgerald are the obvious exemplars. Or, Wolfe should have been an experimenter in technique, like Joyce and Faulkner. Although Wolfe deeply admired Conrad and Joyce, he wrote very old-fashioned novels, a mélange of the picaresque—Fielding, Dickens, Twain—and of the spiritual autobiography—the English romantics, Melville, Whitman.

But if Wolfe's manner is old-fashioned, his matter belongs to our century. When the wisest man in Conrad's *Lord Jim* is asked to diagnose the hero's ailment, he replies: "I understand very well. He is romantic." Conrad's subject, the youthful, romantic egoist, is Wolfe's subject. The hero of *Look Homeward, Angel* has affinities, too, with Fitzgerald's Jay Gatsby and with Faulkner's Quentin Compson in *The Sound and the Fury*. But there is an important difference. These other novelists keep their romantic heroes in check: Conrad and Fitzgerald through a subordinate, ironic narrator; Faulkner through the perspectives of other characters, other points of view. But Thomas Wolfe—Eugene Gant—simply expresses, expresses, expresses his romantic emotions.

I intend to wreak out my soul on paper and express it all. This is what my life means to me: I am at the mercy of this thing and I will do it or die.

Look Homeward, Angel begins with a kind of prose poem:

> . . . a stone, a leaf, an unfound door; of a stone, a leaf, a door.
> . . . we seek the great forgotten language, the lost lane-end into heaven, a stone, a leaf, an unfound door. Where? When?

Like many romantic tales, then, this is the story of a quest, a quest that can never be successfully completed. Just as Gatsby forever pursues the green light, so Eugene Gant's quest finds its symbol in the leaf, stone, and door. Eugene is full of "desire and longing" for some vague perfection never precisely located. As a boy growing up in an isolated provincial town, Eugene often believes his "happy land" lies outside the cup of the mountains, perhaps in the deep South, burning "like Dark Helen in [his] blood," or perhaps in some "golden city." Since the railroad train is his means of escape, train whistles have a special poignancy for him. More frequently, Eugene locates his happy land in the world of imagination, dreams, and artistic creation. He seems to place this in a wonderful cave, entered through an underground passage:

> He groped for the doorless land of faery, that illimitable haunted country that opened somewhere below a leaf or a stone.

Again, Eugene's quest leads toward communication with another person, with his dearest brother, Ben, or with his beloved Laura James. Here, the door leads not to an underground faeryland but rather through the barrier separating personalities. Often, borrowing Wordsworth's notion of a prenatal paradise, Wolfe locates his goal in the past, either in some heaven where he lived before birth or in the actual past of his childhood. Finally, at the very end of the novel, Eugene says that he has found his happy land:

> . . . in the city of myself, upon the continent of my soul, I shall find the forgotten language, the lost world, a door where I may enter.

Self-knowledge, then, appears to be the key to the door. Or rather, the door seems to open upon the individual's inner, buried life.

Although Wolfe asserts that the quest has ended, and although at times Eugene glimpses his goal, the prevailing mood of the hero is frustration. Note that the initial prose poem is less about the quest than about loneliness and loss.

> Which of us has known his brother? Which of us has looked into his father's heart? Which of us has not remained forever prison-pent? Which of us is not forever a stranger and alone? . . . O lost, and by the wind grieved, ghost, come back again.

As a matter of fact, Wolfe's first title for the novel was "O, Lost," and the second, "Alone, Alone." The title he finally chose comes from John Milton's elegy, "Lycidas," in which the poet asks the angel, St. Michael, to look back toward England and melt with pity at the spectacle of a promising young man's death by drowning. While Fitzgerald portrays Gatsby as a young man with an "extraordinary gift for hope," Eugene and Wolfe recognize that utter loneliness is man's lot and that ceaseless change, immutable Time, and Death inevitably frustrate longings for the happy land.

The circumstances of Wolfe's own life make this obsession with change and loss quite comprehensible. One of his earliest memories was the death of his brother Grover, when Wolfe was only four. At six came the wrench of having to leave the warm center of his life, his father's house, for the impersonal, transient chaos of his mother's boardinghouse. Much later he wrote:

> I was without a home—a vagabond since I was seven—with two roofs and no home. . . . I think I learned about being alone when I was a child . . . and I think that I have known about it ever since.

It is hardly surprising that he describes Eugene as "a stranger in a noisy inn." Eugene sees little evidence that anyone else transcends loneliness. He and his brothers and sisters feel only embarrassment when they watch their father's clumsy attempts to embrace their mother: "Aw, Papa, don't." Wolfe used to say that the most tragic event of his life was the death, when he was eighteen, of his favorite brother, Ben. But perhaps even more important was the constant awesome sense of his father's ultimate end, the awareness that the most vital, heroic figure in his life was doomed.

Furthermore, the town in which Wolfe grew up was also undergoing convulsive change. Asheville, North Carolina (Altamont in the novel), is not quite a typical Southern town. Although it underwent the pain of the post-Civil War era, its location high in the Appalachian Mountains gives it a climate that attracted people from the outside world. By the turn of the century, Asheville had become an important health resort and a popular vacation spot. Northern millionaires settled in Asheville, real estate values soared, and the population doubled. Wolfe grew up in an environment that displayed simultaneously Southern defeat and Northern "progress," Southern poverty and Northern materialism. Every year he saw another piece of his cherished past obliterated, until finally his father's tombstone shop gave way to a skyscraper.

Although the themes of loneliness and loss are enormously important to Wolfe, their mere expression does not contribute great significance to the novel. Aching so to be happy and knowing that he cannot, Eugene responds in an adolescent way: he feels sorry for himself. Moreover, the older he becomes the more naked is the self-pity and the less interesting the central character. When Wolfe writes badly, the subject is almost always Eugene.

However, if Wolfe's sense of the inevitability of loss seriously tarnishes the central character of *Look Homeward, Angel*, it also inspires what is truly great in the novel. Conrad defined the writer's task this way:

> To snatch in a moment of courage, from the remorseless rush of time, a passing phase of life.[3]

[3] Preface to *The Nigger of the "Narcissus"* (New York: Doubleday, 1936), p. xiv.

Just as Wolfe's father carved stone monuments to the dead, so Wolfe memorializes his lost past: the earth at her most opulent, his home town in its variety, and his family in their frenetic activity. The Gant family is, of course, the Wolfe family, even to some of the names. In a court case involving real estate in Asheville, *Look Homeward, Angel* was admitted in testimony as a historical record.

What matters, though, is not where these materials came from, but the way in which Wolfe brings them to life. He said:

> My memory is characterized . . . by the intensity of its sense impressions, its power to evoke and bring back the odors, sounds, colors, shapes, and feel of things with concrete vividness.

To the same degree that Wolfe despairs that everything must pass, he jealously cherishes and celebrates what is most imbued with life. Haunted by Time, he describes the earth best in terms of the passing seasons:

> The plum-tree, black and brittle, rocks stiffly in winter wind. Her million little twigs are frozen in spears of ice. But in the spring, lithe and heavy, she will bend under her great load of fruit and blossoms. She will grow young again. Red plums will ripen, will be shaken desperately upon the tiny stems. They will fall bursted on the loamy warm wet earth; when the wind blows in the orchard the air will be filled with dropping plums; the night will be filled with the sound of their dropping, and a great tree of birds will sing, burgeoning, blossoming richly, filling the air also with warm-throated plum-dropping bird-notes.

Whereas poetic accounts of Eugene's loneliness generally contain Wolfe's worst prose, the lyric evocations of the physical world often represent Wolfe's best.

Even more than the earth and its plenty, Wolfe wanted to celebrate the people of his homeland, his family especially, but also the whole range of humanity in the town. Wherever Eugene goes through the streets of Altamont, he *sees* someone. When he glances up at the second story window of a dental building, a tiny breeze blows back the curtains, revealing Dr. H. M. Smathers,

> white-jacketed, competent, drill in hand. He pumped vigorously with his right foot, took a wad of cotton from his assistant, Miss Lola Bruce, and thrusting it securely into the jaw of his unseen patient, bent his fashionable bald head intently. . . . "Do you feel that?" he said tenderly. "Wrogd gdo gurk!" "Spit!"

Though Wolfe can be prolix, he brings to life an array of minor characters with a few striking details of speech, dress, or gesture and with a fine gift for comedy. There is the apparently endless series of predatory, middle-aged females who pass through Eliza's boardinghouse, "Dixieland," and have affairs with the Gant males, from W. O. in his sixties to Eugene in his middle teens. In his portraits of the two best doctors in town, Wolfe combines comedy with deep admiration. We see them not only in their offices but also at 5:30 A.M. before surgery, sitting on stools in the Uneeda Lunch No. 3: McGuire "patiently impaling kidney beans, one at a time, upon the prongs of his fork," the odor of corn whiskey soaking the air about him. "His thick skilful butcher's hands, hairy on the backs," grip the fork "numbly." He speaks in a "barking kindly voice." Coker, the Lung Shark, watches "McGuire's bean hunt with sardonic interest," takes the long cigar out of his "devil's head," and holds it "between his stained fingers." To Ben Gant's irritated plea that McGuire not be permitted to operate in such a condition, Coker responds, "Why, he's just getting hot, son." And the truth is that these two grotesques are humane, expert healers.

Wolfe's greatest triumph in *Look Homeward, Angel* is, of course, the re-creation of his own family, the Gants. Although Eugene at some point hates every member of the family, Wolfe himself loves these creations: "to me . . . they were the greatest people I had ever known. . . . If I could get my magnificent people on paper as they were. . . ." Magnificent they are, and emphatically a *family:* "They had twisted the design of all orderly life, because there was in them a mad, original, disturbing quality." Above all, there is their fantastic energy: they appear to live without need of sleep; they are all compulsive talkers, whether in the slow, deliberate utterances of Eliza, or the idiotic outbursts of Luke, the engineering student: "He was not an electrical engineer—he was electrical energy." In Helen the "hysteria of constant excitement" lurks. Like Eugene, they are all embarked on a quest though, except perhaps for old Gant, none of them seems quite aware of the fact. Helen instinctively gropes "toward a center of life and purpose to which she [can] fasten her energy." Ben, so ironic, disdainful, and independent, tries to get at life by reading the success sermons of millionaires in the *Post*.

Despite their consistent family resemblances, the Gants are all brilliantly defined, their differences made unmistakably sharp. The mother and father live vibrantly in their own right; at the same time, they unobtrusively symbolize the two central, conflicting forces in the novel: the human quest and its inevitable frustration.[4] Wolfe draws W. O. Gant in wonderful broad strokes: the long frame, the large hands, the great blade of a nose, the cold, uneasy eyes, the faint, sly grin at the corners of the thin mouth. Gant, a Northerner in the South, married to a woman he does not understand, longing to carve an angel's head, but unable to, desiring to be a Far Wanderer but tied to his family and home. Gant is "a stranger in a strange land." Sporadically drunk and disorderly, he is nevertheless the artist striving to impose order on a changing world. Gant brings a kind of ritual to their wild family life. Combining Shakespearean rhetoric with Southern political oratory, he delivers to wife and children carefully rehearsed speeches, full of invective, at appointed hours of the day. He yells:

> We will freeze in this hellish, damnable, cruel and God-forsaken climate. Does Brother Will care? Does Brother Jim care? Did the Old Hog, your miserable old father, care? Merciful God!

[4] For a full discussion of this theme, see Louis D. Rubin, Jr., *Thomas Wolfe, "The Weather of His Youth"* (Baton Rouge: Louisiana State University Press, 1955).

I have fallen into the hands of fiends incarnate, more savage, more cruel, more abominable than the beasts of the field. Hell-hounds that they are, they will sit by and gloat at my agony until I am done to death.

Although the hand of death is ever upon him, he remains a fount of energy: he is the great provider, buying whole hogs from the butcher, and a marvelous gardener: "The earth was spermy for him like a big woman." Gant builds roaring fires; his neighbors can tell he is at home by the thick column of smoke from the chimney. He is the source of sexual energy: twice-married father of eight, old rooster frequenting Eliza-beth's brothel, pursuer of colored cooks and middle-aged widows, he is held in high esteem even by the Temperance Ladies of the First Baptist Church. To his children he is simply man as hero:

> swinging violently back and forth in a stout rocker, [he spits] clean and powerful spurts of tobacco-juice over his son's head into the hissing fire.

Eliza is her husband's antithesis. He disdains ownership, spends lavishly, and talks rapidly. She, on the other hand, saves bits of string; has a "powerful germinal instinct for property . . . [; and likes] "to take her time" [and come] "to the point after interminable divagations down all the lane-ends of memory and overtone, feasting upon the golden pageant of all she had ever said, done, felt, thought, seen or replied, with egocentric delight." Her memory moves over the ocean bed of events like a great octopus. To Gant, and at times to all the rest of the family, she seems to symbolize the immutable Time and inert matter that will inevitably frustrate man's romantic quest. Yet she, too, is emphatically human as she stands perpetually over the spitting grease, her nose "stove-red," her hands chapped with hard work and covered with glycerine, her body "clothed in a tattered old sweater and indefinable under-lappings."

Wolfe particularly establishes her humanity in his account of the death of Ben, surely the best prose that he ever wrote. Here is language so accurate that it makes the reader see poor Ben in his last moments, language full of feeling yet seldom sentimental:

> the sallow yellow tint of his face had turned grey: out of this granite tint of death, lit by two red flags of fever, the stiff black furze of a three-day beard was growing . . . it recalled the corrupt vitality of hair, which can grow from a rotting corpse.

Wolfe brings the whole family together for the death: Helen contradicting herself, vibrating between rage at Eliza's ineptitude in the emergency and pity because Ben has rejected his mother; senile Gant, weeping in his rocker at the foot of Ben's bed, and employing his old rhetoric not to eulogize his son but to pity himself:

> O Jesus! I can't bear it! . . . How are we ever going to face this fearful and croo-el winter? It'll cost a thousand dollars before we're through burying him. . . .

Helen actually shaking him in fury right in the death chamber.

> And Eliza, now that [Ben] could deny her no longer . . . sitting near his head beside him, clutching his cold hand between her rough worn palms.

Even when Ben is apparently rigid in death, he asserts his vitality:

> suddenly, marvelously, as if his resurrection and rebirth had come upon him, Ben drew upon the air in a long and powerful respiration; his grey eyes opened. Filled with a terrible vision of all life in the one moment, he seemed to rise forward bodilessly from his pillows without support—a flame, a light, a glory —joined at length in death to the dark spirit who had brooded upon each footstep of his lonely adventure on earth.

But this is not all. Daringly, Wolfe follows the tragic account of Ben's death with a chapter full of eating and of comedy which ends in the funeral parlor of "Horse" Hines, beside Ben's embalmed corpse. Overcome with pride, Hines explains his artistry, how he has tried to do Ben justice. When Luke finds Ben a trifle pale, Hines whips out a rouge-stick and sketches a "ghastly rose-hued mockery of life and health" upon the dead grey cheeks. "Did you ever see anything more natural in your life?" Eugene notes "with a sort of tenderness . . . the earnestness and pride in the long horse-face." But the "dogs of laughter" tug at Eugene's throat, he slides gently off his chair, slowly unbuttoning his vest, languidly loosening his tie. He gurgles helplessly, and Luke looks on all a-grin. That Wolfe should introduce a comic note here is perfectly appropriate. It has been said that the essence of comedy is "human life-feeling." Wolfe, for all his loneliness, self-pity, and despair, affirmed life. He managed to pack a very great deal of this "human life-feeling" into *Look Homeward, Angel.* For this reason and despite countless obvious faults, the novel endures, and Wolfe appears to have conquered his old enemy Time, after all.

19 WILLIAM FAULKNER
The Sound and the Fury

Carvel Collins

When William Faulkner published *The Sound and the Fury* in 1929, some critics thought well of it and felt its author had promise. But most thought it was poor, and the sales gravely disappointed its publishers. Today, more than thirty years later, *The Sound and the Fury* is considered by many to be Faulkner's best novel—and one of the best novels published in the English language in our century.

It is a complex work, comprehension of which was made more difficult by its having appeared considerably ahead of its time. It had to create its own audience—or, more accurately, it had to wait for readers to make a general change in what they expected of fiction. When it first appeared, many readers in the United States demanded that fiction be closely related to the literary naturalism which had developed here after the turn of the century, loosely based on the mid-nineteenth-century practice of such European authors as Zola. Many of these readers assumed that fiction should be rather sociological and rather simple in form, the plots usually being presented in straight chronological sequence, and the books often eliciting in their readers a desire for some improvement of the current social structure.

In *The Sound and the Fury* William Faulkner did not write a book of that kind; instead, as it turned out, he wrote one which would meet the demands of the postnaturalist American readers in the period following the Second World War. Consequently, this novel acquired its large audience in the 1940's; its partisans now view with distaste the earlier, incorrect critical assumption that Faulkner was trying to write a sociological study of the American South but did not know how to go about it. Today large numbers of Faulkner's readers realize that he was aiming at a different target than were Norris, Dreiser, Farrell, and Dos Passos and that he hit its center when he wrote *The Sound and the Fury*. Furthermore, his target is one at which many cultivated readers now want novelists to aim.

The Sound and the Fury, rather than being inexpert literary naturalism, is an expansion of literary naturalism into new territory; its model is the fiction of James Joyce. In *Dubliners* Joyce began to develop and in *Ulysses* he brought to flower what T. S. Eliot, in his famous review of *Ulysses*, called "the mythical method" and which Eliot said, quite accurately, would be the method of many authors in the years to follow.[1]

The major feature of this method, which Faulkner adopted with genius in *The Sound and the Fury*, was simple in concept but extremely difficult in execution. It consisted of keeping the surface of the novel as realistic and accurate in detail as the most naturalistic novel of railroading or coal mining by Zola, while simultaneously making the surface story's events, characterizations, dialogue, and details bear a significant relationship to an underlying myth or pattern. In both *Dubliners* and *Ulysses* Joyce had presented the surface story realistically with what he himself called "scrupulous meanness" while making the events and characters bear a significant relationship—to select but one example—to the events and characters of the myth of Ulysses.

T. S. Eliot has borne out his own prediction that twentieth-century writers would adopt Joyce's method. In play after play he himself has made the seemingly self-contained surface plots and characterizations resonate for many members of his audiences because of their awareness of the significant relationships he has created between the surfaces of

---

[1] "Ulysses, Order, and Myth," *The Dial* (November 1923); reprinted in Seon Givens, ed., *James Joyce*, "Two Decades of Criticism" (New York: Vanguard, 1948), p. 202.

the plays and the older, classic plots and characters which lie below the surfaces. Eliot's experience demonstrates the major problem which such writing has with critics: Eliot said in a speech at Harvard University that when he first revealed how consciously and closely he had based one of his modern plays on a Greek play, there was a general refusal to believe it. Because William Faulkner, in the misleading public statements which he so often made in order to keep his literary privacy, often denied his identical aesthetic method and intention, it is no wonder that some critics have too frequently continued to maintain that he wrote without a plan and certainly wrote without a plan so complex and intellectual. After all, they have his own word for it. He repeatedly said he was a farmer, not a writer.

Faulkner not only wrote *The Sound and the Fury* with Joyce as a model and Eliot as a guide to that model (in ways which will be discussed later), he also wrote *The Sound and the Fury* with little hope that it would be printed. A statement among his literary papers says that his first three published novels were unsuccessful in achieving an audience, yet all he wanted to do was write whether or not he had any audience at all; so he set out to produce a novel with no thought whatever of the public, of editors, or of sales. The result is *The Sound and the Fury*, which now has a large audience and great acclaim.

The surface story of the novel is rather simple. Mr. and Mrs. Compson have a daughter called Caddy and three sons. Mr. Compson is an intelligent and sporadically affectionate but weak and selfish man who seeks in alcohol refuge from nihilism. Mrs. Compson, a selfish woman who has retreated into hypochondria, gives her children no real affection. In part because of lack of support from these parents, their four children lead lives of tragedy or waste.

The youngest child, Benjy, who grows into a huge man with the mentality of a three-year-old, lives in emotional deprivation. His sorrow is the loss of his sister, who has been affectionate toward him in the absence of affection from his hypochondriacal mother.

The chief tragedy of the son named Quentin is that he is

drawn to his sister but repelled from this emotion by social convention and his own weakness. Emotionally and philosophically unsupported by his father and unable to cope with these conflicts, he drowns himself at the end of his first year as a student in Harvard College.

The son named Jason is extremely cruel, continually angry with his family, and furious for years at his sister because of what he considers her loose behavior in general and because, in particular, he blames her for his being only a clerk in a store rather than cashier in her former husband's bank.

The tragedy of the sister, Caddy, is that she sees her family disintegrating, is unable to help her brothers Quentin and Benjy or their father, is abandoned by the man she loves, becomes extremely promiscuous, marries an unpleasant man to give her baby a legal father but is divorced by him when he learns of her pregnancy, and finally becomes a prostitute who cannot return home to her family, which includes her illegitimate daughter.

The technique of the novel led many critics of the thirties and early forties to consider Faulkner careless and out of control. Today the exact opposite is considered true: that *The Sound and the Fury* is one of the most carefully and successfully ordered of great modern novels.

It consists of four numbered and dated sections. The first three are interior monologues, each by one of the three Compson brothers. The fourth section is presented from the point of view of the author as invisible observer. Caddy, the sister, has no section of her own. But she is skillfully made the central subject of each of the interior monologues by her three brothers.

Benjy's monologue, though it jumps about among his memories of more than a dozen significant family episodes ranging through most of his more than thirty years of life, is tightly unified around the theme of deprivation, of emotional loss. His chief loss, to which he continually returns, is Caddy, who was affectionate and supportive but grew away from him as she matured into sexuality and then left home forever. Other losses, which his monologue brings out contrapuntally, include the deaths of his grandmother, his father, and his brother Quentin. Early critics thought Benjy's section difficult because of the way his thoughts skipped about among his memories. But readers today are aware that the sequence of his memories is tightly controlled aesthetically. A sample of the meaningful juxtaposition of Benjy's seemingly random memories lies in the pages of beautifully alternated scenes at the swing in the Compson yard, which show the contrast between, on the one hand, Caddy's compassion for Benjy as she was growing away from him and beginning to be sexually drawn to a young suitor and, on the other hand, her daughter's brutality to Benjy years later when he comes upon her in the swing beside the traveling carnival man with whom she will run away that night forever.

Caddy is the central subject of Jason's monologue too. But his response is the exact opposite of Benjy's desire for her: Jason hates her, and with frenzy. He hates her so much that when Caddy leaves home he devotes his hatred to her daughter, who is daily available in his household to substitute for her absent mother.

Caddy is also the overwhelming central subject of the monologue by Quentin. She seems to be the reason for his decision, before the start of his monologue, to kill himself. As he goes through his day of preparation for that act, his thoughts turn continually to her, and with a duality that contributes to the aesthetic pattern of the responses to Caddy by the three monologists. Benjy in his monologue just wants her and Jason in his monologue just hates her, but Quentin in his monologue, which has a position in the book between the other two, is ambivalent, loving Caddy beyond all women yet at the same time hating her behavior and his own so much that he decides to kill himself.

The styles of the three monologues skillfully reflect these attitudes and situations of the monologists. Benjy, who is unable to speak, has essentially only one style, chiefly based on his mental record of sights and sounds, which he does not directly interpret for us. For example, even his excesses of sorrow often are revealed only by his recording other people's observations that he is moaning. Jason, in his monologue, is usually quite articulate and has essentially only one basic style, a sardonic furiousness expressed in rather conventional syntax and seemingly spoken aloud like a long aside to the audience at an Elizabethan play. Only Quentin's monologue, aesthetically reflecting his ambivalence, has two styles: When he is going ahead with his preparation for killing himself because he hates his situation with Caddy, his monologue is almost as clear and direct as Jason's. But when his mind strays from his preparation for self-punishment and lets his love for Caddy emerge, his monologue changes to a second style, much closer to that of Benjy. Though these variations will disturb those who feel an author should have one style and stick to it, the changes in styles throughout the book are quite meaningful and aesthetically successful.

One of the devices Faulkner learned from Joyce was the interior monologue, to which he gave new shape and function. He also learned from Joyce to use meaningful parallels between the surface story of the novel and some outside pattern or structure, as mentioned earlier.

Though *The Sound and the Fury* contains more than one of these systems of parallels, the easiest one to demonstrate is the parallel between the events involving the Compson children and those involving Christ, especially during the week of His Passion. This parallel in the novel is ironic: to describe it briefly, it emphasizes that the tragedy of the Compsons has its source in a lack of love, because it contrasts their ineffectual lives with the life of Christ in His last days, during which He gave His disciples an eleventh Commandment —"That ye love one another"—and died as the One who Christians believe will save them through His love. In Joyce's *Ulysses* the ironic contrast between the powerful and competent Odysseus of classic mythology and the weaker Leopold Bloom of twentieth-century Dublin adds richly to our conception of Bloom's position; so in Faulkner's *The Sound and the Fury* the ironic contrast between the most dramatically loving days of Christ and the inadequate days lived by the Compsons in the four dated sections of the novel adds to the richness of our aesthetic awareness of the tragedy of their lives.

Three of the sections bear dates in 1928 which turn out to be days in Easter Week of that year: Good Friday, Holy Saturday, and Easter Sunday. The remaining section, Quentin's monologue, bears the date of a Thursday in 1910 which is the Octave of Corpus Christi—a day which celebrates anew the happiest events drawn from Maundy Thursday of Easter Week. So the four sections of the novel have dates related to the four major days in the sequence of Christ's Passion. And the events of the Compson family on each particular day are related to those of the same day in Christian history and liturgy. Many readers are at first skeptical of this, for they have read the novel with great pleasure while having no awareness whatever that such matters lie below its surface. They also have read it in a rather loose way, for attentive readers should be puzzled by the appearance of the precise dates as the headings of the four sections. These dates are Faulkner's surface method of drawing the reader's attention to what lies below, just as Joyce's title for *Ulysses,* a book which does not discuss that mythological character, was his way of alerting the reader to the aesthetic possibilities below the surface of his novel. There would be no function whatever for Joyce's title or Faulkner's careful dates if the presentation of only their realistic surface stories were the sole function of these great works.

In Quentin's monologue, which bears the date of a significant Thursday, Quentin experiences events which suggest many of the events through which Christ passed on Maundy Thursday: after lengthy thoughts of a talk with his father, Quentin is captured by a group of men and taken before a magistrate. In parallel with the major feature of Corpus Christi, which is the carrying of the bread of the Eucharist in procession through the streets, Quentin and the little Italian girl carry bread in their long search for her home. One sample of the meaningful inversion of the parallel which appears throughout the book occurs in Quentin's confrontation with his father: whereas Christ on Thursday asked His Father to take away the cup of suffering and crucifixion, Quentin on Thursday is shown to have asked his father to give him at least the parental support of punishment.

In Jason's section, bearing a date which is that of Good Friday, 1928, Jason appears in inverse parallel to Christ in the Crucifixion of that day. Jason enters upon selfish cotton speculation at the same hour which liturgy has assigned to Christ's unselfish ascent of the Cross; and at the hour of Christ's death on the Cross, the repellent Jason is sold out by his Jewish brokers, whom he vilifies after the fashion in medieval times of vilification of the Jews on Good Friday. Christ's spirit went from his body on the Cross to save worthy souls who were in Hell; Jason hurries from his commercial crucifixion to chase his niece who has said that she will go to Hell. As Jason follows her he says that he will make her carnival lover's red necktie the latchstring to Hell.

Benjy's monologue is dated April 7, 1928, which that year was the date of Holy Saturday, the day which Christ spent in the underworld saving worthy men who had died before his dispensation. Benjy, submerged in his primitive mentality, is involved in events related to those of Holy Saturday, and again the relationship is ironic or inverted. As one example, on this traditional day of the loving christening of children, Benjy's thoughts turn to his mother's unloving act of taking away his original name because it was a name from her family which she selfishly no longer wanted him to bear when she realized that he would never be normal. In Benjy's section he is continually associated with themes of death. But inversely to Christ in the underworld of the dead on Holy Saturday, Benjy is unable to offer any hope for life. And whereas Christ on that day dominated the underworld and its master, Satan, Benjy, helpless, is led about by Luster, that significantly named attendant, whose torments for Benjy even include burning him.

The fourth section, which follows the three monologues, bears the date of Easter Sunday in 1928. On this day when Christ's tomb was found empty except for his abandoned grave clothing, the Compsons find that the bedroom of

Caddy's daughter, who in more ways than one serves often in the novel as her mother's substitute, is empty except for some of her clothing left scattered about after her hurried flight forever from the Compson house. Thus the Compson children on successive days play, in a symbolic inverted way, the role of Christ; and by the end of the novel their combined lives of selfishness, frustration, and defeat have appeared in telling contrast to the life of Christ.

The final section of *The Sound and the Fury* sets up, in contrast to the selfish Compsons, the loving servant Dilsey. Through her, readers see a better way which life might take, and thus they may feel some reduction of the novel's tragedy. But it remains a tragedy, nevertheless, for Dilsey is by no means able to offset the destructive effect of the Compsons' overwhelming emotional failure.

Throughout the book, details such as the use or avoidance of colors, the ringing or silencing of bells, and innumerable phrases of the dialogue and exposition accord in tragic significance with the liturgy for Passion Week. And the total effect, once the reader is aware of this and willing to give it an opportunity to influence his conception of the novel, is to make *The Sound and the Fury* vastly richer. This is not a cheap crossword puzzle or an extraneous, pedantic "hidden meaning"—it is of the essence of the book's technique and aesthetic.

The same is true of other elaborate and consciously executed systems of parallels in the novel: with Macbeth, with Freud's designation of the parts of human personality, and with mythology by way of Sir James Frazer's *The Golden Bough,* Faulkner having read Sherwood Anderson's copy in 1925.

The problem in the thirties and early forties was to persuade critics and readers that Faulkner had competence; now they have accepted that, and the problem is to persuade them just how enormous that competence is in Faulkner's best works such as this. The complexity of *The Sound and the Fury* and the aesthetic rewards of being well acquainted with that complexity are too great to have been more than touched in as brief an essay as this, which can merely attempt to suggest possibilities for increased aesthetic pleasure in this novel. *The Sound and the Fury* seems to come most fully aglow on a third reading. The first reading probably should be mostly in innocence of these underlying elements and fully concerned only with the extraordinarily poignant and moving surface story. The second reading probably should be slower and somewhat pedantic, accompanied by modest examination of the sources of the Christian and other parallels. Then, presumably after some lapse of time, the ideal third reading would reveal the novel in a richer way, with all the vitality of the first "innocent" reading augmented by the resonance from the reader's assimilated knowledge of the no longer submerged parallel elements.

To the reader who responds that he does not want to read any novel which requires three readings for its full effect, one can reply that, though there is no requirement whatever for him to read this or any other novel, he might consider the fact that few devotees of great music feel they get everything from a symphony in the first hearing or that, in the interest of efficiency, they should not listen to it more than once.

Index